TECHNOLOGICAL DEPENDENCE, MONOPOLY, AND GROWTH

TECHNOLOGICAL DEPENDENCE, MONOPOLY, AND GROWTH

BY

MEIR MERHAV

PERGAMON PRESS

OXFORD · LONDON · EDINBURGH · NEW YORK
TORONTO · SYDNEY · PARIS · BRAUNSCHWEIG

Pergamon Press Ltd., Headington Hill Hall, Oxford
4 & 5 Fitzroy Square, London W.1

Pergamon Press (Scotland) Ltd., 2 & 3 Teviot Place, Edinburgh 1

Pergamon Press Inc., Maxwell House, Fairview Park, Elmsford,
New York 10523

Pergamon of Canada Ltd., 207 Queen's Quay West, Toronto 1

Pergamon Press (Aust.) Pty. Ltd., 19a Boundary Street,
Rushcutters Bay, N.S.W. 2011, Australia

Pergamon Press S.A.R.L., 24 rue des Écoles, Paris 5^e

Vieweg & Sohn GmbH, Burgplatz 1, Braunschweig

First edition 1969

Library of Congress Catalog Card No. 68–21747

PRINTED IN GREAT BRITAIN BY A. WHEATON AND CO., EXETER

08 012754 1

In memory of
CARMELLAH MONETA

CONTENTS

vii

PREFACE

THE ideas put forward in this essay as general propositions first arose out of the concern with the problems of economic growth in Israel. The economic structure and performance of that country, which I had the opportunity to study at close quarters for a good number of years, display many of the major symptoms described in this book, except one—that of stagnation, for at least until 1965 the Israeli economy kept up an almost unprecedented rate of growth.

Nevertheless, the danger of ultimate stagnation is never far from the thought of nearly all Israeli economists, for there is a general recognition that the country's rapid growth until now has been sustained mainly by the massive influx of capital transfers from abroad—much of them unrequited—which must before long decline. With unilateral annual transfers of approximately $150 *per capita*, the exceptional nature of this growth needs no further proof. But the unusual factors which so far supported this rapid and continued growth also obscure the structural weaknesses of the Israeli economy and the basic trends at work in it, and dim the awareness of the need to counteract them in time, while the economy still has the resilience and the resources to carry out significant structural changes.

During the last four years, my work in the United Nations gave me the opportunity to acquaint myself with the problems of economic development in many underdeveloped countries, and strengthened my conviction that the tendencies which I thought I could see beneath the surface of prosperity in Israel were much more general. In many other countries which had already gone some way along the road of economic development, notably in Latin America, they could be seen quite clearly on the surface. In the nature of the case, there are great differences between individual countries, but the mechanism which I have tried to outline here in broad strokes seems to provide a coherent explanation for many of the major difficulties of growth which the underdeveloped countries encounter after their initial steps towards industrial development.

An earlier version of this study was submitted as a doctoral dissertation to the Graduate Faculty of the New School for Social Research. I am grateful to my teachers there for their help, but wish to pay a special tribute to Professor Adolph Lowe, whom I knew first while attending his guest lectures in 1953 at the Hebrew University in Jerusalem, and under whom I had the privilege of studying for three valuable years. I owe him not only the student's debt to a great teacher, but also much moral encouragement during the actual writing of this study.

Professors Thomas Vietorisz, Paul M. Sweezy, Joan Robinson, Amartya Kumar Sen, and Nathan Rosenberg read earlier drafts and gave me valuable comments. I am under a similar obligation to my friends Simon Teitel, Drs. Prafullah Sanghvi and Marian Ostrowski at the United Nations, and particularly to Dr. Salvatore Schiavo-Campo, who took the trouble of reading several drafts and commenting on them in detail. Their criticisms saved me from many a blunder, and they are not to blame for those that have remained.

Long before I began to work on this study I was fortunate to have the valuable intellectual companionship of a group of young economists in the Research Department of the Bank of Israel. My colleagues there have long borne with me patiently while I tried out my ideas on them. In the heat of controversy about matters with which we were all deeply concerned my gratitude to them could rarely find expression, and I am happy to acknowledge it here. More recently, I found a similarly congenial environment among my friends in the United Nations, who let me draw upon a diversity of experience, knowledge and outlook that is probably hard to find together elsewhere.

My greatest debt is to Flora Davidov, colleague and the best of friends. Without her, this book would never have been begun; while I was working on it, she unstintingly devoted time and effort to the collection of material for me and to answering endless queries on points of fact. Most of her help, particularly in the programming and collection of data on Israel's competitive structure which had to be left for a separate empirical study, is not directly visible in this essay, but was none the less indispensable for it.

To David Dreiblatt thanks are due for his help in the collection of various data and the preparation of the tables, and to Mrs. Regina Dyer for freely giving me her time to type several drafts of this study.

New York—Jerusalem, 1967 M. M.

INTRODUCTION

THREE-QUARTERS of the human race live in a poverty not far above an animal level of existence. The promise that economic theory holds out to their increasingly articulate desire to rise above that level is that "the country that is more developed industrially only shows, to the less developed, the image of its own future".[1]

This Marxian dictum pervades most of the literature on economic development; quoted out of its context, it implies a universality and gradualism which is hardly consistent with the thinking of its author, but it correctly reflects the widespread conviction that the path from poverty to wealth repeats itself in history—with variations, to be sure, for different peoples and different times, but essentially leading through similar stages and following the same signposts.[2] The laws and generalizations derived from the past experience of the nations now affluent can therefore serve as a lesson for the present and the future of those who are still poor.

Economic development, however, is an historical process, and cannot be understood in terms of equilibrium relations. This has forced many economists to concern themselves once more with the "classical question", and "to explain the expansion of the system through time" rather than the distribution of income and allocation of resources within it. But even this is not adequate, for as Celso Furtado has pointed out, in our times development relates to changes in economic structure which differ in essential respects from those of the past. Even on a high level of abstraction it can therefore not be viewed merely as a repetition of the classical process.[3] Yet the orthodox student of economic development only seldom finds it possible or necessary to follow W. Arthur Lewis and "to work right back to the classical economists before he finds an analytical framework into which he can relevantly fit his problem".[4] Most remain within the fence of neo-classical doctrine, and are content to

1

draw upon "the current reservoir of economic theories, concepts and ideas".[5]

The literary stream that has issued from this reservoir has brought forth a bewildering growth of theories, but hardly any theory of growth. Most of these theories are partial, and some achieve the generality they claim only at the cost of severely limited validity. Some have borrowed to a greater or lesser extent from the analytical framework of the classics; others have almost abandoned the search for the determinants of growth within a postulated capitalist system and have, rather, carried their question further back and asked how a social system capable of self-sustained growth comes into being in the first place. Much of this eclectic quest after the *primum mobile* of economic development has stepped beyond the boundaries of economic analysis proper, and as Albert O. Hirschman says, its results have generally been discouraging—"it has produced an ever lengthening list of factors and conditions, of obstacles and prerequisites".[6] The main reason for this search for elusive extra-economic factors is that orthodox doctrine can neither break out from the conceptual mold of equilibrium analysis nor can it envisage economic growth except within that social order which alone had produced it for so many centuries past, and on the conditions appropriate to it. Traditional doctrine can have no laws for the emergence of a system which it takes for granted, and the search for them must thus remain a futile endeavour.

The starting-point for all these theories, including those that have gone back to the classics, is the assumption of a private-enterprise system with a competitive structure. When the inquiry realizes that the socio-economic structure that is being analysed has little in common with this postulated system and is obviously pre-capitalist, it turns to extra-economic factors in an attempt to answer the question how the actual structure may become transformed into a recognizably capitalist system which possesses the features and functions according to the laws known from the classical model. If, on a higher level of generality, the existence of the basic elements of a capitalist system are presupposed as universal, the need arises to identify the various exogenous factors that inhibit growth.

The automaticity of growth in a private-enterprise system is never called into question. The assumption is always that such a system, if it only has all the proper characteristics, and is not unduly inhibited by "abnormal" or "exogenous" factors, will bring forth economic growth of itself. This is a proposition which cannot be falsified by events, for if growth does not in fact come forth, then evidently the system must be deficient in some of the crucial attributes of a capitalist structure, or else we must look for extraneous obstacles to growth.

In this optimistic view of the growth potential of capitalism, orthodox economics has paradoxically had support in the views of Marx himself as well as in those of some modern Marxist theorists. Marx' own admiration of the immense capacity—indeed, the compulsion—of capitalism to generate growth is well known. And the late Paul A. Baran believed that if only a "complete substitution of capitalist market rationality for the rigidities of semi-feudal servitude" could be brought about, if only a " 'Young Turk' movement of some sort might have succeeded in . . . loosening the hide-bound social and political structure of their countries", if only a "peaceful transplantation of Western culture, science and technology" would have come instead of the destructive impact of Western imperialism, then "this would have served everywhere as a powerful catalyst of economic progress".[7]

This is no doubt true as far as it goes, but it hardly goes far enough. For the problem of economic development does not end with the initial transition from semi-feudal or colonial backwardness to some more or less fully developed modern industrial capitalism, which has already taken place in many underdeveloped countries. This transition is without question a great step forward, but it cannot be evaluated solely in terms of the immediate achievement it represents. Any realistic appraisal of the nature of the aspirations of the underdeveloped countries must conclude that the value of that progress is conditional upon the prospects it holds out for the continuation of economic growth beyond the threshold that separates backwardness in its many social forms from industrial capitalism, however embryonic.

Now even within the framework of the traditional model of competitive capitalism, the analysis of development, from the classics down to the present day, has always contained, in addition to the optimism about the growth potential of the system, also another strand—namely, the concern with the ultimate limits to growth in a private-enterprise system. This concern has nearly always led to the prognosis that, for one reason or another, the system will at some point come to a standstill, if not to decline or complete breakdown. In modern growth theory this is again reflected in the continuing controversy between the post-Keynesians, who are preoccupied with the system's inherent dangers of instability and stagnation, and the adherents of the neo-classical school, who continue to believe in unlimited investment opportunities.

With regard to the underdeveloped countries, such a concern with the possibility of stagnation seems at first sight to be no more than sterile speculation about some ultimate state of the world. But as soon as it is realized that contrary to the common presumption, the historical pattern of growth does not and cannot repeat itself because the classical process itself, as we know it from the past history of the advanced countries, has fundamentally altered the conditions—notably those of technology—for development today, then the problem of stagnation assumes immediate relevance on the theoretical as well as on the policy level. The postulated capitalist structure which theory analyses will function differently according to the point at which it comes upon the historical stage. The question becomes relevant also as soon as it is realized that for many of the underdeveloped countries of today the private enterprise system is not an historically given datum, as it was for the classics, including Marx, and as it still must be for any economist for whom the relevant reality is that of the advanced capitalist countries.

The socio-economic structure of the underdeveloped countries is by definition still preindustrial. The initial position from which they start is not a given pattern of social and economic forces handed down by centuries of evolution through feudalism and mercantile capitalism which, through their complex interplay, laid the basis for the emergence of industrial capitalism, within which accelerated economic growth then comes forth. Their starting-point is, rather, a nationalist movement, a newly-won formal sovereignty, and a concomitant set of social goals which became politically articulated in the process of attaining or consolidating their political independence. Just as politically they wish to equal the sovereignty of their former rulers, so in other spheres of social life they desire to emulate the advanced countries, and they pattern their goals upon the latter's achievements.

Among these goals, that of economic development is the most basic and urgent. The supersession of the present backward socio-economic structure of the underdeveloped countries, whether it is categorized as tribal, semi-feudal, colonial, or by any other term that signifies economic and social stagnation, by a kind of social order that can provide the desired growth nearly always calls for a sharp break with past history rather than for a smooth and natural continuation of its course. The twentieth century, unlike the past, presents the underdeveloped countries with alternatives to the private enterprise system as a means and framework for attaining economic growth. The shape of the new social order that must be set up is far from being taken for granted, but is seen as subordinate to the goal of growth. It is thus still to some extent a matter of choice, even where the legacy of the past has predetermined some of its contours.

Economic growth is certainly not merely an institutional problem; it is always subject to initial constraints which are independent of the social order, and it would be foolish to ignore them or to minimize their importance. Yet the social order, in turn, determines to what degree and how quickly these constraints can be lifted. We are therefore not absolved from asking whether a repetition of the classical process of growth, which took the private-enterprise system for granted and could envisage no other, still holds out the best, or at least a reasonable chance for achieving a high level of development, or whether, given the specific "laws of motion" of such a system and the objective conditions of the point in history at which it begins to function, it is liable to run into some definite limits. And if such limits can be discerned—what are the forces that impose them, and how inevitable are they?

This, essentially, is what this essay is about. The predictions of ultimate stagnation which have always been prominent in the "dismal science" have all referred to tendencies which, whether extraneous or inherent, were supposed to set in only after the system has already attained a high absolute level of economic development. But as Joan Robinson remarked of one version of ultimate stagnation, "a community whose only problem was that they have all the capital that there is any use for, would not really have a great deal to worry about, and we need not wring our hearts by contemplating their troubles".[8] For the underdeveloped countries even a fraction of the present, let alone the "ultimate" level of affluence of the advanced countries is obviously still very much a dream of the distant future. If that affluence could be approached irrespective of the nature of the social system, if stagnation were a correlate only of "economic maturity", there would indeed be little to worry about, and the problem we pose would be academic to the point of irrelevance.

It is, however, the central argument of this study that forces similar to those which, in an advanced private-enterprise system, produce stagnation tendencies only after it has reached a high level of economic development, appear in an underdeveloped country at an early stage of industrial growth, and are likely to stunt it. At the same time, the mechanisms by which the advanced country can counteract or stave off such stagnation tendencies are, in the underdeveloped economy, both fewer and less effective.

More specifically, the argument is that development consists chiefly of the transplantation of an advanced technology into a backward economy which is unable to produce it endogenously, as the outcome of its own evolutionary processes. The adoption of these alien techniques can only take place through the importation of the equipment that incorporates them. But this machinery has historically become adapted to the factor proportions and the scales of output appropriate to the size of the markets and the degree of specialization in its countries of origin. When it is introduced into the underdeveloped countries, which by definition have a low initial level of aggregate demand, the disparity between the scales of output to which it is geared and the extent of the markets, produces, at an early stage of growth, an industrial structure in which technically inevitable monopolies are dominant.*

Spreading monopolization, as the almost immediate result of industrial growth, means that price competition, freedom of

* The term "monopoly" will often be used in a broad, generic sense. Where it is used in its technical meaning, together with terms such as oligopoly, this will be obvious from the context.

entry, constant returns to scale—all the fundamental pre-requisites for the classical process of continual growth in a private-enterprise system—do not exist from the outset. And since the offsetting mechanisms which have in the course of time appeared in the advanced countries have, in the less developed, no time to emerge or are much feebler, their growth is likely to be arrested prematurely.

In general terms it is, of course, no new thing to relate the prevalence of monopoly to the possibilities of growth. Obviously, the erosion of competition has an important bearing on all the major aspects of the performance of the economic system, whatever its level of development—on welfare and efficiency, resource allocation and income distribution, stability and growth, and in the last resort on the viability of the system itself. Monopoly theory has, at least in part, been deeply concerned with the "limits of tolerance of private-enterprise systems with respect to monopoly elements".[9] In some important theories of development, monopoly has been assigned a key role: some have seen it as a major cause of stagnation—as examples, one may cite the whole Marxist school, the work of Joseph Steindl,[10] and, more recently, that of Paolo Sylos-Labini[11]—while others, for instance Schumpeter and his followers, have regarded monopoly as the main engine of economic growth.

All these theories, however, have invariably dealt with the problems that monopoly poses in the *advanced* countries, and many have been more concerned with stability than with growth. The theories of growth and development, by contrast, have remained wholly confined to the competitive assumptions, and the two bodies of literature have remained completely separate.

The reasons for this divorce between the two fields of economic inquiry are not far to seek. As has already been indicated, economic development is commonly viewed as a steady path from "Youth" to "Maturity", in which the underdeveloped countries are supposed to retrace—albeit, perhaps, at a quicker pace—the path through successive and similar "stages of growth" that the advanced countries have followed in the past. In that process, monopoly appeared as a symptom of a late phase, preceded by a long period of competition, and as the end product of its struggle for the survival of the biggest. Therefore, monopoly and the ways in which it may affect the stability and growth of the system has no place in the theory of development, which by definition deals with the stage of Immaturity. This makes the retention of the competitive assumptions not only necessary for orthodox economics because otherwise, as Hicks warned, "the basis on which economic laws can be constructed is . . . shorn away",[12] but it even lends it a semblance of empirical validity.

But if one grants the validity of the assumptions which this study makes about the characteristics of a state of underdevelopment, particularly with respect to the disparity between the scales of output given by technology and the initial size of markets, then the consequences with regard to the competitive structure follow, and the stagnation tendencies which result from monopoly must be expected to appear in an underdeveloped country even more acutely, and certainly earlier, than in an advanced economy. Furthermore, on the basis of the same assumptions it will be possible to argue that whatever validity one may ascribe to monopoly's main defence in the advanced economies—its alleged role as the creator of expansion—this becomes undermined in the conditions of the underdeveloped countries. An application of monopoly theory to the problem of development and its mechanism then leads to the conclusion that monopoly, after the initial spurt of growth in which it establishes itself, is likely to have very destructive consequences not, as Hicks feared, merely for theory, but for something much more important—namely, for the real business of further growth.

It must be emphasized right away that the problem which this essay raises is not merely that of the size of nations; it does not arise simply because there are disparities between a given state of technology and the extent of the market which, as Adam Smith taught us long ago, determines the division of labour. Development has an historical dimension which must be kept in mind, and as I hope to show, it makes all the difference in the world when and in which external circumstances a nation embarks on a process of economic growth. That which was possible for a small country 200 or 100 years ago, even a much bigger country can no longer accomplish today. As Celso Furtado has pointed out, underdevelopment is a "discrete historical process through which economies that have already achieved a high level of development have not necessarily passed".[13] It is not merely the direction and degree of specialization that are at stake, but the very possibility of sustained growth itself. Not only is it far from certain, given the concrete conditions of the present time, that the economic structures known to classical theory, which in earlier times proved so capable of producing continued growth, will function with equal smoothness today, but these circumstances may preclude their very emergence or may distort their shape out of recognition by comparison with the pattern we know from past history.

From what has been said so far it is already evident that most of the issues discussed in this essay relate to industrial growth and its long-run prospects. From this perspective it may perhaps not be necessary to justify in detail why the preconditions for such growth and the role of other sectors are almost completely left out of the account or only touched upon in passing, but a few words may be in order to delimit the scope of this study. The emphasis on industrial growth does not imply that substantial growth cannot be achieved, for instance, through an expansion of agriculture, nor that this may be an indispensable precondition or complement of industrial development. In a closed economy, however, there is a fairly low ceiling to the growth that can be achieved through agricultural expansion, which is limited both on the supply side and on the demand side; and although in the open economy these limitations should, on *a priori* grounds, be less severe, this is generally not the case in practice. Growth therefore turns to industry not only in the longer run, after the potentialities of agricultural expansion have already been exploited, but immediately, and industry is the dynamic sector which sets the pace and pattern of development.

The analysis also disregards the multitude of those growth-inhibiting factors which must be considered as extraneous to a pure capitalist system. This is not to deny, of course, that these factors may be important, perhaps even overwhelmingly so. It may well be that in practice the obstacles raised by feudalism, tribalism, political unrest, traditional inertia, by the scantiness of natural resources and population pressure, or even by the sheer human misery and poverty with all its depressing implications, which development must overcome at the start, are much more important for the foreseeable future than any self-defeating tendencies that a system of industrial capitalism may be discovered to develop. Equally, the impact of foreign interests on development is completely ignored, although it is in many cases indubitable that foreign domination, whether political or in its more subtle economic forms, has more to do with stagnation or with the distortion of economic growth in the underdeveloped countries.

All these highly important factors have been left completely out of account not only because it is necessary to choose a certain level of abstraction at which propositions of some generality become possible, and not only because many of them belong to areas in which economic theorizing has little guidance to offer, but also because this is the frame of discourse established by most of the conventional literature on economic development. The model which that literature holds up as a goal, in theoretical discussion and in policy recommendations, is that of private enterprise in its ideal form. Anyone who wishes to take issue with its predictions must therefore discuss it on its own ground.

From the nature of its subject, this essay must therefore be almost wholly analytical, not an empirical study. Development is structural change over time, and in order to generalize it is necessary to seize upon some basic forces and structural relationships of which one can reasonably assume that they remain invariant under different historical conditions. The technology which all underdeveloped countries must adopt if they wish to achieve growth is the same, whatever their pre-existing structure, and all have in common the small size of their initial markets. If the analysis of their interaction, given the behaviour rules appropriate to a postulated private enterprise system, provides a coherent explanation of the processes under discussion, it is then possible to go from the abstract to the historically concrete, and to define the limits within which the general propositions are valid. Such empirical investigations are a separate task which goes beyond the scope of the present study.

While this essay has thus confined itself to theoretical discussion, a few words may perhaps be said about its subject-matter, the underdeveloped economy that tries to develop the capitalist way. The truth of the matter is that those cases which can be singled out of the enormous diversity displayed by the eighty-odd underdeveloped countries as more or less conforming to the model discussed in the literature are in reality very few. Fewer still have succeeded in attaining a significant degree of economic growth, in which the structure is sufficiently developed so that the trends operating in it can be easily discerned. Often, the picture is masked by the presence of dominant foreign interests, which in many of these countries account for a substantial proportion of total investments.[14] The decisions that affect the operations of such foreign firms, which in good part represent world-wide interests, depend substantially on factors that have little to do with the economies in which they operate.

The private-enterprise economy which grows autonomously, which the literature on economic development analyses theoretically and which it advocates on the policy level, is as rare for a theory which holds that the private enterprise system contains no internal barriers to growth as it is for the opposite view. In an essay on the economic development of Japan, Martin Bronfenbrenner cites that country, together with Israel and Puerto Rico, as exceptional cases of successful development under capitalism in recent times.[15] No detailed knowledge of these three countries is needed to realize how atypical they are. As a matter of fact, both the traditional view and that put forward here relate to a reality which is by and large still in an embryonic stage, and both rely therefore largely on *a priori* argument, at best supported by scattered indicators and fragmentary evidence. In part, the scarcity of empirical material is itself indicative of the inadequacy of the theory of development; but by the same token this is an argument for, not against, the relevance of further theoretical discussion.

Apart from relating the problems arising from a monopolistic structure to underdevelopment, the analysis itself builds with generally familiar blocks and is based upon a highly simplified model, in which the technical conditions have a pivotal role. The first chapter explores the implications of the two defining characteristics of underdevelopment on which the later analysis rests—market size and the structure of demand, and the concept of technological dependence and its effects on the competitive structure. Chapter 2 discusses the relationship between a monopolistic structure and the process of growth, the basic stability of such market structures, and the way in which they affect the directions and scope of investment. Chapter 3 analyses the process of growth under monopoly in the case of a pure *laissez-faire* system, and shows why it tends to stagnate. Chapter 4 takes up the question to what extent such tendencies can be counteracted through government intervention, and discusses the limits of such compensatory action. Chapter 5, finally, turns to the last important avenue of escape from stagnation—foreign trade. It tries to show that growth through trade is inhibited not only by powerful external obstacles, but that the forces generated from within the system also militate against it. Throughout, the central assumption of technological dependence makes it necessary to adopt the framework of an open economy; and the postulate that economic development is an articulate political goal requires that the political framework and its interaction with the economic system must to some extent be included in the analysis.

This essay raises the question of choice between alternative socio-economic systems. Before concluding this introduction it is only fair to state clearly that, like most other people, I also have my own predilections, and no attempt is made to hide them behind a cloak of non-committal presentation and spurious objectivity. Many people argue that alternative social systems—assuming that they are in fact a matter of free choice —are not, cannot, or ought not to be evaluated in terms of economic efficiency alone. I share this belief, but I do not share the view that any of the other criteria for choice of which one may think are, for a society as a whole, independent of the economic structure and its performance in the long run.

The lives of men, at least when they are considered as a group, their attitudes and the values which they come to cherish, are ultimately shaped by the ways in which and the success with which they go about the business of making provision for themselves. At the very least, those values must not be inconsistent with what men do to live together. I do not believe that individual freedom, for instance, however one may define it, can in the long run coexist with poverty; nor conversely, that its absence can in the long run coexist with wealth. A measure of material affluence for the broad mass of the people, and a well-founded hope for more to come in the future, must be considered at least as a *necessary* condition for all the other good things to which a society may aspire.

The underdeveloped countries must attain that minimum level of wealth quickly, lest they sink into even worse misery or lose the substance, if not the appearance, of the political independence that most of them have gained so recently. This is what makes economic development one of the central and most urgent problems of our time. In the concrete circumstances of our age, development cannot be left to the vagaries of the blind forces of the private enterprise system, even when they are buttressed by a good deal of public intervention. Nor do I believe much in "capitalist planning" which, to be effective within its own limitations, depends largely on the predominance of private monopolies—and least of all in the underdeveloped countries where I consider the private monopolistic structure to be one of the main roots of the trouble.

Growth depends on the technical and institutional forms in which a society's economic surplus is created, and which shape the manner in which it is utilized. Since control of the surplus and its mode of utilization depends upon the control of the stock of the means of production, I believe that a system of public ownership is the more rational order and has the greater growth potential. The extent and the specific forms of such public ownership, what it must comprise and how dispersed can be the power which it represents, must differ in each country according to its initial state of wealth, its rate of development over time, and its inherited traditions of social relationships. This implies also a degree of centralized planning that would vary inversely with the level of initial wealth and the rate of progress.

I purposely avoid the term "socialism"; by historical association it inevitably evokes the image of a concrete social system with a specific set of features, and leads all too often to the confounding of the unique and accidental with the general and essential. In the controversy about these matters it is easy to forget that freedom without the means of expressing it is meaningless, and that as means—and primarily those of material existence—become more plentiful, the need for control and restrictions diminishes. The events of the sixties may perhaps make this belief more acceptable than it could be in earlier decades.

But quite apart from such personal preferences, which follow from assigning a dominant place in the scheme of things to economic growth, one is certainly justified in asserting, as a matter of common observation, that economic development stands very high on the list of goals of the underdeveloped countries. Quite often, it seems to outrank any preference for a particular socio-economic structure and the various values and advantages that are alleged to be its exclusive attributes, so long as an alternative system—no less strange to the inherited traditions than industrial capitalism—holds out equal or better promise of rapid and continued growth. Economic efficiency as the chief criterion of choice is therefore defensible as a fair summary description of the "revealed preference" of many of the underdeveloped countries.

Having said this, I would add that I have tried to keep the analysis itself as free from the influence of my extra-economics as I could. Should I have failed unknowingly, at least I have openly stated the bias that may have crept into the discussion. Meanwhile I hope that the argument presented here, for the time being in speculative terms, will draw attention to an important aspect of economic development which has so far been neglected, and will be accepted as a contribution to the understanding of the process, from a viewpoint different from that of conventional development theory.

NOTES AND REFERENCES

1. KARL MARX, *Capital*, preface to the first German edition, Vol. I, Foreign Languages Publishing House, Moscow, pp. 8–9.
2. Much of the literature goes even further and advances one or the other variant of the "advantage of the late-comer thesis", according to which the latecomer will either make more rapid progress than earlier starters, or will even overtake the latter. See the interesting discussion of this problem in EDWARD AMES and NATHAN ROSENBERG, Changing technological leadership and industrial growth, *Economic Journal*, **73**, No. 289, March 1963, pp. 13–31, and the sources quoted there.
3. CELSO FURTADO, *Development and Underdevelopment*, University of California Press, Berkeley and Los Angeles, 1964, pp. 2 and 129.
4. W. ARTHUR LEWIS, *Economic Development with Unlimited Supplies of Labour*, The Manchester School, May 1954, reprinted in A. N. AGARWALA and S. P. SINGH (eds.), *The Economics of Underdevelopment*, Oxford University Press, New York, 1963, p. 401.

5. HARVEY LEIBENSTEIN, *Economic Backwardness and Economic Growth*, John Wiley & Sons, New York, 1957, p. 6.
6. ALBERT O. HIRSCHMAN, *The Strategy of Economic Development*, Yale University Press, New Haven, 1958, p. 1.
7. PAUL A. BARAN, *On the Political Economy of Backwardness*, Manchester School, January 1952, reprinted in AGARWALA and SINGH, *op. cit.*, pp. 76–78, and *The Political Economy of Growth*, Monthly Review Press, New York, 1957, p. 162. See also pp. 151 ff.
8. JOAN ROBINSON, *The Rate of Interest*, Macmillan & Co., London, 1952, p. 161.
9. WILLIAM FELLNER, *Competition Among the Few*, Alfred Knopf, New York, 1949, p. vi.
10. J. STEINDL, *Maturity and Stagnation in American Capitalism*, Basil Blackwell, Oxford 1952.
11. PAOLO SYLOS-LABINI, *Oligopoly and Technical Progress*, Harvard University Press, Cambridge (Mass.), 1962, Part III.
12. J. R. HICKS, *Value and Capital*, Oxford University Press, London, 2nd ed., 1946, pp. 83–84.
13. CELSO FURTADO, *op. cit.*, p. 129.
14. See, for example, *Foreign Capital in Latin America*, United Nations, New York, 1955, and KEITH B. GRIFFIN, Reflections on Latin American development, *Oxford Economic Papers*, **18**, No. 1, March 1966, p. 2.
15. MARTIN BRONFENBRENNER, Some lessons of Japan's economic development, 1853–1938, *Pacific Affairs*, **34**, No. 1, Spring 1961, pp. 26–27.

CHAPTER 1

UNDERDEVELOPMENT, MARKET SIZE, AND TECHNOLOGICAL DEPENDENCE

UNDERDEVELOPMENT has many facets, and the literature on the subject abounds with descriptions of its various attributes.* In its most immediate and straightforward sense most people understand it as synonymous with material poverty, as measured by a low *per capita* income, and as a lack of capacity to break out of stagnation. Viewed from the supply side it is, according to Celso Furtado's definition, "a state of factor unbalance reflecting a lack of adjustment between the availability of factors and the technology of their use, so that it is impossible to achieve full utilization of both capital and labour simultaneously";[1] it denotes that there exists an unutilized "set of possibilities of achievement".[2]

Material poverty, however, may mean many things even in the everyday sense of the term. For our present purpose we are interested in those of its aspects which represent that set of initial conditions from which all economic growth must start. Three of these are central to our analysis, and will be taken up in that order: the existence of a social goal of economic growth, the framework for growth afforded by the initial size of markets, and the technical incapacity to produce the capital goods required for modern technology. The latter, which makes development almost wholly dependent on imports of capital goods, is what we mean by "Technological Dependence".

---

* In a list compiled by Harvey Leibenstein, the number of economic and technological attributes alone of underdevelopment which are most frequently mentioned in the literature, runs to no less than twenty-five.[3]

16

DEVELOPMENT AS A POLITICAL GOAL

The notion of underdevelopment implies more than appears at first sight, for in addition to being a descriptive statement of fact it also has a distinctly evaluative connotation—it implies that the state so termed is undesirable. It always refers to a political entity, to a nation, and when a country describes itself as underdeveloped, it articulates a collective economic goal. The point in making this distinction is of course not for the sake of mere terminological refinement, but to emphasize an aspect which is all too often overlooked in conventional theory with its predilection for thinking in terms of individuals and their welfare, rather than in terms of nations—namely, that the term underdevelopment has a clear *political* content, both from the viewpoint of how it is regarded within a given country, and from the viewpoint of one nation compared with another.

In most current development theory there is an implicit assumption that whenever we speak of underdeveloped versus developed countries, we refer to a family of nations, or rather to collections of individuals called nations, which existed from time immemorial, and some of which somehow succeeded in "taking off" to accelerated growth while others remained backward until modern communications enabled them to compare their poverty with the riches of the advanced countries and aroused their discontent, whereupon they "decided" to set themselves the goal of economic development.

This largely fictitious image of history and reality obscures much of the real meaning of the term underdevelopment. The areas and populations which nowadays make up the underdeveloped countries have, of course, always been poor, and sometimes poorer than they are now; but they have not somehow just recently awakened from a state of blissful or miserable isolation from the rest of the world which "took off" and passed them by, but have for ages been an integral part of the worldwide economic system established and dominated by the advanced countries—and until some two decades ago mostly under the direct political rule of the latter. It is only the attainment of national sovereignty that reveals openly the disparity between the wealth of the advanced countries and the poverty of their periphery, and only in the process of attaining that national independence was the discontent with that poverty enunciated as a political goal.

The problem of underdevelopment thus has an essentially political content; within each country, it stands for a certain set of demands upon the given social structure, and versus other countries it is cast in a nationalist mold. In the latter respect there has been a drastic change in the world in the last decade and a half. Much of the current thinking about economic development is still dominated by the reality that stood before the eyes of theorists and policy-makers up to the early fifties, which was primarily that of the larger Latin American countries and those Asian countries which had by then achieved national independence. The dissolution of the former colonial empires has since then wrought a profound structural change in the world. For although it remains true that one country, India, is equal, in terms of the number of individuals whose welfare is involved, to the whole of Africa and Latin America combined, this is not how the problem of underdevelopment presents itself in the political reality of the world. There, it is nations rather than individuals that count.

The emergence of a large number of new independent countries has fundamentally changed the characteristics of the "typical" underdeveloped country. The most obvious change, compared with the situation up to the end of World War II and shortly afterwards, is that most of the countries that have since then achieved independence are very small in terms of population, and often also in terms of territory and resource potential. The size distribution shown in Table I.1 illustrates the changes that have taken place since 1950—the average size of the underdeveloped countries is two-thirds smaller, and the median country is now only about half as large as fifteen years ago. Among the member states of the United Nations, the number of underdeveloped countries (not counting the socialist countries and the poorer countries of Europe) has grown from forty-two in 1950 to eighty-five in 1965, and instead of fifteen countries with populations of less than five million people (on the basis of their 1965 populations) there are now forty-five such small countries—more than half of all underdeveloped countries, and nearly two-fifths of all countries.

Many of these countries had formerly belonged to what might

TABLE I.1. *Frequency Distribution of Underdeveloped Countries,*[a] *Member States of the United Nations, in 1950 and 1965, by Population in 1965.*

Size class	Number of countries		Total population in 1965, millions	
	1950	1965	1950	1965
0– 5 millions	15	45	38	115
5–10 ,,	8	15	55	108
10–15 ,,	4	8	45	93
15–20 ,,	2	3	33	49
20–30 ,,	5	5	122	122
30–50 ,,	4	4	142	142
50–100 ,,	1	2	81	138
over 100 ,,	3	3	677	677
Total, all countries	42	85	1193	1444
Median	—	—	9	5
Arithmetic mean			28	17
Geometric mean			9	5

Source: *Statistical Yearbooks* of the United Nations.
[a] Excluding the socialist countries and the less developed countries of Europe.

be called the backwaters of the colonial empires, from which the former rulers had extracted little that required any significant participation by the indigenous population, and in which they had invested even less. As a consequence, these countries have had even less opportunity to benefit from that limited adsorption of modern skills, knowledge, techniques and institutions, and from that small measure of industrialization and progress which was sometimes the by-product of colonialism in some of the older underdeveloped countries. Our subsequent analysis will show that the obstacles to growth which these countries encounter tend to be even higher in the case of the newer and generally smaller countries. The important point to note here is that on the international plane, the political goal and claim for development of each of these countries is, in principle, equal, and it is in these terms that the development problem presents itself to the world in general.

From the viewpoint of the claims upon the performance of the social structure which the acceptance of a goal of growth represents within each country, that goal provides a criterion by which the existing socio-economic system is judged. This raises a difficult problem for orthodox economic doctrine and its policy recommendations, for that doctrine was hardly ever called upon to question its basic framework until it was confronted by the problem of underdevelopment. On the contrary, its entire conceptual apparatus is designed to take the private-enterprise framework and its behaviour patterns as given and not, so to say, stand outside it and judge its performance. It is perhaps not superfluous to devote a few more passages to this political aspect of underdevelopment and its implications, if only because most conventional theory excludes the political framework from its considerations.

The underdeveloped countries generally emerge as politically sovereign nations as a result of more or less severe struggles with the former colonialist powers. Even where there was no outright political domination, for example in Latin America or in Iran, the new goal of economic progress evolved through conflicts in which the same colonial powers were deeply involved. It is therefore not surprising that in these countries capitalism, far from being viewed as that benign and growth-promoting system depicted in economic doctrine which all nations are supposedly equally free to adopt and enjoy, should more often be identified with colonialism, and that it should be held responsible for their present backwardness. What John P. Lewis says of India is probably true for many parts of the under-developed world: "In India 'capitalism' is a bad word because it has historically been linked to colonialism."[4] There is therefore, to say the least, much less readiness to accept at face value the merits of an idealized version of private enterprise, of which these countries have no historical experience but which, on the contrary, usually appeared to them in quite a different guise.

One would therefore not have been surprised to find the private enterprise system viewed with a good deal of scepticism even if it had been the sole contender for the role of the growth-promoting social system. This, however, is no longer so. Capitalism is being challenged, at least where economic growth is concerned, by socialism—not as an abstract scheme, but as a concrete reality which is able to offer an alternative partial or complete model. The private enterprise system is thus challenged to stand up and be measured in terms of its long-run growth potential. This poses problems for economic theory and practice alike that have little precedent in the development of the advanced countries.

In the developed countries, the present economic structure is the result of a secular process in which the various elements of the entire social system became adapted to each other. Social and individual aspirations, legal and political institutions, in fact the whole social fabric, came in the course of centuries to correspond with the underlying productive system in such a way as to be in accord, at least in their major aspects, with the system's "achievement possibilities". The new nations, by contrast, appear upon the world stage as political structures which reflect not their *present* economic and social make-up, but rather one which is essentially foreign, and to which they can as yet only aspire—often as a fairly distant goal. The very political systems of these countries are largely adoptive and imitative rather than endogenously evolved, and the disparities between them and the underlying economic structure set up stresses in which the one or the other may easily give way.

People in the new countries often associated the colonial and imperialist subjection from which they emerge with their poverty and backwardness. The alleviation of that poverty therefore becomes the primary task—indeed, almost the *raison d'être*—of national independence. Even highly autocratic governments must pay at least some heed to such popular demands for better living standards, and must assuage at least the worst ills of backwardness, if only out of fear for the stability of their rule.*

This creates a situation in which the political goal of economic development is logically and historically prior to individual motivations. The former are in no sense the sum total of the latter but, on the contrary, it is the collective goal that circumscribes the economic aspirations of individuals, conditions the forms in which they are expressed, and even brings them forth. At the stage of national emergence the pattern, the structure, and the rate of economic development are in the proximate sense determined by the political system, and not vice versa.

Economic development as the material concomitant of political independence can thus hardly be understood adequately in terms of a theory that views it as resulting more or less automatically from the random action of individuals who pursue their own ends, action that will come forth of itself if only the necessary conditions for it are created. Even in the advanced countries, of course, the business of stability and growth has everywhere become far too important to be left to private businessmen; it has become a political objective of first-rank importance. Few economists would nowadays restrict the role of the State to that of a mere umpire, and be content to leave growth to come about of itself through the interaction of individual preferences. But equally, few have abandoned the idea that whatever growth will be achieved, must come about through the "animal spirits" of private entrepreneurs. Hence much of the discussion in the literature on development about the causes of the lack of a "proper entrepreneurial atmosphere", a "favourable business climate" in the underdeveloped countries, and about the ways to create it.

* The land reform and other measures of economic development, introduced by the Shah of Iran after the Mossadegh government was ousted and he was reinstated in 1953, are a case in point. Another example is the development policy followed in the 1950's by the government of Fulgencio Batista in Cuba. These examples could easily be multiplied.

Whatever may be the truth in the case of the advanced countries, for the underdeveloped countries one can certainly defend the proposition that the State as such has its own preference function, which cannot simply be deduced from the preference functions of individuals as usually conceived. [5] This is not to say that the State is independent of the social and economic groups and classes which it represents, and of the goals which their members hold as individuals. What is meant is that a dual set of goals tends to develop even where the State represents only a narrow social class; and that two possible sets of objectives—for instance, that of a certain minimal rate of growth, and that of creating and maintaining the conditions which, from the viewpoint of the dominant class, may be the most favourable for the private benefit of its members—may become so contradictory that a collective choice may have to be made between them.

Such a dual system of preferences presents the possibility of choice. It is particularly important in the early stage of development, before the social structure has hardened into forms which predetermine the path which the country is free to follow subsequently. At an early stage of development it is still much easier to shape the pattern of development, without having to break down existing social, political, and economic structures in violent upheavals. The very progress of development in one or the other direction, however, narrows the choice open to society as a whole.

The possibility of social transformation is therefore inherent in the existence of a generally accepted political goal of economic growth, as long as it has not become superseded by the particular goals of vested interest groups. While it remains alive among wide strata of the population, it acts as a check on particularistic goals and interests, and sets the lower limit of the progress that is politically acceptable.

POVERTY AND MARKET SIZE

The political goal of growth sets the lower limits that must be attained; the potentialities given by the available technology together with the initial level of income, that is to say, broadly speaking, by the extent of the market, determine the upper bounds of the development possibilities open to a country. From the statement that an economy is poor it follows tautologically that its market is small, and that narrow limits are thereby set to the extent to which modern techniques, which generally involve large-scale production or a high degree of specialization, can be applied initially. This seems so self-evident that the implications are rarely thought worthy of detailed discussion. The emphasis put in this book on the contradictions arising from the unavoidable application of a given (generally large-scale) technology to limited markets makes it useful to look a little more closely at the problem of the extent of the markets, if only to illustrate the extent of the disparities that exist in this regard between the developed and the underdeveloped countries.

The vast differences between the levels of income in the developed and the underdeveloped countries are well known and need not be described again here in detail. A few summary data are cited in Table I.2. Of the many familiar reservations that can be made with respect to such data perhaps only one that is of relevance for this study may be singled out: The national accounts estimates impute money values to the output produced by the subsistence sectors, and thus create a grossly exaggerated impression of the real size of the market economy in the underdeveloped countries. The extent of the money demand for goods is therefore in reality much smaller than the national income data would suggest. The field of expansion for modern industry which the initial demand affords is thus much narrower than is indicated by comparisons of national income.

In addition to this crude quantitative disparity between the developed and underdeveloped countries there are also highly important qualitative differences, for material poverty also has far-reaching implications for the composition of income in terms of specific goods. It is a generally accepted empirical observation that consumers' wants follow a hierarchical order, that the marginal propensity to consume a specific good falls with rising income. This behaviour constant, known as Engel's law, has the result that variations in levels of income express themselves only partially as differences in the quantities consumed of similar goods. Their main effect is to alter the composition of the consumption basket. This has been observed not

	Gross national product		Population (thousands)	Share in world total, per cent		Index of inequality[a]
	Per capita, in dollars	Total, in million dollars		GNP	population	
A. Levels of per capita GNP: $						
0– 100	73	100,597	1,387,324	8·7	49·7	18
101– 300	198	94,588	477,343	8·2	17·1	48
301– 600	489	245,446	501,641	21·3	18·0	118
601–1200	971	204,177	210,247	17·7	7·5	235
over 1200	2387	509,819	213,578	44·2	7·7	577
B. Regional distribution:						
AMERICA: U.S.A. and Canada	2521	475,561	188,609	41·2	6·8	609
Rest of America	310	59,212	191,082	5·1	6·8	75
OCEANIA: Australia and New Zealand	1315	15,673	11,921	1·4	0·4	318
Rest of Oceania	45	126	2,790	n.	n.	11
EUROPE: Non-socialist countries	826	247,800	299,934	21·5	10·7	200
Socialist countries[b]	549	173,425	316,032	15·0	11·3	133
ASIA: Middle East[c]	178	17,411	97,848	1·5	3·5	43
Rest of Asia, non-socialist	116	94,248	814,390	8·2	29·2	28
Rest, socialist countries	72	47,761	658,823	4·1	23·6	17
AFRICA: All countries	112	23,410	208,694	2·0	7·5	27
C. World total:	414	1,154,628	2,790,133	100·0	100·0	100·0

[a] *Per capita* income (GNP) as a percentage of world average GNP.
[b] Including the whole of the U.S.S.R.   [c] Including the United Arab Republic.
Source: MIKOTO USUI and E. E. HAGEN, *World Income 1957*, Massachusetts Institute of Technology, Cambridge (Mass.), 1959 (mimeographed).

only as the normal pattern of consumers' behaviour within a given country, but a similar picture has been shown also by comparisons of consumers' expenditures in different countries with different levels of income.[6]

The statistical problems involved in these researches do not concern us here; the broad picture that emerges confirms what common sense suggests: that the difference between poverty and wealth is one of kind as well as quantity, and that the higher the income, the greater is the diversification of demand. This is true both for individuals in a given country and for aggregate consumption in different countries. The higher the income, the wider is the range of goods consumed, and the satisfaction of the basic necessities, which are similar in the different countries, is also increasingly shifted to more refined, more highly processed goods. In the lower income groups and in the poorer countries the budget share of food, for instance, is therefore high and that of manufactured goods and various services is low, and within these broad groups the simpler products are preponderant.

These consequences of poverty for the composition of demand imply that the markets for those categories of goods which are typically produced by advanced industrial methods, and which therefore represent the margin of growth, are in fact much narrower than the mere comparison of income levels would indicate. The estimates of apparent consumption of manufactured goods given in Table I.3 may perhaps serve as a crude approximation to the disparities in the size of the domestic markets for manufactured goods between the developed and the underdeveloped countries.

Even though the data of this table include imports of various commodities, such as a wide range of capital goods, that cannot feasibly be produced in the underdeveloped countries, and thus have an upward bias, they illustrate the fact that even the markets of the more populous underdeveloped countries are exceedingly small by comparison with the advanced countries. Pakistan, with a population approximately equal to that of Japan, has a market for manufactured goods which is barely one-thirtieth as large. Brazil, a relatively developed country, has a market which is about half as large as that of the Netherlands, although her population is nearly six times as big. India,

TABLE 1.3. *Apparent Consumption of Manufactured Goods,*ᵃ *Selected Countries, 1958 (millions of U.S. dollars)*

Country	Population (thousands)	Gross value of production	Imports	Exportsᵇ	Apparent consumption of manufactured goods	
					Total	Per capita
Developed countries						
Australia	9846	10,191	1682	1430	10,443	1060
Denmark (1960)	4515	3819	1477	1176	4120	912
Japan	91,760	32,488	2051	2818	31,721	346
Netherlands	11,186	12,351	2964	2110	13,205	1180
United Kingdom	51,842	82,301	7578	8636	81,243	1567
United States (1961)	183,756	369,994	13,897	18,837	365,054	1986
Underdeveloped countries						
Argentina (1954)	18,611	3640	889	546	3983	214
Brazil	62,725	5609	1092	353	6348	101
Colombia	13,522	1550	349	91	1808	133
India	397,540	3618	1430	807	4241	11
Israel	1997	1093	351	79	1365	683
Mexico (1955)	30,015	6132	791	524	6399	213
Morocco	10,330	568	392	265	695	67
Pakistan	89,136	803	230	60	973	11
Philippines	24,010	815	553	349	1019	42
Thailand	21,474	772	370	68	1074	50
Tunisia	4836	112	148	145	115	24

ᵃ Domestic production plus imports, minus exports.
ᵇ Excluding tea, unroasted coffee, cocoa beans and butter, and rice.
Sources: United Nations, *Statistical Yearbook 1964, Yearbook of International Trade Statistics, Demographic Yearbook, and Yearbook of National Accounts Statistics 1964.*

with all her vastness, has a market about as large as that of Denmark, a nation with slightly more than 1 per cent of India's population.

The size of the markets indicated by these figures is, of course, no rigid magnitude, even initially. In many underdeveloped countries the substitution of products of modern industry for those of the traditional artisanate and for imports can still go further, often substantially so. Nevertheless, the initial markets would clearly remain very limited even if an additional margin of expansion were taken into account, and the disparities between the developed and the underdeveloped countries are probably larger the further away we go from the basic necessities of life to the more highly processed commodities.

In addition, there are forces at work which make for the further fragmentation of these narrow initial markets. The well-known "demonstration effect" that emanates from the advanced countries not only creates a pressure for a higher *absolute* level of living, but modifies also the *specific ways* in which people wish to satisfy their traditional wants. Demand tends to become more diversified even without a rise in income, and if the traditional goods are to be replaced by new products, it will be a more varied collection of such goods that will be demanded. This has the result that from the point of view of the opportunities which the initially small market presents for mass production methods, it tends to become further broken up into proportionately even smaller markets for specific goods.

The diversification of potential demand that occurs as a result of the demonstration effect thus has a two-fold consequence. First, it specifies the types of industries that can be set up, and sets the limits to the choice of products that is acceptable within the given structure of domestic demand.* This is particularly obvious in the case of import substitution, where the structure of demand has been established by the previous imports, and the possibilities of deviations in terms of quality, design, or function are limited.[7] Secondly, it establishes the absolute size of the markets for particular commodities, and thereby

---

* The question to what extent development is limited by the structure and scale of the domestic market, and to what extent it can be oriented towards exports, must be deferred for the time being. At this stage of the discussion, the argument, of course, refers only to the domestic market.

determines the scale at which new industries can operate initially. This scale will evidently be much smaller than in the advanced countries.

TECHNOLOGICAL DEPENDENCE AND SCALE OF PRODUCTION

The obverse of the deficiency of real demand in the underdeveloped countries is, on the supply side, their low capacity to produce. This is the familiar impasse of underdevelopment, its "low-level equilibrium trap".[8] Much, if not indeed all, of development theory is in the last resort about the ways in which this trap might be sprung.

The outside observer often finds some aspects of the stagnation in which the underdeveloped countries are caught almost incomprehensible. Even a layman, armed with no more than an everyday knowledge of Western civilization and technique, can easily point out many glaringly obvious possibilities for raising productivity. Some of these would seem to require no more than the simplest of means, and hardly any real capital. The failure to exploit them therefore appears to be utterly irrational, and if it can be explained at all, it seems necessary to fall back on psychological and institutional factors.

When this approach is not adopted, and as in this essay, the analysis starts by taking economic rationality as given, it generally concentrates on capital formation as the crucial growth-determining factor. But like other aspects of the development problem, capital formation also cannot be discussed in terms which are simply taken over from the reality of the advanced countries. It is not enough to consider the quantitative aspect of the overall allocation of income between consumption and savings, or that of the equalization of intended saving with intended investment. The discussion of the factors involved in mobilizing savings and increasing the formation of real capital is inadequate, for capital formation also has a *physical–technical* aspect. In the advanced countries it may be permissible to take this for granted, but not so in the underdeveloped countries. This aspect relates, on the one hand, to the structural interrelationships of the different parts of the productive structure and, on the other hand, to the techniques at its disposal.

The structural interrelationships of the growth process, which occupy a central place only in the Marxian derivative of classical growth theory, have seen a partial revival in modern economics, in the linear programming and input–output approaches to analysis and planning, and also in post-Keynesian growth theory. In these modern theories, however, the technical structure of the economic system is not accorded a causal role, but serves mainly as a technique for dealing with more or less disaggregated partial or general equilibrium models. It is not a central tool in the analysis of the growth process itself, and the ability of the system to effect inter-sectoral adjustments in any direction, in response to price signals and other overall parametric changes, is taken to be unrestricted by technical factors.[9]

Underdevelopment, however, is characterized by a *structural incapacity to produce the capital goods required for growth*, for as Celso Furtado has pointed out, development is not the endogenous transformation of a preindustrial economy, but the implantation of an accelerated growth process through the adoption of foreign techniques.[10] These techniques are embodied in physical capital goods which cannot be produced domestically. This incapacity is what is meant by the term "Technological Dependence" in the title of this study. It has two major consequences. First, because it consists necessarily of the imitation of techniques evolved in the advanced economies with their vastly larger markets, it is a decisive determinant of the competitive structure. And secondly, because the needed capital goods must be imported, it tends to create a constant insufficiency of effective demand through the leakage of domestic savings into imports of producers' goods.*

The importance of real capital formation, in the technical–physical sense, becomes evident as soon as one considers the widely observed phenomenon that the savings ratio as such is in many underdeveloped countries. It is often quite substantial therefore not necessarily the absence of an economic surplus as such that chokes off growth, but the structural inability to convert these savings into investments. Hence the familiar phenomena of conspicuous consumption, of hoarding, of capital flight,

* This assumes, of course, that the level of exports is independent of the level of overall investment. See also footnote on page 28.

and of various other forms of sterilization of the surplus generated by the economy. Much of this unproductive disposition of potential savings must be interpreted as a rational response to the absence of more attractive and productive alternatives, which results from the characteristics of the technical structure of the existing productive system. [11]

Some theories of development have, as already mentioned, seized upon these surface manifestations of the inability to produce growth, and have interpreted them in institutional, sociological, or psychological terms. Such explanations may sometimes be more or less valid in their own right, but economic theory is hardly particularly competent to deal with them. At best, economic theory can issue a call for help to the other social disciplines, which are as likely as not to be equally hard-pressed for satisfactory answers. It seems a more fruitful approach to retain the time-honoured assumptions of market rationality, and to take a closer look at the objectively given determinants of the ability to convert savings into productive capacity. This is neither more nor less than the technical capacity for self-sustained growth, and as Marx observed long ago, the use that can be made of the economic surplus depends on the material structure of the productive system. [12]

In the imaginary world of a closed economy, without market imperfections and with given savings, the rise in output would be limited only by the rate of technical progress. In the classical model each entrepreneur, facing given prices for factors and goods, must innovate to increase his profits. Since all entrepreneurs try to do the same thing, the constant pursuit of profit and its instrument, innovation, becomes compulsory for each; those who fail are driven to the wall, and others take their place. [13] As long as the system remains competitive in the classical sense, that is to say as long as there are no barriers to entry, the only limits to innovation for the individual firm are the rate of advance of technical knowledge and, at any given time, the amount of resources over which it can obtain command.

There is no need to go here over the familiar ground of the classical model except to note that, as innovation becomes diffused through the system, the typical size of plant tends to increase,* and at the same time, competition ensures that the fruits of rising productivity are distributed in the form of higher real incomes. Thus the expansion of the market, in real terms, parallels the increase in the scales of output of individual plants, leaving the competitive structure largely unaffected.

This rise in the scale of output with the widening of the market, which would occur even if no firms were to grow at the expense of others, is further accentuated by concentration. As some firms innovate and increase their scale of output, their temporary advantage over competitors will often become permanent and irreversible, and they will attain a size which accounts for a significant share of the industry. Barriers to entry will appear, and with the decline of competition, the rise of productivity will still depend on technical progress, but the rate of innovation, the rate at which new inventions are in fact introduced, will now become, for each firm, a function of the size of its own market, of which it has become aware by virtue of its large share in it.

Whether we take the expansion of the market or the rate of technical progress as the independent variable, there will be a tendency for the scales of output typical for an industry to correspond to the size of its market. The main difference, in terms of historical development, is that in the advanced countries, in which concentration has taken place, this parallelism exists at a much higher level of output than in the mythical competitive economy of the early nineteenth century. Nowadays, vast markets go together with immense plants and even larger firms and complexes of interlocked firms. It is in these that the bulk of all output and employment originates, and they are the locus of the demand for new capital

---

* It is, of course, the same thing to say that an innovation is factor-saving for a given output as that it is output-increasing for a given quantity of factors. If all factors are taken to be perfectly divisible, then there is no *theoretical* necessity for plant size to increase. The factors set free by innovation could move into another industry. In reality, however, technical progress is almost invariably bound up with an increase in the scale of plant, and in so far as it relates to organization, also of the firm. In addition, there are economies of scale, which are conceptually distinct from technical advance, although in practice they are difficult to separate. Both together produce a trend of rising scale even if, with a widening market, the industry remains competitive.

goods and determine the scale of production to which these capital goods are geared.

The point which must be borne in mind is that technical progress is not scientific knowledge in the abstract, nor even engineering know-how as such. As an economic category, it is scientific and technical knowledge which is embodied in tangible producers' goods, primarily in *machines*, that counts for most purposes, and the technical and demand conditions that determine their physical characteristics.*

These machines are produced by capitalists, like any other goods, and are therefore adapted to the requirements of the markets in which they are sold. With the secular expansion of markets and scales of production, the plant and equipment comes to be designed for the large-scale dimensions of its users— the producers of the next stage of fabrication. Although older techniques, designed for a smaller scale of output, may for a while coexist with the newer, their reproduction ceases as old equipment wears out, and demand for both replacement and net investment shifts to more modern plant. The design of the capital goods currently produced thus becomes increasingly adapted to the demand for the latest technical methods and scales of production. Older techniques gradually fall into oblivion and, after a lapse of time which may not be much greater than the normal lifetime of the equipment, become extinct.[14]

Nor is this process simply a passive compliance of equipment producers with the demand from its users. Their own competitive advantage lies in being able to offer goods which, at constant cost to their customers, will yield them a greater value —a larger physical output. In short, the techniques and scales of production appropriate to earlier stages of industrial development—sometimes no more remote than twenty or thirty years ago—pass out of existence as part of the operative current stock of knowledge and practical arts. Producers no longer make the equipment, engineers no longer know the techniques, and workmen no longer have the skills for the older processes.

* There are, of course, forms of technical knowledge which are "disembodied", but these are relatively unimportant in the underdeveloped countries, or are of a type that already presupposes the existence of a productive apparatus capable of utilizing them. For all practical purposes, technical progress and knowledge can be considered as incorporated in plant and equipment.

History has wrought a tremendous gap between the present techniques of production in the industrialized countries and those appropriate to markets of a size that may perhaps have existed in Europe a hundred, or possibly even 200 years ago.* There is abundant evidence for this intuitively obvious development, but its implications for the problem of development have largely been overlooked. Victor S. Clark's voluminous *History of Manufactures in the United States*,[15] for example, contains a wealth of material which illustrates the vast increase in the scale of output in the first half of the nineteenth century, even before the revolution in land and sea transportation during the second and third quarters of the last century. The railway and the ocean-going steamship not only accelerated this process by drawing together formerly separate markets, but they were also a prime factor in the development of the production of machinery as a specialized industry.

It is not often remembered in the literature on economic development that the specialized production of machinery is a relatively late phenomenon, and that in the early stages of industrialization of today's advanced countries the producers of final commodities built their own machines, in their own workshops, to their own designs, and in accordance with the requirements of their production of the final goods. In the United States, for example, we are told by Nathan Rosenberg that the "growth of independent machinery-producing firms occurred in a continuing sequence of stages roughly between the years 1840–1880".[17] He adds that this growth reflects the increase in the extent of the market for machines—itself a function of the size of the market for the final goods produced by them—and that, in addition to the accretion of technical skills which accompanied the process, there emerged eventually "a pattern of product specialization by machine-producing firms which

---

* The following rough comparisons may illustrate this point. The gross national product of the United Kingdom grew approximately fourfold during the nineteenth century, and rose by another two-thirds until 1952. Since 1800 the total increase was thus about six and a half times. This would make her gross national product, in constant values, nearly twice as big in 1800 as that of Pakistan or Turkey in 1953, about three times that of Egypt, Chile, Colombia or Venezuela, about a third larger than that of Brazil, a fifth larger than that of Mexico, and about comparable to that of Argentina in 1953.[16]

was closely geared to accommodating the requirements of machine users". One might add that it had probably much to do with shaping those very requirements, for the specialization of machine production made the directions of technical progress in the production of final goods dependent upon the advances achieved in the former.

The immense and continual advance of technology since the Industrial Revolution, which constantly reduced the ratio of volume and weight to power and speed of machines, further increased the effective size of the market by reducing the costs of transportation per unit of capacity, thus reinforcing the improvements in the means of transportation themselves, until today the entire world has been drawn together into one market for capital goods, which is dominated by three industrial countries—the United States, Western Germany and Great Britain, who account for some 70 per cent of total world exports of capital goods.[18] The displacement of bulky, low-power machines by smaller and more powerful prime movers, the progress in precision engineering which constantly reduced the weight and bulk of machines, the development of interchangeable-part production which made it possible to transport knocked-down equipment and to reassemble it on the spot (and which reduced the costs of maintenance), together with the simultaneous improvements in land and sea transportation, both increased the specialization of machine production and accelerated its further progress.[19]*

The speed of these technical advances and their importance has not declined, and progress continues along the same lines. Once this specialization has taken place, the diffusion of techniques becomes more rapid because they are now incorporated

---

* The magnitude of the changes that occurred in the bulk and weight of machines may perhaps be illustrated by the following example—one out of many—given by Clark of the size of machines used in the middle of the last century: "The large low-pressure engines had enormous cylinders. Those in a Fall River boat, built in 1854, were nearly 9 feet in diameter and 14 feet long. A machine-shop in Philadelphia was equipped to bore castings 16 feet in diameter and 18 feet long. Some blowing engines built at that city for coal mines had a 10-foot stroke and their walking-beams were supported on cast-iron pillars 30 feet high. The Corliss Engine Works, at Providence, made geared fly-wheels 25 feet in diameter, that weighed 32 tons when turned, finished, and cogged."[20]

in mobile goods rather than dependent on largely immobile factors such as the skills needed for custom-built equipment. But by the same token, the producers of final goods have become completely dependent upon the suppliers of the equipment they require. The latter, in fact, to a large extent set the pace and direction of the technical progress of the former.

Within a unified national market, these developments were thus a powerful engine of progress; in the theory of international trade, which knows no boundaries except as impediments to factor mobility, they are still so regarded. But when the units of reference are separate national entities, this specialization—which is the defining characteristic and exclusive province of the advanced countries—implies a dependence which, far from promoting the autonomous development of the underdeveloped countries, militates against it. Even if they had the necessary markets and the skills to develop their own production of equipment, the combined effects of the developments described above would deprive them of the protection of transport costs in the production of machinery, since by comparison with final goods, the freight costs as a proportion of final value are lowest for this class of commodities.[21] The first-comers in this field thus have an advantage on this count alone.

This trend of rising scales of output, and the concomitant specialization, has not abated in the more recent past. Technical progress continues to reduce the bulk and to increase the speed and precision of machines, at the same time as it increases its degree of specialization, in correspondence with the requirements and opportunities of constantly expanding scales of production of the goods produced by these machines. Developments such as modular engineering, numerical control, miniaturization and micro-electronics, the introduction of continuous-flow and automated processes in more and more branches of production are all based upon the possibility of catering to ever-larger markets and are geared to rising scales of output. From time to time, it is true, there is a technical breakthrough which reduces the scale of the minimum productive unit. The development of continuous steel casting and, most recently, of new techniques of copper casting, are cases in point. After a century of constantly rising size of plant, the new techniques reduced the size of the smallest indivisible unit by a factor of ten. But soon after such a breakthrough the trend of increasing scale usually re-establishes itself, and plant size begins to grow once more on the basis of the new technique. The more usual case is that a new technical development involves a higher degree of specialization, and thus requires larger and continuous runs of production.

A recent statistical study of the rise of average production scales in American manufacturing industry by Saul S. Sands[22] shows that between 1904 and 1947 the average quinquennial growth rate for manufacturing industry as a whole was 15·4 per cent; the average scale of output, in physical terms, was nearly three and a half times as large in 1947 as in 1904. In a sample of forty-six industries for which data were available for the whole period, the highest five-yearly increase was 89 per cent, and only one industry showed a decline. For thirty-five other industries, for which data were available only for a shorter time span, the highest growth rate was 135 per cent, and only three industries showed a fall in average scale of establishment. Sands' results are reproduced in Appendix Table I/A; he rightly contests the view expressed by John M. Blair, that the new techniques invented since World War I permit a reduction of the largest indivisible factor of production and thus a smaller optimal size of plant.[23]

The interrelationships between the size of markets, technical progress, the degree of specialization, and the scales of output to which equipment is geared involve many complex issues, and have important implications for the process of growth which lie outside the scope of the present analysis.[24] Whatever the ultimate causes may be, the underdeveloped countries depend for their growth on the techniques of the advanced countries, and the consequences of the scales of capacity determined in the latter for the competitive structure in the former are immediately obvious: their narrow markets cannot sustain more than a few firms in each line of production. The available technology puts a floor under the size of almost any plant that still represents a significant shift from the traditional to modern techniques of production. For the moment, we must defer the question whether the range of choice between different scales of plant that this technology allows is wide enough to make the adoption of modern techniques compatible with the maintenance of a competitive structure. First, we must take a look at the closely related problem of economies of scale, which will become especially important with respect to foreign trade, to which we shall turn in Chapter 5.

ECONOMIES OF SCALE AND COMPETITIVE STRUCTURE

Much of the general economic literature, including that on the monopoly problem, draws no clear distinction between economies of scale in the strict sense, that is to say rises in output which are greater that the increase in qualitatively unchanged factor inputs, and rises in productivity which for reasons of indivisibility involve a larger scale. Both are usually subsumed under the term "economies of scale", and in what follows we shall use the same rather loose terminology.

The existence of economies of scale in this sense is often taken for granted as a matter of common knowledge, since it has always been part of the almost self-evident empirical generalizations of economic theory.[25] Yet surprisingly, the admission that economies of scale are a general phenomenon continues to meet with much reluctance—perhaps because of the danger which their implications have for most of established theory—so that the verdict is sometimes "not proven",[26] and some writers even define them away altogether.[28]

The problem has in recent years received renewed attention in connexion with the various schemes of regional integration, for which the assumption that there are widespread economies of scale is, of course, basic. The empirical evidence for individual industries is widely scattered, and mostly based on engineering data; more comprehensive empirical studies are few and rarely permit firm conclusions with respect to the scales of output which are relevant for a comparison between the developed and the underdeveloped economies. Bela Balassa, in his *Theory of Economic Integration*, has provided a survey of the available literature, both on so-called internal economies of scale, and on external economies and the relation of both to market size.[28]

For the underdeveloped countries, in particular, the data are very sparse, although the volume of engineering estimates of costs for different levels of output has been growing in connexion with studies carried out for programmes of regional integration, particularly in Latin America. There is in any case little doubt that the theoretical and empirical discussions of economies of scale, as applicable to the advanced countries, have limited relevance for the range of outputs that are usually feasible in the underdeveloped countries.

Although we have argued that the underdeveloped countries' dependence on the technology that is available from the advanced countries sets a lower limit to the scale of production they can adopt, this does not mean that this scale is unique. For many industries, there is a range of choice between different techniques, and consequently different scales of output and levels of cost. For various fairly obvious reasons, entrepreneurs in the underdeveloped countries will only rarely adopt the upper end of the range of the technically possible scales of output. Thus, Joe S. Bain's findings for the United States, that the evidence for the existence of economies of scale is in some industries inconclusive, are largely irrelevant for smaller markets. [29] Bain's data, on the contrary, provide indirect support for the hypothesis that even scales of output much smaller than those prevailing in the United States would not only have higher costs, but would at the same time still be very large in relation to the markets of most underdeveloped countries. The constancy of costs with respect to size in certain industries in the United States, and presumably also in other advanced countries, says nothing about the shape of the cost–size function in ranges of output lower than those surviving in the advanced countries.

There can be little doubt that, at least within the range relevant for the underdeveloped countries, economies of scale are substantial in most sectors of modern manufacturing, and also in other economic sectors. In this respect it makes no difference whether we speak of economies of scale in the strict sense of the term, or of the possibility that the underdeveloped economies may not have fully exploited all the available techniques, some of which may become economic only at scales of output greater than their present markets would allow.

Both economies of scale proper, and the shift to more advanced techniques, produce the same effect as far as the competitive structure is concerned; the scales of production are generally significant in relation to the size of the markets. But while the availability of techniques involving still larger scale provides, so to say, a reserve of applicable monopoly power in the home market, the failure to adopt them—which may well be rational from the standpoint of the individual entrepreneur, given the domestic factor prices, the attainable share of the market, and other factors—raises the level of costs above those of the same industries in the advanced countries. The under-developed economy thus falls between two stools: the discontinuity between the traditional, pre-industrial and the modern techniques, as determined by the scales of production to which the imported machinery is adapted, is large enough to make for monopoly in the home market, but the range of choice is sufficiently wide so that other factors, of which more will be said later, will restrict it sufficiently to raise the cost level above that of foreign competitors.

Some comparisons may illustrate the disparities that are involved. It stands to reason that the variability of techniques and scales of output is probably greatest in those industries which supply universal basic needs, for these exist in one form or another at all levels of economic development. Examples are: bread-baking, slaughtering, food preservation, carpentry, construction, spinning and weaving, shoemaking, and others of a similar nature. The textile industry is prominent in the group of manufacturing sectors with which, for better for worse, a process of industrialization often begins. Two studies of different types of mill-versus handloom-weaving in India carried out by Amartya Kumar Sen[30] and by the Nederlandsch Economisch Instituut[31] are instructive on this point.

The data provided in these studies permit the rough estimate that annual output for a plant with fifty handlooms and weavers, working one shift per day (a technique which is already far in advance of the primitive bamboo loom) would be about 100,000 yards. A mill with fifty powerlooms, working two daily shifts with twenty-five workers each—by no means a large mill —would produce about 2·5 million yards of cloth a year. The data permit no firm conclusions with respect to the difference in capital costs between the two types of mill, but labour costs in the large mill are about one-seventh of those in the smaller. A study of economies of scale in the cotton-spinning industry, prepared by the Economic Commission for Latin America, found that while in the range of 1000 to 13,000 spindles labour costs fall from 16·6 cents per kilogram of cotton to 5·7 cents, capital costs go down from 36·5 to 21·8 cents per kilogram.[32]

The evidence that can be found in engineering estimates and feasibility studies for various industries supports the argument that, on the one hand, the higher private profitability of more advanced techniques and their associated large scale presents the private entrepreneur with an irresistible attraction, and on the other hand, that these techniques generally fall in the range of outputs where they account for a significant share of the available markets. If this is the case in the relatively unsophisticated industries, such as food processing or spinning and weaving, it is even more pronounced in those modern types of manufacturing activities, such as chemicals, steel-making, aluminum and others which are based on continuous-flow or large-batch processes. Some data on the cost-size ratios for selected industries are given in Appendix Table I/B; they show uniformly that both capital costs and labour costs decline rapidly with size of output. For each level of output, the capital-labour ratio is fixed within a relatively narrow range. Such possibilities of variation as exist relate mainly to the ancillary processes, but the shifts that are relevant in reality are those from one technique and size class to another.

If economies of scale are as universal as is indicated, then it may be expected that the ranking of industries in terms of size would be similar in different countries. Various factors, such as large differences in relative factor prices, the age of the industry, the organizational, technical and managerial capability of entrepreneurs, or transport costs, will produce a scale effect, but an industry which is characterized by large scale in one country will be relatively large-scale also in another country. Smaller markets will then contain fewer plants, and other things being equal, will display a higher degree of concentration. Such a tendency has been noted by a number of students of industrial concentration.*

* If concentration is a function of elapsed time, as well as technology and other factors, the older industry will, *caeteris paribus*, be more concentrated. Empirical investigations which cannot take this into account are therefore unlikely to reveal any systematic differences in the degree of concentration in markets of different size, since the age of the industry and the size of the market may act in opposite directions.

International comparisons of concentration and firm size are beset with considerable statistical difficulties. Many judgements in the literature often seem to be based on general impressions rather than firm empirical evidence, and when measurement is undertaken, the conclusions depend very much on the specific measures and concepts used. Thus, the conclusion of P. Sargant Florence that American industry is approximately as concentrated as British industry,[33] as well as the opposite view of Gideon Rosenbluth, have recently been contested by W. Geoffrey Shepherd, who finds the evidence inconclusive either way.[34]

Rosenbluth's comparison of concentration in the United States and Canada is one of the best known in the literature.[35] He found that Canada's higher degree of concentration was to a considerable extent explainable as the result of her smaller market, despite the fact that Canadian firms were smaller. The number-reducing effect of the small market was not fully compensated by the size-reducing effects of different relative factor prices and other factors. Rosenbluth attributes the tendency of plant size to be similar in the two countries to their cultural affinity and geographic proximity, which make for a similarity of demand structure and of preference for techniques. His findings are therefore not applicable in the same way to the underdeveloped countries, where such affinities do not exist. The similarity must therefore be attributed to technology, the major common denominator.

International comparisons of absolute sizes of plant are even more difficult to find. John Jewkes compared firms in the United States, Great Britain, Germany, Australia and Canada, and concluded that in the first three of these countries the prevailing average size of firm, measured by employment, tended to be similar.[36] The use of the arithmetic mean for such comparisons is open to serious objections, but even so, equivalent data for the underdeveloped countries are almost non-existent. A recent comparison of size structures in Indian and Japanese manufacturing industries, by Shigeru Ishikawa, shows that the weight of the large firms in total industry was considerably higher in India than in Japan. He concludes that the higher degree of concentration in India may be the result of the fact that the smaller Indian market prevented the growth of small and medium-sized firms.[37] In general, the correlation between the extent of the market and the degree of concentration within a given country seems to be well established through several inter-industry comparisons of concentration,[38] and the same probably holds between countries.

There can be little question that the main determinant of plant size, and thereby of the competitive structure, is technology. A study by Simon Teitel shows that there is a high degree of similarity in the ranking of industries in different countries according to the average size of establishment, measured by gross value added.[39] He compared rankings for Burma, Canada, Colombia, Finland, India, Israel, Japan, Peru, the United Kingdom and the United States, and obtained a coefficient of concordance of 0·71, which was found significant at the 1 per cent level. This similarity of ranking strongly indicates the influence of technology, which makes itself felt despite all the various scale effects, such as the highly different relative factor prices in the different countries.

Data on the size distributions of establishments in the underdeveloped countries are available only for a few cases, and are often not comparable in terms of the classification systems used and their coverage. A rough comparison nevertheless indicates that the size distributions are also fairly similar. Everywhere the bulk of output is concentrated in a small number of establishments, and these tend to be more similar in size to the typical plants in the more advanced countries than the average of all plants.

The arithmetic mean, which for obvious reasons is the most commonly used measure in such comparisons, is a very inadequate yardstick of size for the examination of the technological determinants of the competitive structure. The problem of measurement of concentration, and the limitations of any single measure of such a complex phenomenon, have been discussed *ad nauseam* in the literature, and there is little point in going into them here. Granted that any single statistical measure has only limited significance, the question which we should like it to answer for our purpose is: What is the *absolute* size of establishment in which output "typically" originates? The unit of our inquiry is output, employment, assets, rather than the legal or technical entity of the firm or plant, as is the case in most studies of industrial concentration.

The index proposed by Jürg Niehans seems the most appropriate for our needs.[40] This index, which is closely related to Herfindahl's index of concentration,[41] measures the area above a modified Lorenz curve, in which the usual relative shares of establishments are replaced by their absolute shares.* It is an average weighted by the share of each establishment in the total, and is sensitive not only to differences in their size, irrespective of weight (as is, for example, the quadratic mean) but up to a certain critical value it will register an increase in the size (and therefore in the weight) of small establishments as a *decline*—thereby indicating that the size of the *typical* plant, where most output originates, has fallen.

A comparison of the size distributions of manufacturing industry for some developed and underdeveloped countries, for which data could be obtained, shows that the ranking of industries by size of "typical" establishment is highly similar in different countries. For the United States, the United Kingdom and Western Germany the coefficient of concordance of rankings according to the Niehans index was $0 \cdot 90$; that for the four underdeveloped countries, Colombia, El Salvador, Israel and the Philippines, was $0 \cdot 60$, and a similar coefficient was found for all seven countries together. All these coefficients were found to be significant at the 1 per cent level (see Table I.4). This strongly indicates that the size of the "typical" establishment is chiefly determined by technical factors. As stated before, differences in relative factor prices as well as other causes undoubtedly have a scale effect and, perhaps more importantly, are also likely to express themselves in different weights of industries.

If technology determines the size of plant, then it is not surprising to find that the degree of concentration in the underdeveloped countries is as high, if not higher, as in the advanced countries, even though their industries are much "younger"

---

* The formula for this index, for data grouped by size classes, is

$$I = \frac{a_1 \cdot a_1}{k_2 \, A} - \frac{a_2 \cdot a_2}{b_2 \, A} - \cdots \frac{a_n \cdot a_n}{b_n \, A} = \frac{\Sigma \, a_j^2 / b_j}{A},$$

where a_j is output, employment, etc., of size class j, b_j is the number of establishments in the size class, and A is the total. The formula for Herfindahl's index, for ungrouped data, is $\Sigma \, a_j^2 / A^2$.

TABLE I.4. *Ranking of Industries According to Niehans' Index of Firm Size, for Gross Output, Selected Countries*

Country	Industry															
	Food, beverages, and tobacco	Textiles	Paper and paper products	Printing	Apparel	Wood and wood products	Furniture	Leather	Rubber	Chemicals	Non-metallic minerals	Basic metals	Metal products	Machinery	Electrical machinery	Transportation equipment
Germany (1960)	6	12	11	13	14	15	16	8	3	4	9	2	10	7	5	1
United Kingdom (1958)	3	11	7	9	13	15	16	14	5	4	12	1	10	8	6	2
United States (1958)	7	12	9	8	15	16	13	14	5	3	11	2	10	6	11	1
Colombia (1962)	6	4	3	9	12	16	14	8	3	7	10	1	13	15	5	1
El Salvador (1956)	1	2	13	4	10	11	14	9	7	5	3	12	15	6	16	8
Israel (1958)	6	7	8	14	9	10	15	16	5	1	4	2	11	12	13	3
Philippines (1960)	3	5	8	13	15	12	16	14	2	1	4	6	10	11	9	7

Kendall's coefficient of concordance: for the first three countries: 0·90
for the last four countries: 0·60
for all seven countries: 0·60

Using an F-test, all three coefficients were found significant at the 1 per cent level (the F's obtained being 18, 4·5 and 9, respectively).
Sources: Published census data, and unpublished tabulations for size distributions obtained by request from the Statistical Bureaus of Colombia, El Salvador, and the
Philippines.

TABLE I.5. *Percentage of Number of Establishments Accounting for Over 40 per cent of Gross Output, by Industries, Selected Countries*

Country		Food	Textiles	Paper	Printing	Apparel	Wood	Furniture	Leather	Rubber	Chemicals	Petroleum	Non-met. min.	Basic metals	Metal prod.	Machinery	Elect. mach.	Transp. eq.
Germany	Firms	3·3	5·7	5·9	2·6	6·1	2·3	11·0	4·1	5·8	2·5	3·5	5·9	3·6	3·9	3·1	5·6	6·6
	Output	53·3	50·7	48·2	44·6	44·9	44·0	58·3	49·2	70·6	66·6	47·9	63·9	67·5	49·6	46·3	55·7	86·3
United Kingdom	Firms	2·8	14·4	5·7	2·4	15·2	9·4	15·4	6·6	3·8	2·9	1·5	12·7	5·5	3·1	4·6	3·4	2·3
	Output	49·4	54·5	55·0	52·0	63·2	57·3	54·8	44·4	52·0	46·4	51·1	71·1	62·3	49·2	53·2	47·6	52·2
United States	Firms	2·9	5·3	4·0	1·4	9·1	2·6	7·6	4·1	1·3	2·2	4·2	2·8	2·3	3·2	1·7	3·0	2·0
	Output	46·0	41·1	42·5	44·9	47·9	42·8	59·0	55·3	47·6	54·1	58·3	46·3	60·2	47·3	50·1	52·4	60·5
Colombia	Firms	3·4	9·7	3·0	4·0	5·3	12·7	3·4	5·3	9·4	8·6		2·7	12·9	6·9	19·8		3·1
	Output	50·1	68·9	54·1	45·2	58·4	57·6	44·0	44·5	89·8	55·7	78·2	62·1	79·8	45·1	53·2	56·5	50·0
El Salvador	Firms	3·4	3·3	66·7	9·5	8·4	13·3	28·6	23·3	40·0	23·1		3·4		18·8	7·8		11·1
	Output	65·0	42·5	76·2	78·7	46·4	61·4	63·1	64·1	62·8	51·0		57·2		39·7	55·0		57·2
Ireland	Firms	4·6	15·1	13·2	7·1	13·8	10·4	30·4	13·8		21·0		6·3	33·3	10·6	11·5	9·4	33·7
	Output	49·4	58·6	62·6	60·4	55·7	49·2	66·1	43·8		70·4		64·4	90·7	56·4	44·9	50·8	94·7
Israel	Firms	3·0	3·9	4·9	2·3	3·0		3·0		4·1		5·9	3·3	4·2	4·1	5·6		1·4
	Output	46·5	51·8	65·2	46·8	51·5		49·9		56·3		64·0	58·3	71·5	46·2	58·1		52·8
Malaya	Firms	4·6			16·4	22·3	19·5	11·0	5·9	4·9	8·9		9·3		6·7	18·6	5·8	19·7
	Output	55·8			51·9	48·6	52·0	43·7	52·6	58·9	52·8		55·1		51·6	61·8	52·8	51·7
Philippines	Firms	1·3	15·2	22·5	5·7	20·9	11·2	17·6	14·6	14·7	4·5		1·6	14·7	10·4	6·3	10·7	2·9
	Output	47·3	59·4	63·2	51·4	67·4	46·1	63·1	46·1	72·9	52·5		45·4	75·0	62·8	70·4	53·9	46·3

Sources: As for Table II.1.

and there has been less time for some firms to grow at the expense of others. The technology on which the underdeveloped countries depend brings their industries into the world in an already concentrated state, without ever passing through the stage of anything akin to atomistic competition. This high degree of concentration is evident even at the level of main sectors of industry, as can be seen from Table I.5, which shows the percentage of the total number of establishments that account for 40 per cent of output or more. In over one-half of the cases, no more than 10 per cent of the firms accounted for at least 40 per cent of gross output; in over one-third of the cases they were responsible for more than half the total output.

Perhaps even more than the concentration by relative shares is the small *absolute* number of establishments in each industry, for when the major share of output and employment is controlled by a small number of firms it is no longer important, as Paolo Sylos-Labini has rightly pointed out,[42] what the precise "degree of concentration" is. From all relevant viewpoints, an industry in which, say, six firms control one-half or two-thirds of output is just as monopolistic as one in which that share is held by three firms. In such situations, the comparison of concentration ratios and their changes over time amount to little more than pedantry. They no longer have any real economic significance. The data shown in Table I.6 indicate that, if the number of dominant firms is so limited even for the main sectors of industry, there can be little doubt that market structures in the underdeveloped countries are almost without exception oligopolistic or monopolistic.

It might be objected that the small number of firms or establishments that predominate in the underdeveloped countries represents no more than a stage of transition. Monopoly, in other words, exists only in the trivial sense that where an industry is new, there can by definition be only a small number of firms. Why monopoly, once established, tends to be a stable structure, and the number of firms is therefore not likely to grow appreciably up to the point where competition might effectively prevail, will be discussed in the next chapter. For the present it will be sufficient if it is accepted that a high degree of concentration is characteristic of the industrial structure in underdeveloped countries. This seems to be true for countries

TABLE I.6. *Number of Establishments Accounting for Over 40 per cent of Gross Output, by Industries, Selected Countries*

Country	Food	Textiles	Paper	Printing	Apparel	Wood	Furniture	Leather	Rubber	Chemicals	Petroleum	Non-met. min.	Basic metals	Metal product	Machinery	Electr. mach.	Transp. eq.
Germany	426	374	105	161	326	146	561	13	23	163	9	95	153	300	170	168	85
United Kingdom	253	1191	90	175	1257	511	606	121	21	103	7	634	155	312	550	88	80
United States	1215	407	213	498	2658	966	768	457	59	248	67	415	194	799	501	239	134
Colombia	114	44	3	7	111	50	12	7	6	40	2	28	4	37	50	7	19
El Salvador	58	2	2	4	21	2	10	7	2	6	} 15	3	1	3	2		4
Ireland	40	30	7	10	52	14	42			29		6		17	6	5	30
Israel	37	25	6	10	25	} 42		33	5	18		15	4	34	34	19	6
Malaya	72	15	16	46	45	117	51	7	8	14		23	5	39	57		14
Philippines	34			22	385	37	60		5			13		29	6	10	6

Sources: As for Table II.1.

which differ widely in their degree of development, thus already indicating that the phenomenon is not transitional, but a structural constant, the root of which lies in the objective technical constraints under which development must take place in these countries.

COMPETITION AND THE CHOICE OF TECHNIQUE

Most conventional growth and development theory ignores the problems that arise from the disparity between market size and a technology which is subject to scale restrictions from the supply side. We must therefore ask: Is this tendency to adopt relatively large-scale techniques really necessary, or is it merely the result of market imperfections and distortions of the price mechanism? Is there in fact that much rigidity, or is it more true to say that there is considerable scope for choice which might be influenced by appropriate overall and indirect policy measures? The neo-classical school, in particular, finds it especially congenial to deny such rigidities, for this makes it easier to retain the assumption of flexibility in factor proportions which it needs to establish the possibility of stability in the model of an advanced economy.

Choice may relate to two different things: to the choice of industries, and to the choice of techniques within industries. As for the former, our discussion of the demand structure in the previous chapter shows that it makes little sense to speak of development, and then turn around and to postulate that the demand structure should remain unchanged. It is an old-established theorem of international trade that demand is more diversified than production, and the structure of demand in the underdeveloped countries tends to approximate that of the developed countries long before the absolute levels of per capita income begin to grow closer or before the productive system has become adapted to that demand. The commodities that are demanded, and thus the industries that will be put up, are therefore broadly given.

This leaves us with the problem whether there is much scope for choice between different techniques for producing given commodities. We have previously argued that since the production of equipment is geared to the large markets of the advanced countries, and because of competition in it, there is a certain lower limit to the scale of output that can be adopted, and that this is generally large in relation to the size of the market. But even without supply constraints on scale of output, competition will induce each entrepreneur to avail himself of the most productive techniques he can obtain, within the limits of his resources of ability and capital. The spectrum of techniques available to the entrepreneur in an underdeveloped economy includes all those that have been developed by the advanced countries, insofar as they can be freely bought in the market. The technical progress of the entrepreneur in the underdeveloped economy is not limited, like that of entrepreneurs in an advanced economy, to the rate of invention and scientific advance in his own country or in other similarly advanced economies. He has the advantage of the latecomer, and can make much greater *relative* advances than the entrepreneur in the advanced economy. Limitations of finance may prevent him from choosing the most productive technique which is available; the limited demand which he can anticipate, uncertainty, a higher relative cost of capital, his own lack of technical and organizational knowledge, and like factors, may combine to produce a scale effect. Despite these limitations, the entrepreneur in the underdeveloped country will have a choice of much more productive techniques, already tried and proved in practice elsewhere, than those which could be brought forth indigenously.

If the entrepreneur wishes to survive in the competitive struggle, he can therefore not rely on the slow advances that the autonomous development of his own economy may offer; he must have recourse to the techniques, to the machines that incorporate them, and to the scales of output for which they are designed, that can only come from the advanced countries. The underdeveloped country, one might say, is a case of "Economic Growth with Unlimited Supplies of Technical Progress"—but it depends for that progress on the advanced countries.

It is a familiar argument that this will hold only to the extent that market prices for factors do not reflect their true social cost. If the market price for capital were to reflect correctly its real scarcity, so the argument runs, entrepreneurs would no longer choose the more capital-absorbing, large-scale techniques, and would prefer those which need less capital and are correspondingly smaller in output. Therefore, the scale of plant need not be disproportionately large in relation to the size of the market, and there would be no reason why monopolies should arise.

In discussions about the choice of techniques it is often not clear whether one refers to the goal of maximizing employment or to that of maximizing output. As for the first, it is an obvious proposition that where capital is scarce the greatest amount of employment can be created by spreading capital as thinly as possible—at least in the short run. But it should not be overlooked, as John P. Lewis put it concisely, that much of the argument in favour of labour-intensive techniques rests "on the assumption that employment goals can ever be divorced from output and income goals. Any society, if it could rid itself of enough technique and capital, could keep every one of its ambulatory members fully employed grubbing for roots and berries." [43]

Our discussion here is not concerned with employment goals, but centres on problems of output. From this point of view the argument in favour of labour-intensive techniques often erroneously identifies large-scale production, which is usually capital-intensive, with the use of more capital *per unit of output*. It seems plausible to think that a technique which, with a given amount of capital, employs more workers than another that requires the same amount of capital, will also yield a larger output. If this were possible, rational maximizing behaviour would lead entrepreneurs—other things being equal—to adopt it. But in reality there are indivisibilities which prevent this, and although the more capital-intensive technique, which as a rule goes together with large-scale output, may require a large absolute amount of capital, it often also uses *less* capital per unit of output if operated close to capacity.

It is obviously desirable for a capital-poor economy to save on the use of capital, and it would seem that this could be most easily achieved by raising its price.* But in practice the issue is

---

* We assume here for simplicity, in line with much of the literature, that there are only two factors of production—capital and labour. In fact, it may be skilled labour that is the scarcest factor, and in order to economize on it it may be necessary to use more capital. [44]

less one of substitutions *within* a given production-possibility set-up than of shifts from one set-up to another. Where the adoption of a more capital-saving technique requires a shift to a larger scale of production, or where economies of scale in the strict sense are present, a higher price of capital will make it more difficult to concentrate the large lumps of finance required for big undertakings. A higher price of capital will then result in a greater fragmentation of the total social capital which, being spread more thinly, would have a lower marginal productivity, and would therefore yield a lower rate of capital accumulation for the economy as a whole.

For the reasons set out earlier, the choice of technique is in reality restricted on the supply side. The available equipment is far from "factor-appropriate", and at least with respect to the core processes it usually puts a relatively high floor under the scales of output that can be adopted. It is these processes that determine relative market shares, the level of costs, and thus the competitive structure. In the ancillary processes and in auxiliary services there may be a wider choice of techniques and of factor proportions, with favourable effects on employment, but this is largely irrelevant for our argument. This supply-determined restriction to a relatively large-scale production tends to be particularly characteristic for many of the more modern commodities, those which enter demand as a result of the demonstration effect, as well as of many intermediate goods. Many of these are themselves the products of an advanced technology, and small-scale, labour-intensive techniques for their production, irrespective of costs, hardly exist.[45] With regard to most of what is properly called modern industry it makes little sense for the economic theorist to talk about techniques adapted to the factor proportions of the underdeveloped countries when the technicians do not know, and producers who are oriented primarily to the markets of the advanced countries, have little incentive, to make the equipment for them.[46]

The alternative to the adoption of modern techniques of production, which involve discontinuous shifts from lower to higher production functions and are as a rule associated with relatively large scales of output, is to rely on whatever gradual progress might be made in the course of time—probably a very long time—from the starting-point of the traditional techniques, which are by definition "factor-appropriate". But this means little more than to be back in the same low-level equilibrium trap from which the underdeveloped countries wish to escape; in the last resort this argument boils down to saying that the product-mix, that is to say the structure of production and demand, should change as little as possible. For all practical purposes this kind of reasoning relegates growth to a never-never land.[47]

In addition to these supply restrictions on the choice of technique there are also factors on the demand side which push in the direction of large scale. The marginal-productivity approach with which we have taken issue here usually overlooks the dynamics of competition in a private enterprise economy, and tends to forget the behaviour postulates appropriate for such a system. Development theorists who take this line of reasoning often conduct their argument in terms that almost make one suspect that what they have in mind is some kind of centrally planned, not a private enterprise economy in which the driving force is private profit maximization.

In the pursuit of private profit, it may be well to recall, the individual capitalist is compelled by the constant threat of his rivals to search out the most productive technique he can attain. The only way known so far to raise productivity is to make and use more and better, i.e. *technically* more efficient, machines, not less and worse. If factor costs are equal for all firms, any individual entrepreneur can gain a competitive advantage over his rivals only by introducing more and better machinery. More and better machinery means more output per worker—and thus an increase in scale. This the individual entrepreneur will do even if output per unit of capital remains constant or, at the limit, even if it falls, so long as total average cost is lower than with the older technique. Thus, even if market prices correctly reflected relative factor scarcities at some point of time, competition would bring about a continual rise in the scale of production, and, as some firms became entrenched in their market positions, also of concentration.

It would have mattered little if this push towards larger scales of output and rising concentration which stems from the forces of competition would have been only that secular concomitant of a high degree of economic development as we know it from the advanced countries. But the point at issue is that in the underdeveloped countries the same forces make for the *initial* establishment of a highly concentrated industrial structure. In the developed countries there are sometimes cases where a technical breakthrough permits the immediate capture of a significant share of the market, but usually the establishment of a dominant market position is the outcome of a prolonged competitive struggle, only gradually attained and often precariously maintained. In the underdeveloped countries, by contrast, entrepreneurs have available to them a wide range of techniques and scales of output which permit the immediate establishment of dominant market positions. But when this is the case, the whole marginal productivity approach breaks down, for it rests on the assumptions of perfect competition. Factor proportions will be adjusted to changes in relative prices—if this is technically possible—only if commodity prices are given.

When technology in relation to market size makes it possible to attain a dominant market position, this is obviously no longer so, for the dominant firm can then fix the price of the industry's products. The price of capital is given by its yield, by profits— and these will *caeteris paribus* be highest where the degree of monopoly is maximized. Capital, which accounts for the indivisibilities without which monopoly cannot be maintained, then becomes the *cheaper* factor of production for the firm which can establish itself as a monopolist. In other words, once monopoly becomes possible, the conventional remedy for what is considered as a misallocation of resources, namely that of making capital dearer, may not only fail to achieve its purpose, but may have the opposite effect: It may result in the diversion of capital from the competitive sectors to the monopolistic sectors and firms, and to the *intensification* of its use there, so long as there are still unexploited possibilities of technical progress or economies of scale.

The highly concentrated industrial structure of the underdeveloped countries can at least in good part be attributed to these factors, although there are undoubtedly also others which have been excluded from our analysis. There can be little question that there is a substantial backlog of still unexploited, yet more advanced techniques which entrepreneurs in the underdeveloped countries can obtain with relative ease from the advanced countries. These permit the establishment of monopolistic positions in most of those markets that lend themselves to the introduction of modern methods of production—that is to say, practically in the whole field of possible economic development, not excluding the capitalistic agricultural sector. Existing monopoly positions can therefore be strengthened with relative ease if an incentive to do so is provided by a change in factor prices.*

THE IMPORT-DEPENDENCE OF INVESTMENT

We now turn to the second major consequence of technological dependence mentioned at the beginning of this chapter. If the markets for final goods are limited in the underdeveloped countries, then those for the equipment necessary to make them are even narrower, by comparison with the scales of production which prevail in the advanced countries. The number of units of any one type of machine that will be demanded in an underdeveloped economy is small not only because the market for the final goods for which it is needed is restricted, but also because the existing stock of capital is small and generates little demand for replacement.

Thus, even if the necessary technical knowledge and the skills for the domestic production of equipment were available, there would be few economic incentives to do so. There is no need to labour this point: it is obvious that one of the outstanding features of underdevelopment is the inability to produce the machines for modern industry. Wassily Leontief recently compared the industrial structures of several underdeveloped

---

* Fei and Ranis, in their *Development of the Labor Surplus Economy*, have compared the growth processes of Japan and India with respect to the relative use of capital and labour and found that whereas the former first went through a "capital-shallowing" stage which lasted until World War I and then turned into a "capital-deepening" tendency, the latter "embarked on a policy of capital deepening in her industrial sector" "almost from the outset". This would tend to support our argument with respect to the difference of the technological gap which a country finds at the beginning of its growth process, for the gap between Japan and the more advanced countries of the period 1853–1914 was much smaller than that between India and the advanced countries after 1949.[48]

countries, as described by their input–output tables, with the structure of the United States, and showed that the shortfall of self-sufficiency (i.e. domestic production of requirements) of the underdeveloped countries is greatest in the sectors of machinery and basic producers' goods.[49] Had it been possible for Leontief to take into account that even such production of machinery, electrical equipment, metal products, or chemicals as is recorded in these data is heavily weighted with consumers' goods, the results would have been even more striking. The share of metal products and basic metals in total manufacturing industry in the underdeveloped countries is generally not over 10 to 15 per cent, compared with 30 to 40 per cent in the advanced countries.[50]

To these bottlenecks on the supply side one must add the disincentives coming from the demand side, irrespective of market size. Private entrepreneurs are generally unwilling to risk their entire operation by substituting domestic, untried and often really inferior equipment for imported machinery, and governments wanting to encourage investment and development are also reluctant to deter potential investors by forcing upon them domestic capital goods. Various other factors which need not be discussed here in detail also work in the same direction.

The underdeveloped countries, then, depend for their development upon imports of producers' goods. Their dependence, roughly measured by the share of imported capital goods in gross domestic fixed investment, is on the average close to two-fifths, as can be seen from Table I.7. The changes in the import-component of gross fixed investment over the period covered by these estimates are insignificant even for individual countries. They are probably more the result of accidental fluctuations in the composition of investment in the years compared than the consequences of any systematic changes of the productive structure. We may therefore take the import-dependence of investment as a structural constant.

Now this technologically determined dependence on imports, which is strengthened by various demand factors, means that the domestic output and employment generated by a given amount of investment will always be diminished proportionately to the share of imports in total investment expenditure— the investment multiplier will be reduced. This is so irrespective

TABLE I.7. *Share of Imports of Capital Goods in Gross Domestic Fixed Investment, 1950–1 and 1958–9,*[a] *in per cent, Selected Underdeveloped Countries*

Country	1950–1	1958–9
Ireland (1952–3)	42	55
Greece (1952–3)	31	41
Ecuador	26	34
Philippines (1952–3)	35	40
Thailand	34	39
Peru (1951–2)	33	37
Brazil	26	30
Chile	30	33
Israel (1955–6)	33	36
Cyprus (1953–4)	48	51
India	28	30
Venezuela	31	33
Colombia (1951–2)	33	34
China (Taiwan) (1954–5)	31	31
Honduras (1952–3 to 1957–8)	36	36
Panama (1952–3)	38	37
Rhodesia and Nyasaland (1954–5)	43	42
Portugal (1952–3)	53	52
South Africa	32	29
Argentina (1951–2)	22	18
Mexico	41	36
Morocco (1951–2 to 1957–8)	38	32
Jamaica	49	36
Turkey (1951–2 to 1959)	40	25
Average, all countries	35·5	36·0

[a] Except where other years are indicated.

Source: United Nations, *World Economic Survey 1961*, New York, 1962, p. 24.

of whether exports are constant or increasing, for changes in the volume of exports are independent of this aspect of investment; if they can increase, they will, whether investment is import-dependent or not. The export sector is the economic equivalent of the producers' goods sector in the advanced economy, for it provides the foreign exchange for which the producers' goods can be imported. But it is in this respect the *differentia specifica* of underdevelopment that there is no necessary technical and economic interdependence and complementarity between the export sector and the consumers' goods sector as there is between the latter and the producers' goods sector in the advanced economy.

Consider the familiar model of the circular flow in an economy which possesses both sectors. Investment increases the demand for, and the output of, producers' goods, and the income thus generated in turn raises the demand for the products of the consumers' goods sector, up to the limit of its capacity. With full employment of resources and constant technique, further investment can take place only through a rise in the savings ratio, i.e. a fall in demand for consumers' goods and a shift of the resources so set free to the production of capital goods. The sectoral interdependence also means that an increase in demand for producers' goods can ultimately only come from an expansion of the consumers' goods sector, which requires additional machines and raw materials to produce a larger quantity of goods.

In this model, the two sectors operate in the same market, and behind the market exchanges between them there stands a real exchange of functionally and technically different kinds of goods. Since the two sectors complement each other technically they must, for any given technique, stand in a certain proportion to one another if the system is to remain in equilibrium.* If that proportionality is upset for one reason or another, it is likely to be restored in a destructive manner.

In the underdeveloped economy, by contrast, no such interdependence exists. The relevant distinction here is between a domestic and an export sector, both of which depend for their expansion upon imports of producers' goods from abroad. The two sectors are not necessarily complementary to each other; the link between them is at most competitive—they may compete with one another for factors in the domestic market. The specific relationship between these two sectors will be discussed

---

* This is the main point of difference between the conditions of equilibrium in Adolph Lowe's growth model[51] and that of Harrod. The latter requires only the equality of intended savings with intended investment. The proportionality condition, however, is crucial, for it destroys Harrod's argument of the basic instability of equilibrium growth. Lowe shows that equilibrium, if once attained, is likely to be highly stable. This is, of course, not to say that there is any great likelihood that a *laissez-faire* economy will achieve equilibrium growth in the first place. See also Chapters 4 and 5.

further in Chapter 5, but this much is already obvious: They can develop in a divergent manner, for the level of output and employment, and consequently also of investment, in the export sector is independent of the level of demand in the domestic sector (but not vice versa, since the demand for producers' goods that originates in the domestic sector is ultimately limited by the import capacity provided by the export sector). Whether the demand for foreign exchange that comes from investment can increase the supply of exports via a fall in the exchange rate depends to a great extent on demand conditions in foreign markets. The expansibility of exports limits the amount of investment that can take place. It is reasonable to suppose that the price-elasticity of supply of exports will be low* or, in other words, that the increase in domestic income and employment generated by an additional volume of exports will be small in relation to the rise in the price of foreign exchange that is necessary to call it forth. This steep fall in the exchange rate will, on the other hand, reduce the profitability of investment by driving up the domestic price of the imported capital goods.

The underdeveloped economy differs from the open developed economy in that its supply elasticity of producers' goods is practically zero.† The advanced economy, even if it imports capital goods, can respond to an increased demand for imports and a falling exchange rate by substituting domestic products for the former imports. Since its domestic production of capital goods has a positive supply elasticity, it can shift the income and employment effects of investment homeward. The underdeveloped country can never do so as long as its technological dependence persists. To put the same thing in different words: the specialization of the advanced economy is one of *choice*, while that of the underdeveloped is one of *necessity*.

To sum up. Technological dependence leads, on the one hand, to the emergence of a monopolistic structure because the scales of output that must be adopted to introduce modern methods of production are large relative to the extent of the initial market; and on the other hand, these markets will be only partially expanded through income generated by investment, since a large proportion of the capital goods must be imported.

* For a more detailed discussion see Chapter 5.
† This is strictly true only for the imported producers' goods.

In addition, the monopolistic structure itself will restrict the volume of investment, as we shall see later, so that the two effects reinforce each other: Investment is less than what it could be with the existing resources, and such investment as takes place expands domestic income only fractionally; and vice versa—the insufficient expansion of the domestic market reduces the incentive to invest.

NOTES AND REFERENCES

1. CELSO FURTADO, *Development and Underdevelopment*, University of California Press, Berkeley and Los Angeles, 1964, p. 142.
2. HARVEY LEIBENSTEIN, *Economic Backwardness and Economic Growth*, John Wiley & Sons, New York, 1957, pp. 9–11.
3. *Ibid.*, pp. 40–41.
4. JOHN P. LEWIS, *Quiet Crisis in India*, The Brookings Institution, Washington D.C., 1962, p. 203.
5. For a development of a theory of such dual preference systems under socialism, see JAN DREWNOWSKI, The economic theory of socialism: a suggestion for reconsideration, *Journal of Political Economy*, August 1961. A similar argument can be made out for non-socialist systems, although the State preference function there is likely to be less clearly articulated and more narrowly circumscribed. Often, goals may be proclaimed as a concession to public opinion, while the particular interests of the actual ruling classes are either indifferent to their implementation or, still worse, prevent it in practice. This is evidenced in the frequent vocal declarations in favour of economic development by the governments of some underdeveloped countries, which are, however, not backed up by any visible action to achieve the declared goal.
6. See, for example, H. S. HOUTHAKKER, *Some Problems in the International Comparison of Consumption Patterns*, Memorandum B-10, Research Center in Economic Growth, Stanford University, July 1961; and MILTON GILBERT and IRVING B. KRAVIS, *An International Comparison of National Products and the Purchasing Power of Currencies*, O.E.E.C., Paris, 1954, pp. 113–19.
7. The demand-creating role of imports has been emphasized by ALBERT O. HIRSCHMAN, *The Strategy of Economic Development*, Yale University Press, New Haven, 1958, pp. 120 ff.
8. R. R. NELSON, A theory of the low-level equilibrium trap, *American Economic Review*, December 1956.
9. For an excellent analysis of the differences between the Keynesian and the Marxian aggregates which is pertinent to this problem, see SHIGETU TSURU, Keynes versus Marx: the methodology of aggregates, in KENNETH KURIHARA (ed.), *Post-Keynesian Economics*, Rutgers University Press, New Brunswick (N.J.), 1954, especially pp. 336–44.
10. CELSO FURTADO, *op. cit.*, p. 142.

11. See the interesting discussion by NATHAN ROSENBERG, Capital formation in underdeveloped countries, *American Economic Review*, **50**, No. 4, September 1960, particularly p. 708 and p. 713.

12. KARL MARX, *Capital*, Vol. I, p. 581.

13. For a classic formulation of the coercive nature of the process of competition, see KARL MARX, *Capital*, Vol. I, Foreign Languages Publishing House, Moscow (no date), p. 592.

14. See also WERNER BAER and MICHEL E. A. HERVÉ, Employment and industrialization in developing countries, *Quarterly Journal of Economics*, **80**, No. 1, February 1966, pp. 88–107.

15. VICTOR S. CLARK, *History of Manufactures in the United States*, McGraw-Hill Book Co., New York (3 Vols.), particularly vol. 1, ch. xvi.

16. See PHYLLIS DEANE, The Industrial Revolution and economic growth: the evidence of early British national income estimates, *Economic Development and Cultural Change*, Vol. V, No. 2, January 1957; other data taken from COLIN CLARK, *The Conditions of Economic Progress*, 3rd ed., MacMillan & Co., New York, 1957, pp. 136–9, and United Nations, *Yearbook of National Accounts Statistics 1964*, New York, 1965, pp. 389–91.

17. NATHAN ROSENBERG, Technological change in the machine tool industry, 1840–1910, *Journal of Economic History*, **23**, December 1963, p. 418.

18. See ALFRED MAIZELS, *Industrial Growth and World Trade*, Cambridge University Press, Cambridge 1963, p. 276.

19. ROSENBERG, *op. cit.*, footnote.

20. CLARK, *op. cit.*, p. 506.

21. CARMELLAH MONETA, The estimation of transportation costs in international trade, *Journal of Political Economy*, **47**, February 1959, p. 58. These estimates for the percentage of freight costs in the c.i.f. value of Germany's imports in 1951 show that metals and metal products have the lowest freight factors, with machinery at the very end of the scale.

22. SAUL S. SANDS, Changes in scale of production in United States manufacturing industry, 1904–1947, *Review of Economics and Statistics*, **43**, November 1961, pp. 365–8.

23. JOHN M. BLAIR, Technology and size, *American Economic Review Supplement*, **45**, May 1958, p. 151. Blair's view, which is often repeated, confuses the capital-saving character of new inventions with a fall in total output per productive unit.

24. For an interesting recent attempt to come to grips with this much neglected subject, which contains many suggestive ideas on the relationship between specialization and development, see EDWARD AMES and NATHAN ROSENBERG, The progressive division and specialization of industries, *Journal of Development Studies*, **1**, July 1965.

25. See, for example, United Nations, *Measures for the Economic Development of Underdeveloped Countries*, New York, 1951, p. 23, and also *Processes and Problems of Industrialization in Under-Developed Countries*, New York, 1955, p. 14.

26. See CALEB A. SMITH, Survey of the empirical evidence on economies of scale, in *Business Concentration and Price Policy*, National Bureau of

Economic Research, Princeton, 1955, pp. 213 ff. It ought to be added, however, that while Smith finds the empirical evidence in general "indefinite and disappointing", he concludes that within the small to medium range of firm size average costs fall if factor costs are held constant. See pp. 230–8.

27. For a somewhat bizarre attempt to define economies of scale out of existence, see Professor Milton Friedman's comments on the article by Caleb A. Smith cited above. One of Friedman's arguments is that "if *ex post* costs are defined to equal receipts *ex post*, then cost per dollar of output is necessarily one dollar, regardless of size". All we can then know, he continues, is that capital costs vary with size, which may merely reflect systematic differences in factor combinations according to size. It is a consoling thought that the problem which plagued Marshall, and that is at the root of all monopoly theory, is now finally solved, and that the search for empirical evidence of economies of scale has produced so little only because, according to Friedman, "foolish questions deserve foolish answers . . .".

28. BELA BALASSA, *The Theory of Economic Integration*, Richard D. Irwin, Homewood (Ill.), 1961, chapters 6 and 7. See also, by the same author, *Economic Development and Integration*, Centro de Estudios Latino-americanos, Mexico, 1965.

29. JOE S. BAIN, *Barriers to New Competition*, Harvard University Press, Cambridge (Mass.), 1956, chapter 3. See also the critical review of the literature on economies of scale there, pp. 56–57.

30. A. K. SEN, *Choice of Techniques*, Basil Blackwell, Oxford, 1956, pp. 102 ff.

31. Nederlandsch Economisch Instituut, *The Economics of Mill versus Handloom Weaving in India*, Rotterdam, 1956 (mimeographed).

32. United Nations, Economic Commission for Latin America, ROGER HAOUR, *Economies of Scale in the Cotton Spinning Industry*, New York, 1965 (mimeographed). See also K. N. RAJ, Employment and unemployment in the Indian economy: problems of classification, measurement and policy, *Economic Development and Cultural Change*, **7,** April 1959.

33. P. SARGANT FLORENCE, *The Logic of British and American Industry*, Routledge & Kegan Paul Ltd., London, 1953, pp. 132 ff.

34. W. GEOFFREY SHEPHERD, A comparison of industrial concentration in the United States and Britain, *Review of Economics and Statistics*, **43,** February 1961, p. 70.

35. GIDEON ROSENBLUTH, *Concentration in Canadian Manufacturing Industries*, Princeton University Press, Princeton, 1957, chapter iv.

36. JOHN JEWKES, The size of factory, *The Economic Journal*, **62,** June 1952, pp. 237–62.

37. SHIGERU ISHIKAWA, A comparison of size structures in Indian and Japanese manufacturing industries, *Hitotsubashi Journal of Economics*, **2,** No. 2, March 1962, pp. 50 ff.

38. See, for example, R. EVELY and I. M. D. LITTLE, *Concentration in British Industry*, Cambridge University Press, Cambridge, 1960, pp. 86 ff and 104 ff., or Rosenbluth's study for Canada, pp. 40 ff.

39. SIMON TEITEL, *Criteria for the Development of Manufacturing Industries in*

Developing Countries, New York, 1966 (mimeographed). This paper is part of a Ph.D. dissertation now in preparation.

40. Jürg Niehans, *An Index of the Size of Industrial Establishments*, translated and republished in *International Economic Papers*, No. 8, New York, 1958, pp. 122–32.

41. Orris C. Herfindahl, *Concentration in the Steel Industry*, unpublished Ph.D. dissertation, Columbia University, New York, 1950.

42. Paolo Sylos-Labini, *Oligopoly and Technical Progress*, Harvard University Press, Cambridge (Mass.), 1962, pp. 7–8.

43. John P. Lewis, *op. cit.*, p. 52.

44. For a recent analysis of this problem, see Werner Baer and Michel E. A. Hervé, *op. cit.*, pp. 97 ff. See also Hirschman, *op. cit.*, pp. 145 ff.

45. In a recent article comparing the industrial structures of different countries on the basis of their input–output tables, Wassily Leontief states that "the choice of alternative technologies hardly exists. The process of development consists essentially in the installation and building of an approximation of the system embodied in the advanced countries . . .", *Scientific American*, **209**, No. 3, September 1963, p. 159.

46. Compare, for example, the following statement by Joan Robinson: ". . . the so-called underdeveloped economies . . . would do better by developing efficient techniques of using man-power than by imitating capital-using techniques evolved in 'advanced' economies which enjoy conditions of scarcity of labour" (*The Accumulation of Capital*, Macmillan & Co., London, 1956, p. 132). This well-meant recommendation, which is so often found in the literature on development, overlooks the simple fact that if the underdeveloped countries were able to develop such indigenous techniques, they would not be underdeveloped in the first place. Economic history knows no examples of such adaptation of techniques except at a stage of development which is already high, and in cases where the social structure provided for a continued supply of cheap labour to a relatively advanced capitalist sector. This was apparently the case in the development of Japan, where the agrarian structure maintained an elastic supply, at least of unskilled labour, for a long period. In an entirely different manner, but with similar end results with respect to a "capital-shallowing" pattern of growth, this was true of Israel where mass immigration provided the elastic labour supply.

47. The argument here goes further than that of R. S. Eckaus in his well-known article, The factor proportions problem in under-developed areas, *American Economic Review*, September 1955, reprinted in A. N. Agarwala and S. P. Singh, *The Economics of Underdevelopment*, Oxford University Press, New York, 1963, pp. 348–78. Eckaus assumes that factor proportions are fixed by technology, but that the scale of production is not so fixed. For his purposes these assumptions were sufficient, but they imply the variability of the composition of national output (the product-mix), which is limited only by the structure of demand. What is suggested here is that the constraints on the scale of output further accentuate the rigidity of the factor-proportions.

48. JOHN C. H. FEI and GUSTAV RANIS, *Development of the Labor Surplus Economy*, The Economic Growth Center, Yale University, Richard D. Irwin, Homewood (Ill.), 1964, pp. 125 ff.
49. WASSILY LEONTIEF, The structure of development, *Scientific American*, **209,** No. 3, September 1963, pp. 162–3.
50. See United Nations, *The Growth of World Industry*, 1938–1961, New York, 1963, tables on the structure of industry.
51. ADOLPH LOWE, Structural analysis of real capital formation, in *Capital Formation and Economic Growth*, National Bureau of Economic Research, Princeton University Press, Princeton, 1955, pp. 581–634, and particularly pp. 610–22.

CHAPTER 2

MONOPOLISTIC STRUCTURES AND GROWTH

WE HAVE argued in the preceding chapter that the under-developed economies have only limited alternatives to the adoption of techniques and scales of production which evolved in the advanced economies in adaptation to their large markets and factor proportions. It follows that the transplantation of such methods of production to an underdeveloped environment tends to create monopolies even in industries which in the advanced countries are more nearly competitive in structure; and *a fortiori* in those industries where monopoly is for technical reasons the rule also in the developed countries.

If this is so, the question arises whether Joan Robinson is right in saying that there is no necessary connexion between monopoly and the rate of growth, which she ascribes to the "animal spirits" of entrepreneurs. These, however, may not be a parameter, but rather themselves subject to change and to the constraints which are rooted in the technical and competitive conditions of the system.[1] It is in any case difficult to accept the proposition that the conventional theories of growth and development, which base their whole analysis on the assumptions of a competitive structure, remain valid even if these basic postulates must be dropped. We must therefore turn to the theory of monopoly and examine its propositions for their relevance to the problem of economic development, and then discuss some of the main features of monopolistic structures as they affect the process of development. For the present study the chief interest lies in those forces within monopolistic structures which tend to work towards stagnation as against those which make for further growth, and this is the subject of this and the next chapter.

MONOPOLY THEORY AND GROWTH

We do not intend here to review the extensive literature on monopoly theory, but it will be useful to devote some space to a discussion of its main outlines in order to clear the ground and to emphasize the points of departure from conventional doctrine.

The literature on the monopoly problem may be roughly classified into three categories. The first contains the whole corpus of so-called anti-trust literature, which generally criticizes monopoly from the standpoint of the competitive model inherited from the classics. It may consider monopoly to be inefficient in terms of that model, or it may grant its superior efficiency; but according to the democratic maxim that power corrupts and is therefore dangerous and evil in itself, it is primarily concerned with the political and social dangers held to be inherent in the concentration of economic power. The writings which belong to this group derive most of their theoretical content from the other two categories which are more directly of interest for our purpose.

The second class, which has most of its roots in Marx, is best known from the work of Schumpeter, and is mainly concerned with the secular trends operating in a highly developed capitalist system. The common feature of the works that belong to this category is that they see monopoly as the irreversible product of an historical process, as the result of the basic forces which set the capitalist system in motion. The outlook of these writings, which include those which regard monopoly as causing secular stagnation and the ultimate breakdown of the system as well as those who, on the contrary, view it as the mainspring of progress, is thus essentially dynamic. Its main problem is, as Schumpeter put it, not to see how capitalism administers existing structures, but rather how it creates and destroys them.[2] This is, of course, also the central problem of this study, but it is posed in the context of the chances which monopolistic structures afford for an escape from backwardness, and thus assumes a different orientation. Instead of asking about the ultimate viability of the capitalist system under monopoly, the question is whether in such a structure a high level of economic development is likely to be attained in the first place.

The third category of monopoly theory or, more properly, of the theory of imperfect or monopolistic competition, is essentially an outgrowth of the competitive model; the very titles of the two works which introduced it reveal this clearly.[3] At its inception the theory represented a rebellion against the useless abstractions of orthodox doctrine from economic reality, but being a direct descendant of Marshallian short-period analysis of the individual firm and industry, it did not challenge the basic assumptions of conventional theory on the macro-economic level, and could therefore be grafted on to it.

W. Arthur Lewis has called Keynesian theory "one long, important, and fascinating footnote" to neo-classicism,[4] and the theory of imperfect competition is the other. It is hardly an accident that while Keynesian theory attacked the automaticity of full-employment equilibrium of the neo-classical model at the aggregate level, the theory of imperfect competition shook the structural foundations of the competitive model at the level of the individual firm. Both "footnotes", however, only qualified the main body of the neo-classical text; they did not contradict it. Moreover, although born of the same dissatisfaction with what traditional theory was able to contribute to an understanding of economic reality in the thirties, the two bodies of theory were never systematically linked with each other in accepted doctrine. Macro-economic analysis, including neo-classical and post-Keynesian growth theory, went on blithely assuming a competitive structure—if not a perfect one, then at least one that was "workably" competitive—while the theory of imperfect competition saw a world of monopolies and oligopolies and never raised its eyes from the individual firm and its behaviour. The classical and neo-classical consistency of micro-economic and macro-economic analysis had broken down, but the consequences that follow from this breakdown are rarely recognized.

A theory of development is by definition causal-historical; the more explicitly so the more it is policy-oriented. It must be based upon a model in which, to quote Joan Robinson, "we specify the technical conditions obtaining in an economy and the behaviour reactions of its inhabitants, and then, so to say, dump it down in a particular situation at a particular date in historical time and work out what will happen next. . . . To build up a causal model, we must start not from equilibrium relations but from the rules and motives governing human behaviour."[5]

The theory of imperfect competition has been singularly unsuccessful in its thirty-year-old search for determinate short-run equilibria, and has nothing to say with respect to the functioning of the system as a whole. Its method is that of static, short-run analysis, and its object is to determine the functional relationships that hold in the prevailing system—not to reduce these to their causal determinants and thereby to inquire into the laws of emergence and change of the system itself. But it is precisely its preoccupation with the "rules and motives governing human behaviour" in a set of non-competitive economic relations which has sharpened our insights into the changes in the behaviour patterns that occur under monopoly, and which must be taken into account when a causal-historical point of view is adopted. The static micro-economic concepts of the theory, in particular, can be extended to an understanding of the investment process—the crucial determinant of growth. Moreover, perhaps the theory's very lack of success in solving those problems which it set out to investigate has recently led to a shift of attention away from the behaviour of the individual firm, and back to the objective determinants of a monopolistic structure itself, taken as a whole—namely to technology and market size. These two, together with capital accumulation, are also the main elements of a theory of development.

Given its assumptions, the theory of imperfect competition cannot explain these elements adequately, but its method can provide a useful point of departure for their analysis. The structures to which this theory refers, and which are investigated by the empirical studies that took their lead from it, are those of individual product markets. The basic unit of investigation is the commodity, which is distinguished from others by the difference in the elasticity of consumers' demand for it: "All that monopoly means . . . is that the output of the individual producer happens to be bounded on all sides by a marked gap in the chain of substitutes."[6] The "producer" here is defined by the product—he is, so to say, a commodity which makes decisions.

Now all demands, considered together at a point of time, are complementary to each other, and are therefore marked by "gaps in the chain of substitutes". At the same time each specific good is to some extent substitutable for another. There is no objective criterion for deciding how marked the gap between substitutes must be so that a given market may be regarded as monopolistic. A chain is made up equally of links and of gaps between them; from a distance, it will not appear very different from an unbroken string, and if looked at from close up, nothing but individual links and gaps between them will be seen. It is therefore not difficult to conclude either that all products are, in the last analysis, subject to monopoly, or that because ultimately all commodities must compete with one another for the sovereign consumer's expenditure, competition after all remains "workable", and is a fair description of economic reality.

The commodities and the "firms" that are defined by them, on which this theory focuses its attention, are obviously not the *dramatis personae* of the economic process, but merely the objects through which that process takes place. Decisions about the variables which concern economic theory in general, and development theory in particular, are made by *concrete* firms— by capitalists, entrepreneurs. These decisions are supposed to be made in response to autonomous shifts and changes in the demand for goods and the supply of factors. But real firms, it has always been known, typically produce more than one commodity and therefore operate in different markets. These market operations are differentiated, but their motivating force and end result is not—for it is the pursuit and accumulation of profits, of an *undifferentiated* flow of money, that is the purpose of the whole activity.

In the competitive model it was possible to abstract from the multi-product nature of real firms without damage to the theory. Under imperfect competition, however, this can no longer be done even for short-run analysis, for decisions in one product market are no longer independent of the conditions in other markets. When the long run is considered, the assumption of the single-commodity firm in imperfect competition becomes altogether untenable because, as will be argued in the next chapter, such a firm cannot remain confined to one market but must expand beyond it through diversification. The abstraction from the multi-product firm is, under imperfect competition, not an acceptable first approximation, but becomes a forced short-run assumption which ignores the essential feature of monopolistic rivalry—that which has been put forward as its main defence from the viewpoint of its role in long run growth: Product differentiation and diversification.

Short-run, static theory is blind to this feature because it has always been preoccupied with the search for determinate cost–revenue equilibria. The differentiation of products through selling costs or advertising, and to some extent also through changes in design or raw materials, could still be accommodated in the framework of short-run analysis. But empirically most of the product differentiation that matters involves a change in physical specifications, that is to say in the way the product is produced. Different production functions must mean a change in inputs, and particularly those of producers' goods— and that means investment, which is by definition excluded from short-run analysis. This is even more true of diversification, which means not the modification of existing, but the production of entirely new goods, which differ from the old in their physical characteristics and are destined for new markets.

The manner in which the theory of imperfect competition and the empirical studies which it inspired find a way out of the difficulty that, after its own dethronement of price competition as the main equilibrating mechanism of the system, product innovation has become the dominant mode of monopolistic rivalry, is by falling back on its definition of the firm: The expansion of the firm's activities into another market through differentiation and diversification merely means that we have a "new" firm—which will be considered in its own turn, in isolation from all other markets and firms. This may tell us something about monopoly in individual markets and is necessary, but far from sufficient, for understanding the ways in which monopoly elements affect the functioning of the system as a whole, and particularly its growth.* The rules that govern the

* What matters here is the expansion of the same firms from one market into another, and the interlocking of different sectors of the economy in powerful blocks of unified control, for it is these that determine the level and the direction of investment and thus of aggregate growth. It is easily understandable that once this *modus operandi* of monopoly is ignored, one should

behaviour of the real firms thus become a will-o'-the-wisp. The forces which erect barriers to their further growth in their original markets and which impel them to search out others, and the limits to such investment and growth, remain largely hidden from sight.

Conventional theory, with its substitution of the motions of inanimate commodities for the motives of men, and the timelessness of its statics in which all relationships are simultaneous and reversible, is evidently inadequate for an explanation of growth. Theory must, in its treatment of monopoly as in aggregative analysis, work its way back across the tradition of Marshallian short-period analysis of the firm to the classical framework. It must focus its attention on the functioning of entire structures and on the determinants of their emergence.

THE STABILITY OF MONOPOLISTIC STRUCTURES

If it is granted that monopolies are technically inevitable in underdeveloped countries, it would seem to follow almost automatically that after the initial stage of growth in which the monopolistic structures become established, more or less marked tendencies of stagnation will set in. This may come about through any one of several possible mechanisms, of which it is more difficult to find a precise description in the literature than it is to find arguments that they are, or can be, counteracted.

The strongest defence of monopoly is the well-known Schumpeterian argument which holds that monopoly is not only inherently capable of widening its own markets through constant innovation, but that innovation—and thus expansion—will not come about unless there is an expectation that a monopoly position and the profits that go with it can be obtained. Such an expectation must be confirmed by results, by the materialization of the expected profits, if innovation is to go on. Therefore the

---

find, as many empirical studies have done, that the concentration ratios of isolated industries are often stable over time. In fact, it is not difficult to show that if a small group of oligopolists is represented simultaneously in different markets, monopoly in the meaningful sense may increase while the degree of concentration need not, and may even decline.

existence of monopoly is a condition for progress, and monopoly profits are the mainspring of growth. The validity of this argument against theories of monopolistic stagnation in the advanced economies is not the primary concern of this study. But even if one grants this defence for the case of the developed economies, the question remains whether it does not rest on special assumptions which are not tenable in the conditions of backwardness. It is indeed the contention of this study that whatever the merits one may ascribe to innovation and diversification as a counterweight to stagnation tendencies in the advanced countries, it will not only fail to have a similar effect where technological dependence and small markets combine, but is even likely to accentuate such tendencies. The following chapter will try to support this argument in detail, but first it is necessary to show that the monopolies and oligopolies that will appear in the conditions of underdevelopment are generally stable structures which, once established, strongly resist change.

The proposition that, for a given set of factor prices and demand elasticities, it is technology and market size that will determine the structure of the market, which this study applies to the problem of underdevelopment, is essentially identical with the central argument of the theory developed by Joe S. Bain,[7] Paolo Sylos-Labini,[8] and Franco Modigliani.[9] Despite its apparent adherence to conventional concepts, this new development of oligopoly theory is a radical departure from traditional doctrine because it abandons the usual preoccupation of oligopoly theory with the conjectural variations in market behaviour within a *given* group of firms and concentrates, instead, on the *conditions of entry* as the determinant of market behaviour and of long-run equilibrium. In other words, instead of analysing the various possible "moves and countermoves" with respect to price and output within a given structure, the Bain–Sylos–Labini–Modigliani theory is concerned with the *determinants of emergence of the structure itself.*

The key concept of the new theory is "the condition of entry", the term used by Bain to define the advantages of established firms over potential entrants. As Bain points out repeatedly, this is a structural concept, and is defined by reference to the minimum attainable average cost for the most efficient scale of firm, at an optimal rate of capacity utilization. This level of costs, and the related efficient scale, are determined by technology, while entry into an industry always involves investment. Thus, although both Bain and Sylos-Labini conduct their analysis in static terms, the introduction of this new concept* serves as an important stepping-stone to a dynamic approach, for it hinges on the process of investment. This obviously makes it highly relevant for a discussion of the problem of development, provided that some account can be given not only of the long-run equilibrium of price, output, and industry structure, but also of the structural factors that influence investment itself. First, however, it seems useful to follow this theory and to see, without going into a detailed recapitulation of the formal analysis, how it comes to the conclusion that oligopolistic structures display a high degree of stability, and what determines that stability.

Sylos-Labini's question is not—as customary in traditional oligopoly theory—how price and output are adjusted from some initial level in response to changes in the parameters, but rather how the prevailing levels of price and output come to be what they are in the first place. It is of course the same thing to ask how the corresponding market structure comes to be established—how many firms there will be and what their sizes will be if technology and demand are given. As Sylos-Labini points out, this is a long-term problem,[10] since it takes into account changes in the plant and equipment of existing firms as well as possible changes in the structure of the industry in consequence of the entry of new firms. The demand curve and its elasticity which this theory considers is no longer the "imagined" demand curve of the individual firm within a *given* oligopolistic structure (that is, a conjectural schedule of a state of expectations), but once more the Marshallian *industry* demand curve which is objectively given to any and all firms by the tastes and reactions of consumers.

Sylos-Labini assumes that the established firms will adopt a hostile attitude towards potential entrants. They will not restrict their own output and thus yield the entrant a share in the market. Equally, potential entrants assume that the established firms will react in this manner, and they behave accordingly.

* New, that is, only within the framework of traditional oligopoly theory. Both the Marxian and the Schumpeterian analysis have put such structural changes in the centre of their argument.

The same behaviour rule holds for internal changes in the industry—in the face of price changes, for example, firms will not restrict their output so long as the prevailing price is higher than their direct cost. Only those obstacles to entry are considered that can be erected by the established firms through price and output variations.

Assume now that potential entrants to the industry have access to a long-run cost function (that is, a technology) which is at least equal to that of the least efficient of the established firms, so that the prevailing price will be equal or higher than the highest long-run minimum average cost of any of the existing firms. Entry would then occur only if the feasible output of the potential entrant was an insignificant proportion of the existing market size. If, however, there are economies of large-scale production, such that in order to achieve at least the highest minimum average cost now prevailing in the industry it is necessary to produce and sell a quantity which is significant in relation to the existing industry output, then "anybody proposing to enter the market must reckon not only with the present size of demand, but also make some estimate of the market's capacity to absorb an additional quantity of goods— either (a) at lower prices if the market is stationary, (b) at the ruling price if the market tends to expand, or (c) at lower prices if the market tends to expand but the entrant wants to speed up its expansion".[11]

If the market's absorptive capacity can be increased only by a reduction of price from the prevailing level to one which is lower than the long-run average cost attainable by the potential entrant, then the ruling price will be an entry-preventing price. The highest entry-preventing price will be set with respect to that scale of output and its associated level of long-run minimum average cost, in relation to market size, that is represented by the potential entrant who poses the most immediate threat of entry. In other words, the entry-preventing price and its corresponding "critical" industry output are determined, on the one hand, by the array of cost functions of the established firms, and on the other hand it must be set to correspond to an industry output such that the additional output of the potential entrant will reduce the price below his own long-run minimum average cost. The barriers which the established firms can erect

against new entrants thus depend upon the relationship between their own technology and that of the potential entrants,
given the elasticity of industry demand.

There is thus a lower and an upper limit to long-run equilibrium price and output. The former equals the long-run minimum average cost attainable for the industry, as determined by
technology, and represents the hypothetical levels of price and
output which, given the demand function, would prevail under
perfect competition. The upper limit is the entry-preventing
price and its corresponding output which is determined in relation to the scale of output and cost level of the potential entrant.
These long-run equilibrium prices and industry outputs are
determined by factors which can be ascertained objectively and
are, at least in principle, measurable: by long-run cost and
demand functions. They are independent of the conjectures,
expectations, decisions or actions of the firms. If there are
economies of large-scale production, as must be assumed if an
industry has an oligopolistic structure, then the internal structure of the industry will also be determinate. And if such a
structure should tend to perpetuate itself at the prevailing price
and output levels, then the rate of accumulation possible within
it and the maximum possible rate of growth, for a given savings
function, will also be determinate if there are no limits to
investment opportunities.

As Modigliani observes, the industry structure that will
establish itself need not be the most rational one for the given
array of possible cost functions and the existing demand function. It is possible that technology and demand should permit a
more rational structure, one that would be able to produce the
given output at a lower total social cost than the existing structure. If it is assumed that within the range of outputs represented
by the size of the markets in the underdeveloped countries there
exists, for many industries, a large still untapped reservoir of
more efficient techniques, the question arises: What are the
forces within an oligopolistic structure that prevent it from
moving steadily towards a more rational structure, until the
entire market is occupied only by the smallest possible number
of large-scale, efficient firms which its size can sustain? In other
words, if the available technology and initial market size preclude a competitive structure, are there forces at work that will

make an oligopolistic structure perpetuate itself and thereby prevent the rationalization of output through monopoly?

Sylos-Labini shows that in the absence of major changes in technology and market size there is little likelihood that an oligopolistic structure, once it has become established, will transform itself from within. Its internal structure, the market shares of the existing firms, is established by the range of existing techniques, given the demand function, and it is a long-run equilibrium structure. Price wars may occur, but they are rare interludes and represent the move from one equilibrium structure to another in response to a major change in the parameters. The final equilibrium structure, for any given set of technical and demand conditions, depends not only on the initial conditions but also on the path followed in attaining that equilibrium. In the sequence of possible changes, each stage is a set of initial conditions for subsequent stages, and modifies the final outcome. Thus, if small, relatively inefficient firms are the first to enter the market, the subsequent entry of more efficient firms may be precluded, and vice versa. The larger the absolute size of the market, the greater is the likelihood that structural changes will be brought about by price wars; the tendency will be for the average size of firm to be larger, and for the equilibrium price to be lower. Conversely, the smaller the market, the more restrictive are the constraints imposed by the given technology, and the less scope does it afford for an increase in efficiency through the process of competition among the established firms. The more likely, therefore, is the initial structure to perpetuate itself.

In a limited market, changes in the structure can be expected to come about only if a potential entrant is willing to pursue an aggressive price policy to force his entry. In the abstract there is, of course, nothing to prevent this from happening if more efficient techniques of production are available, but in reality it is not very likely to occur. The outsider would have to enforce his entry through a price struggle which may last a long time and which may be risky since its final results can hardly be foreseen with accuracy. If he can expect to obtain a monopoly position after successful entry, he is more likely to attempt the struggle than if he must expect to share the market with others; also, if the potential entrant, in his turn, must expect to have to ward off later entry by firms still more efficient than himself, he is unlikely to incur the costs of such a price war, which he cannot then be confident of being able to recoup later. In the conditions of the underdeveloped countries another factor must be remembered: the established firms are generally likely to be domestic firms, whereas those potential entrants who have the edge of efficiency over them will often be foreign. In these conditions, institutional barriers to entry will often be created if the economic barriers are insufficient.

At this point it may be useful to point to one assumption of the Bain–Sylos-Labini–Modigliani theory which is reasonable for the advanced countries, but may have to be relaxed for the case of the underdeveloped economies, namely that the same array of techniques is equally accessible to the established firms and to those outside the industry. If potential entrants have access to a technique with long-run minimum average costs which are lower than those of any of the established firms (for example, a foreign firm which has access to a more efficient production technique than those of any of the existing firms), the entry-preventing price may be depressed by this overhanging threat of entry. From a welfare point of view the price and output so established will be closer to the "competitive" level, and therefore closer to the social optimum; but at the same time profits, and thus the rate of accumulation, will be depressed. It is sufficient, for this to happen, that there should be only a *threat* of entry; entry need not actually occur.

In such a situation, the outside threat of entry may induce a higher degree of concentration than would otherwise obtain. A larger share of the market will fall into the hands of the more efficient producers who are able, by virtue of their lower costs, to forestall this potential entry, and their rate of capacity utilization will be higher than it would otherwise be. But at the same time their monopolistic profits will be reduced. Although the utilization of resources within the *existing* structure will be more rational from a social point of view, the lower prices and profits and the larger output that will obtain in such a situation will also, by the same token, be more "efficient" in preventing entry. This means that it will retard the *transformation* of the existing productive structure by barring the entry of firms with better, lower-cost techniques; and profits and accumulation being lower, it will also slow down transformation from within the industry.

As Modigliani points out, the Sylos-Labini analysis shows that under oligopoly there may be several determinate equilibria, and the existing one may not be optimal from the social point of view.[12] As already indicated earlier, there may exist a "more rational" structure that would permit the same output to be produced at a lower total social cost, or a larger output at the same total social cost, even though all such oligopolistic or monopolistic structures depart from the conditions of Pareto optimality. But any move towards such a "more rational" structure is likely to be retarded, if not precluded altogether, by the very fact that the less rational structure is stable. From the point of view of aggregate accumulation this means that the actual surplus produced by such a structure will always be less than the potential surplus. The upshot of the argument is that where economies of large-scale production are present, the smaller market pays the penalty of being small not only by being unable to sustain efficient techniques initially, but also by being unable to transform an existing—from a social point of view less than rational—structure into a more rational one.

Because of limitations of financial, organizational, and technical resources, because of the uncertainty of investing in new markets, and because of the dynamics of growth itself, it is in practice not very likely that an underdeveloped economy will evolve the most rational structure that technology and market size potentially permit. Generally, it will not be, say, monopoly or a highly concentrated oligopoly of a few large firms that will be established, but a less rational oligopolistic structure, with relatively inefficient techniques, smaller and more plants, a lower output and a higher equilibrium price. The rigidities introduced into the economic system by oligopolies are all the more severe the more widespread they are throughout the economy, the more they restrict each other's expansion.

If the techniques effectively accessible to indigenous entrepreneurs in underdeveloped countries are markedly inferior to those at the disposal of potential foreign rivals, and the threat posed by them depresses the rate of profit, the underdeveloped economy may find itself in the worst of all possible worlds: oligopoly and its attendant rigidities are technically almost unavoidable, and these structures are highly stable and resist progress towards higher efficiency from within. At the same time, the constant threat of entry by foreign rivals, having access to superior levels of technique and backed up by vastly greater resources, forces the level of profits down in an effort to bar their entry; while this is beneficial from a welfare viewpoint, it has the result that the oligopolies fail to yield the above-normal profits usually associated with such market structures.

When the dominant firms are, as is so often the case, subsidiaries of foreign firms, the situation is still worse. Once entrenched, they are much better placed than native entrepreneurs to prevent further entry, both of other foreign rivals and even more easily so of indigenous entrepreneurs, except when the latter are given special institutional preferences. If the existing market structure makes it unprofitable for such firms to continue to invest in the markets in which they operate, they can easily shift their investments elsewhere, particularly to their home country, rather than accept a lower marginal rate of profit as local firms might have to do.

But granted that there will be little expansion from within of the markets in which oligopolies have become entrenched, what is there to prevent growth from going on, and markets from expanding all round, through the development of new industries, through diversification?

DIVERSIFICATION: THE DEFENCE AND RATIONALE OF MONOPOLISTIC RIVALRY

Sylos-Labini's theory deals only with undifferentiated oligopoly and has been criticized on that account, particularly with respect to his pessimistic conclusions in regard to the effects of oligopoly on the distribution of the fruits of technical progress and growth. The critique of his stagnation theory alleges that because he fails to take account of product innovation, i.e. diversification, he overlooks the most important way in which investment under oligopoly can continually widen its own field of expansion. His fears of stagnation are therefore held to be exaggerated.

Now it is indeed true that rapid, even accelerating diversification is perhaps the most outstanding feature of the productive structure of the advanced countries. This is true not only in the aggregate but also on the level of the individual firm. It is therefore all the more extraordinary that conventional theory should so largely have closed its eyes to the determinants of that aspect of monopoly which Schumpeter had raised to the rank of its main defence: its alleged role as the engine of progress and continual expansion. Perhaps Schumpeter's final conclusions with respect to the viability of capitalism came, albeit through a different route, too close to the grim Marxian prophesies; perhaps his defence of monopoly was, as Joan Robinson has remarked of his eminent follower, John Kenneth Galbraith, too cynical to be generally acceptable.[13] Whatever the reason, conventional theory has been unable to break out of its static framework and to account satisfactorily for diversification. It has consequently also given little stimulation to the empirical study of this phenomenon.* The only attempt at a theoretical analysis of diversification so far is Edith T. Penrose's penetrating *Theory of the Growth of the Firm*,[14] which is in many respects the logical complement of the oligopoly theories developed about the same time by Bain, Sylos-Labini and Modigliani, and provides some of the missing links which are necessary to incorporate the latter into a theory of development.

Within the fold of conventional economic literature, the latest and most comprehensive study of diversification so far is Michael Gort's *Diversification and Integration in American Industry*,[15] which cites only two earlier studies in the same field— the first by Willard L. Thorp in 1924,[16] and the second by Walter F. Crowder in 1941.[17] Gort finds that in 1954, firms having establishments in more than one census industry (at the 4-digit level of the Standard Industrial Classification Code) accounted for one-quarter of 1 per cent of the number of firms, but contributed 38 per cent to total employment. Judging by the evidence cited by M. A. Adelman, the share of this small fraction of all firms in total *assets* can be assumed to be well over 50 per cent.[18]

---

* There is, of course, a wealth of material in the history of business enterprises and in the literature on business administration, but this does not deal with diversification from a theoretical viewpoint.

In the manufacturing sector alone, Gort finds that multi-industry firms were 1·3 per cent of the total number, but this small fraction accounted for 53 per cent of total employment. If multi-plant, rather than multi-industry firms are examined, these percentages become 3 and 64 respectively. It is thus abundantly clear that the diversified firm is the most outstanding feature of a modern industrial structure. Gort also finds, not surprisingly, a positive association between diversification and size, as well as concentration ratios. Even more important is his finding that in the period covered by the study—1929 to 1954— there was an *accelerating* trend of diversification, and that new activities tended to be more remote from the original activities in terms of production processes or final uses of the products.[19]

It matters little that Gort's own explanations for the phenomenon he has seen and measured are inadequate or meaningless.* The real explanation strikes the eye as soon as one moves outside the orbit of the conventional static and atomistic approach. It is that the diversification Gort has observed in his painstaking study is the characteristic, one may even say the only possible, *modus operandi* of monopolistic rivalry. It is its only long-run escape from diminishing investment outlets.

The validity of the defence of monopoly that seems to lie in this expansion through diversification could be contested even for the case of the advanced countries. This study, however, is not concerned with the long-run viability of advanced capitalist systems under monopoly, but with the development prospects of the industrially backward countries. These differ from the advanced economies precisely in those structural features which apparently make it possible for the latter to maintain continued growth. One can therefore assume a "strong case" and admit, for the sake of argument, not only that under oligopoly and monopoly diversification is a real escape from stagnation, but that in the long run it is the *only possible outlet*.

---

* In his foreword to Gort's book, Stigler sees the causes of diversification in that "businessmen wish to achieve a greater stability of operations than specialization allows . . . or that (they) seek entry to young, rapidly growing industries . . .". This is much like saying of human reproduction that, because parents have children, this remarkable phenomenon must be due to a "preference" of mature humans to associate with young, rapidly growing members of the species.

But the degree to which oligopolistic firms can avail them-selves of this opportunity—in other words, the degree to which they can continue to invest at all—depends on the same factors which, in the underdeveloped economy, bring about oligopoly in the first place: technological dependence and market size. We shall argue that, given the assumptions made earlier about the attributes of underdevelopment, the investment opportuni-ties presented by diversification are not only narrow from the outset, but tend to shrink rapidly in consequence of the market restrictions engendered by oligopoly and monopoly, and as a result of the dependence upon imports of capital goods. At this point is it necessary to take a closer look at some of the deter-minants of diversification.

For an analysis of diversification it is necessary to introduce a distinction with respect to the concept of the firm which is due to Edith T. Penrose.[20] In conventional price theory, it will be recalled, the firm is defined by its product—a clearly defined commodity with a specific demand function.[21] In the static analysis of perfect competition or of pure monopoly this concept will serve, but for an analysis that goes beyond static equilibria it is inadequate. As soon as we come to deal with problems such as investment, innovation, or concentration, our concept of the firm has to come closer to reality and must refer to the real actors in the economic process. The distinction between these two concepts of the firm—the abstract personification of a single commodity of price theory, and that entity of real life which is meant in common parlance and in economic history, business literature, or in the literature on monopoly—is rarely made clear in the general economic literature.

The basic behaviour postulate for our analysis will be long-run profit maximization, which is equivalent to asset maximiza-tion.[22] Also, in the manner of the classics, we shall be con-cerned with competition as an ongoing process, and not as a state of equilibrium. For better distinction, it may perhaps more appropriately be called "rivalry".[22] This rivalry prevails among economic entities who constantly strive to augment their profits, i.e. entities who control investment. Since a stock of capital is an accumulation of investments over time this is equiva-lent to saying that firms are economic entities defined by having effective ultimate control over a certain aggregate of assets.

The firm is only instrumentally a maker of specific goods or a seller in a specific market. Products are differentiated according to the particular human wants they must satisfy, but the satisfaction of human wants is the last thing on earth that interests the firm, except as a means to the end of accumulating un-differentiated profits. The specificity of products or markets is, from the point of view of the firm, a constraint due to indivisibilities, to the specialization of the physical assets into which profits must be converted before they can produce more profits, or to the limited knowledge and skills of the owners of the firms.

Conventional theory is agreed that in a monopolistic structure price competition, if not completely evanescent as an instrument of rivalry, is at least of secondary importance. Sylos-Labini's analysis brings out clearly that generally it occurs only as a prelude to structural changes induced by fairly drastic changes in the external conditions—the size of the market, technology, the elasticity of demand, or factor prices. Any change in one or more of these has to be substantial to induce price rivalry. Once the structure has again become stabilized, price competition will once more decline into insignificance. This is likely to be particularly true where the prevalence of monopolistic practices has diffused its typical attitudes towards "accepted" modes of rivalry throughout the socio-economic system. Not only will it then tend to disappear in the monopolistic industries themselves, but as these become important in the economy their specific business ethic, the ideological superstructure which arises on the basis of their economic reality, will increasingly influence the typical modes of rivalry also in relatively competitive industries and in the social system in general. Collusion and conformity, interspersed with short bursts of sharp strife, take the place of active competition and continual rivalry; administration and authoritative direction supplant the self-regulating, anonymous mechanism of the market and its analogues in other spheres of social life.

Abstention from price competition, and a general attitude of "live-and-let-live" become the general rule, and such restraints of competition often obtain, in the economic as well as in other spheres, the sanction of the State. Where historical circumstances have left a legacy of co-operation among capitalists, for example by having united them in a national struggle for independence, the erosion of competition may be strengthened by ideological elements not directly traceable to the economic basis. The existence of an active development policy by the government operates in the same direction. The application of the rule of equality before the law to the disbursement of legal and other privileges or to the administration of various kinds of economic controls all have the effect of making the firms prone to combine, in the first place, *vis-à-vis* the government. Combination, however, does not end there any more than it remains confined to social intercourse, as Adam Smith observed long ago, but embraces other activities as well. Tendencies towards combination and collusion are thus likely to appear even in industries where economic conditions, considered by themselves, would lead one to expect a state of competition.

But the decline of price competition, the most conspicuous and direct form of rivalry, does not mean the abolition of rivalry itself. This remains the driving force of the private-enterprise system, and only its outward form changes. An oligopolistic structure in a specific market, as well as non-economic ideological factors, impose upon the individual firm a pattern of behaviour that is fundamentally alien to the laws of a private property system. That system requires a continual effort by each to augment his own property at the expense of all others. Individual businessmen no doubt act upon their honest conception of the "proper" business ethic, but in reality their behaviour is shaped by the constraints of the industry structure in which they are situated. These compel a spurious co-operation, an unstable truce, in regard to one mode of rivalry or with respect to some specific market, but thereby they only sharpen the competitive struggle in other areas or through other means. The accumulation of capital is the only end and purpose of the capitalist firm; if it fails to do so continually it will cease to exist. Therefore, if it cannot expand in its original industry because the structure there prevents it from extending its activities, it must go into new products and new markets.

What then are the alternative forms of rivalry open to the firm, bearing in mind that the struggle is ultimately for the size of the capital under its control, for the power and prestige it confers in a private-property system, and not merely for an income flow of profits which is somehow conceived as akin to wages? The monopolistic firm can maximize its long-run profits, as long as it confines itself only to its original industry, in two ways: it can attempt, like the firm in atomistic competition, to reduce its costs through the introduction of improved methods of production, and it can try to influence the shape and position of its demand curve. Let us examine what this implies in the long run for the instruments by which the firm competes for the increase of its capital, by comparison with the atomistic market structure.

In atomistic competition cost-reducing innovations will give the firm a temporary advantage over its rivals; with the same total costs as before it will be able to produce a larger output. Since its output accounts for a negligible share of the market, it will be able to sell all it produces without experiencing a fall in the ruling price. A larger volume of sales will yield greater profits for an unchanged amount of capital. Sooner or later, however, the innovation will be imitated, or a different innovation will be introduced by another firm, and with the general increase of industry output, market price will fall—ultimately, by the full extent of the average cost reduction achieved in the industry as a whole through the innovation. Those firms who failed to follow the innovators and remained at the higher cost level will be driven out, and the initial excess profits of the innovator will be eliminated by the price fall.

What will meanwhile have happened to capital and to the structure of the industry? The capital of the original innovator will have become augmented by the excess profits he has been able to obtain temporarily; marginal firms unable to follow in his footsteps will have made losses, their capital will have diminished, and some will have been squeezed out. Some firms will have gained strength at the expense of others, and to that extent a tendency of concentration will have appeared. But as long as the market continues to expand and the process of innovation remains randomly distributed among the many firms through time—sometimes one, sometimes the other firm innovating and reaping extra profits—there will be no barriers to entry and the industry will remain competitive.

The average size of firms will grow in this process, because cost reduction through technical progress must be accompanied by an increase in scale since firms will not divest themselves of capital to produce the previous volume of output but will, rather, keep their capital constant and expand their output. Nevertheless, since the fruits of technical progress are passed on to the consumer in the form of lower prices, the market keeps expanding at the same time that the average size of firm grows, and no firm will therefore attain a size which represents a significant share of the market. Neither sheer size nor differential access to technical progress, nor any other difference between firms, will constitute barriers to entry.

Where will the competitive firm of this textbook image invest its accumulated profits? Since its market share is minute, there are no practical limits to the further expansion of its original output. If the original plant is of optimal size in the given state of technique, the firm may establish an additional unit in the same industry. It may, however, equally well invest in a different industry. Its choice will be governed solely by the prospective rates of profit in the various industries, and neither the elasticity of demand nor the market structure in which it is situated will restrict it in any way. The only constraint is, on empirical grounds, the specialization of the firm-*cum*-entrepreneur to a specific industry; but with a sufficiently large size of the market and correspondingly larger firms, an increased division of managerial and entrepreneurial functions also becomes possible.

This, roughly, is the conventional picture of the competitive firm. Even this turns out to be quite different, as Edith T. Penrose has shown, when the firm is viewed dynamically. She introduces an important distinction between economies of size and "economies of growth".[24] The latter are the "internal economies available to an individual firm which make expansion profitable in particular directions". These arise because the process of production always involves experience and learning, so that even if at some initial stage the firm had achieved a perfect balance of processes, this initial bundle of resources could never remain completely specialized even with invariant external conditions. In fact, however, external conditions change constantly, so that even if there was no process of learning, they would soon "despecialize" the firm.

In the ongoing process of production both internal and external changes will combine to create imbalances of processes and resources. The firm will become aware that its available resources permit of additional uses, either by introducing the product so far made into new markets for different uses, or by using the same complement of productive facilities to make a physically different product, or a combination of both. At any given point of time the firm will find itself in a sub-optimal position with respect to its rate of utilization and the allocation of its resources, and consequently with respect to its maximization of profits. Change therefore exerts constant pressure for further change.

The tendency towards diversification is therefore immanent in the dynamics of production itself, irrespective of the nature of competition or any structural barriers to entry. The process of production is the application of resources which remain invariant throughout their lifetime by men who learn and thus change constantly, to a continually changing external environment. It is a dynamic process which involves a recurring creation of imbalances, of "loose ends". The discovery and the development of such partial excess capacities—in the sense of being able to produce more, and particularly *different* goods with a given bundle of resources—usually requires some marginal addition of productive facilities to complement the original set-up. Since the existing stock of resources is largely specialized and characterized by indivisibilities, the restoration of the balance through contraction is impossible: it would result in loss. This leaves only the possibility of balancing through additions of new resources. But as soon as these are applied to production, new imbalances are generated; the process never comes to an end—as soon as the balance is restored for one purpose, a new imbalance appears.*

These tendencies towards diversification which are inherent in the growth process of the firm even when considered in isolation become reinforced to the point of being the dominant form of growth whenever there are, in addition to these "economies of growth", also (a) economies of large-scale production, and

---

* Penrose quotes the following illuminating statement by an industrial engineer in charge of product development in a firm: "Every time we make something, we have something left over, and have to find something to do with that. And when we find something to do with it we usually find that leaves us with something else. It is an endless process."[25]

(b) constraints on further expansion in the original industry. An oligopolistic or monopolistic structure imposes such restrictions on expansion, and therefore pushes investment into new lines of activity.

THE CASE OF DIVERSIFICATION
UNDER MONOPOLY

Consider, first, the usual static model of the firm in a monopolistic position. Such a firm has basically three choices for the investment of its accumulating profits (assuming for the time being that its demand curve is independent of its cost curve): it may invest in (a) cost-reducing innovations; (b) expanding its capacity without change of technique; and (c) product innovation. The first of these three alternatives only postpones, so to speak, the problem of investment outlets that arises when a firm must take into account that the demand curve is downward-sloping, and the second reduces in the long run to the third.

With a given demand, it is irrational for a monopolistic firm to invest in the expansion of capacity of its original product if average cost remains unchanged, except as a measure to forestall entry or to initiate a struggle for a bigger market share. Since it is by assumption aware of the negative slope of the demand curve, the firm has presumably set its output where marginal cost equals marginal revenue. With a given demand curve, the marginal revenue schedule remains unchanged, but investment in additional capacity will raise the long-run marginal cost curve. The loss resulting from such a course of action would therefore be even greater than if the firm had attempted to increase output and sales from existing capacity.

Given an unchanging demand curve, and ignoring investment in cost-reducing improvements which only raise the same problem at a later stage, there remains only investment in new products. This may take the form of vertical integration or of lateral diversification. Neither of these are, of course, likely to appear in a pure form, that is to say as expansion into products that are totally unrelated to the firm's productive resources or existing markets. This is so because, as Penrose has emphasized, there will always be at least *some* resources that are not utilized to their full technical capacity. The existence of indivisibilities, as well as the continual internal creation of "excess ability" through the learning process, constantly hold out the incentive of increasing the output–capital ratio through the better utilization of such partially employed resources. The new products are therefore likely to have some technical propinquity to the original activity, or to be related to it through market similarity.*

The tendency towards diversification is likely to be stronger, the lower the elasticity of demand in the original product, the greater the excess capacity, and the lower the degree of specialization of the firm's productive facilities. It is not implausible to expect all three of these factors to combine in the conditions of an underdeveloped economy: the price-elasticity of demand for any particular commodity probably tends to be low in a low-income demand structure where goods are more likely to be complementary to each other rather than close substitutes; with limited markets and constraints of technical indivisibilities as well as for a number of other reasons, excess capacity is likely to be prevalent; and where simpler and less mechanized techniques are chosen, equipment is likely to be less specialized than with a higher degree of mechanization and technical sophistication. The main factor working in the opposite direction is a yet unstable competitive structure (which, however, is not likely to last long), or an expanding and highly income-elastic demand.

The closer the firm is to the model of the Chamberlinian monopolistic competitor, the greater will be the push towards diversification, for the tangency of its cost curve to the demand curve means that it has unemployed resources that call for utilization in another product precisely because they cannot be put to profitable use in the original industry. Once diversification has set in, it is likely to produce further diversification as a result of the creation of new imbalances, new partial excess capacities and "excess abilities", and in consequence of the wider spread of the field in which external change and internal learning can take place.

* Market similarity, whether it means complementarity of products or a range of close substitutes, will have the by-product that the firm's monopolistic position will be strengthened because it will control a greater span of related products. Integration, which brings under the firm's control the inputs which it formerly had to buy from other firms, has a similar effect.

The investment outlets provided by the firm's original industry will thus be limited by the rate of change in the shape or position of the demand curve. The more elastic its cost function with respect to volume of output, the higher will be the rate of capacity utilization for any given demand curve. If the demand curve now shifts, there will be a strong inducement to expand capacity in the original line of activity. If the absolute accretion to demand that the firm can expect is small relative to the size of the optimal plant and to the magnitude of the investible capital at its disposal (whether internally accumulated or provided from the outside), the firm will have to search for investment outlets outside its original industry. The higher the average level of income in the economy, the more elastic with respect to price is the demand for any individual commodity likely to be; and the more rapidly income grows, the more likely is the demand curve for the specific good to shift, as long as its income elasticity remains positive. The greater, therefore, the scope for undiversified investment. Also, the higher the level of average income, the larger are the markets for individual goods, and the less therefore the likelihood of excess capacity due to technical indivisibilities.

What can be said about the tendencies towards diversification in the case of the pure monopolist? If there is an increase in demand, the monopolist may by definition expect the total increment to accrue to him. He can therefore expand his primary output at the rate at which demand rises. It is reasonable to assume, on empirical grounds, that the rate of accumulation will usually exceed the rate of growth of demand. A profit rate of, say, 20 per cent is not very high, judging by the available data on monopolistic profits; on the other hand, it would be very unusual to find a growth rate of 10 per cent for total income together with an income elasticity of $2 \cdot 0$ for the monopolist's product, which would be necessary to make these two rates equal. With such a high income elasticity of demand the monopolist would be hard put to prevent entry. Generally, therefore, the monopolist will have to turn to diversification as an outlet for his accumulated profits—assuming, to repeat, constant technique and independence of demand of cost curves.

THE CASE OF OLIGOPOLY

In the case of oligopoly the situation is more complex, and the investment opportunities afforded by the original industry are likely to dry up even sooner than in the case of the pure monopolist. The individual oligopolist cannot expect the total increment of industry demand to accrue to him alone. According to Tibor Scitovsky, who analysed this problem,[26] three alternatives arise for such a firm if the plants operated by the existing firms are of optimum size: (a) the firm may expect to obtain only its proportionate share in the additional industry demand, and will thus be forced to invest in sub-optimal plant to maintain its share in the expanding market; (b) it may instal optimal plant, but acquiesce in its partial utilization or try, simultaneously, to encroach upon the markets of its rivals; and (c) it may postpone investment until its individual share in the market will enable it to operate an optimum-size plant at the usual rate of capacity utilization.

It is easily seen that all three alternatives lead to a fall in the profit rate, or carry the risks involved in an attempt to upset the existing distribution of market shares. As can be seen from Sylos-Labini's analysis, the latter will hardly be undertaken unless the changes in technology and market size are very substantial. Sylos-Labini's theory also shows that it is more likely that the expansion of the market will induce entry: the smaller the absolute increase, and the greater the economies of large-scale production of the leading firms, the more likely is the entry of additional *small* plants. Their entry will, in turn, preclude the further expansion of the larger firms in the same industry. Thus, even an expanding market is not likely to upset the stability of an oligopolistic structure unless the absolute extent of the expansion is very considerable.

The escape from this limitation on expansion is diversification. A strong oligopoly which is not immediately threatened by entry might conceivably keep supply inelastic for a while, by a tacit agreement to let sleeping dogs lie, not to encroach upon each other's market shares, and jointly postpone investment until the installation of optimum-size plant becomes feasible for all. This, however, would require a most improbable degree of collusion and would imply the possibility of joint long-range planning. With expanding demand, prices and profits would meanwhile rise, and this would only aggravate the insufficiency of investment outlets in the same industry in the next round. Before long, then, the oligopolistic firm will have to turn to other industries. The larger the scale of its original operations, the less likely is it to be constrained by specialization in terms of access to production techniques, knowledge of markets, or commercial conditions in general; the greater, therefore, will be its opportunities and inducements for further diversification.

In reality there will always be improvements in methods of production, not only through investment in new capacity, but also as a result of the replacement of worn-out equipment with newer, more efficient units. This may result in a substitution of capital for labour, but generally it also results in an expansion of scale and an increase in the output–capital ratio. If the cost advantage of the new techniques is considerable, this may upset the existing industry structure, but when this is not the case, or where the same technique is accessible to several oligopolists, and the scale of output is restricted by demand conditions, part of the firm's depreciation funds will be set free and will join the accumulated profits in the search for investment outlets outside the original industry.

With stable market shares and where technical improvements involve larger-scale plant, an oligopolist will thus have less opportunity and incentive to invest in technical progress in his original industry than the monopolist. Since he must share any accretion to demand with his rivals, the reduction of costs that might be obtainable at capacity levels of output would be nullified by a lower rate of utilization. In the case of oligopoly the need to diversify will therefore be much stronger, and will set in earlier, than in the case of a monopolist, even where the market expands.

With a demand curve which is independent of the cost curve, the urge to accumulate will sooner or later lead to diversification in any non-competitive industry structure. The greater the rate at which demand for the industry's output increases in relation to the rate of accumulation, and the larger the absolute size of the increment to demand in relation to the optimum size of plant, the later will diversification appear. The higher the rate at which aggregate demand expands as a result of factors exogenous to the industry, the greater will be the opportunities for diversification, since demand itself expands by way of becoming more diversified. The greater the dominance of the monopolistic structures in the economy, the larger the share of aggregate demand which they supply, the fewer the investment outlets provided by autonomous shifts in demand, the stronger will be the tendency for investment to depend primarily on diversification.

INVESTMENT IN SELLING COSTS

Apart from investment in productive capital goods, whether in the original industry or in another, the monopolistic firm has two further outlets for its accumulated profits: investment in financial assets, or in an attempt to change the demand function for its original products.

For the individual firm investment in liquid assets may be a rational course of action: financial flexibility may be more advantageous than investment in fixed assets if risks are great or if the expected rate of profit on alternative investments is low. Such an increased liquidity preference, of course, spells stagnation if it becomes general. If there were no constraints arising from the factors we have emphasized throughout, namely technology and the structure and size of the market, there would of course be no reason why aggregate growth should cease. Profits which find no profitable investment in the industry in which they originated could be deposited with the banking system, and be lent out to other investors. The same would happen if the monopolistic firms were to invest in financial assets other than money. The original accumulators of the profits would merely forego control over part of their accumulated capital, which would be put at the disposal of new investors through the intermediary of the capital market, and would thus flow into new industries. From the aggregate viewpoint there would be continued growth through the diversification of the productive structure.

This presupposes that the impediments to continued investment by way of diversification by the original owners of the investible capital themselves are to be found on the supply side, so that they are unable to avail themselves of investment opportunities which exist outside their industries. Otherwise there would be no reason why they should lend out their capital to others and presumably accept a lower rate of return. Such situations do, no doubt, occur, particularly in the early stages of industrial growth, but in practice their importance is not very significant. Furthermore, in an underdeveloped economy, where the capital markets are generally rudimentary and where risk and inflationary pressures make lenders unwilling to invest in fixed-value assets, it is unrealistic to assume such a mobility of capital. It is much more likely that the absence of investment outlets will result in capital flight or in investment in non-reproducible assets, such as urban real estate or agricultural land. From the point of view of the economy as a whole this again would mean stagnation or even retrogression.

The monopolistic firm may use its accumulated profits to try and change the shape and position of the demand curve for its original product, both in the short and in the long run. A change in variable costs, such as by incurring higher sales costs, advertisement, or some forms of minor product differentiation which involve no substantial changes in production processes, is from the viewpoint of the seller merely a substitute for price competition—although not so from the viewpoint of the consumer.* To the extent that it becomes established throughout the industry, it will result in a general rise in costs, which may or may not be passed on to the consumer; the result with respect to profits is indeterminate. In any case, such differentiation will be subject to diminishing returns, so that even if this policy is initially successful in expanding demand and output, the accumulating profits will ultimately find no further investment opportunities in the original industry. If such costs of product differentiation become diffused throughout an industry without substantially expanding total industry demand, profits will fall, and if learning by experience is taken into account, this form of inter-firm rivalry will decline or will be established at some

* The informative value that advertisement may have for the consumer in an underdeveloped country is probably much less than in an advanced economy, where sales costs and advertisement may help, within limits, to extricate the consumer—at least in the relatively well-to-do classes—from his *embarras de richesses*, and in genuinely difficult choice situations.

tacitly agreed level. Competition will then again be forced into diversification.

In the conditions of an underdeveloped economy it is in any case reasonable to rule out such minor product differentiation as an important form of rivalry, at least for goods of mass consumption. Most product differentiation of the kind referred to here depends on a high level of affluence and literacy, both of which do not exist in an underdeveloped economy.* Product differentiation there will have to be more tangible to have an appreciable effect, and substantial differentiation generally requires a change in production processes and is thus equivalent to a mixture of sales costs and diversification proper.

The extension of credit to consumers is another variant of investment in financial assets. A shift of the short-run demand curve through the extension of consumers' credit would enable the firm to expand sales from existing capacity as well as to augment capacity. Much of what has been said before about investment in financial assets in general applies to this case as well. But in addition, if the extension of consumers' credit is intended to provide outlets for an increase of productive capacity, it may result in a fall in the marginal rate of profit. Unless consumers' debt interest were as high as the profit rate on capital invested in productive assets—which may in practice often be the case—the overall capital-output ratio would rise and the rate of profit would fall.

In the short run this is a feasible alternative if the diversion of part of the accumulated profits into consumers' debt is combined with improvements in production methods which lower the capital–output ratio and thus set free part of the capital necessary to produce a given output. In the longer run, the additional investment outlets provided through this route must necessarily exhaust themselves. The extension of credit beyond a certain level is fraught with a high degree of risk, and cannot exceed a certain ratio to the rise in consumers' real current income. Moreover, the stimulation of demand through credit extension or any other means is always easier for new products than for old. The firm would therefore have an incentive to

---

* Except for the industries that cater to the demand of the high-income groups, which may easily become the "dynamic" industries. See next chapter.

diversify even if it were to divert part of its profits to the creation of consumers' credit in all possible lines of production. Like minor product differentiation, expansion through the extension of consumers' credit is probably not very important in the underdeveloped economies. One has only to remember the conditions necessary for it—a highly developed legal system, a smoothly functioning financial structure, sophisticated marketing methods, and, above all, price and cost stability, to see how far-fetched it must usually be in practice.

In a monopolistic structure, whatever its particular form and whatever the short-run alternatives initially adopted by an individual firm, there is a long-run tendency towards diversification as the only possible form of growth and as the dominant form of rivalry among firms. Each round of further investment in the original industry brings diversification another step nearer, each innovation which is successful in raising short-run profits only accelerates the accumulation of the capital which will have to search for new investment outlets. To the extent that the expansion of aggregate demand lags behind the rate of accumulation—which will happen wherever investment expenditure leaks into imports—the competition among individual capitalists for the existing demand will become keener and will lead to the growth of some and the wiping out of others. Part of the social capital will be rendered valueless, and the higher efficiency of the winners will only partially offset the loss to society of productive assets that results from this struggle for the survival of the biggest. Increased concentration, in turn, tends to further accelerate this process. Alternatively, and particularly where the size of firms is absolutely small and the volume of discrete profit accumulations is of an order of magnitude comparable with the traditional consumption levels of their owners, the system may settle down to a low-level equilibrium in which profits are largely consumed.

DIVERSIFICATION IN THE UNDERDEVELOPED ECONOMY

In an advanced economy the creation of additional income through the development of new industries will in part counteract the inherent tendencies of a monopolistic system to stagnate.

As long as we do not inquire too closely into the nature of the new demands created and satisfied in this manner, and as long as we accept the diversion of resources into uses and pursuits which in large part serve the function of maintaining the existing system, the post-Schumpeterian defence of monopoly will hold within wide limits, and the system will remain viable. Nevertheless, the implications of the workings of such a structure and the mode of competition which it imposes for the directions and limits of growth, through their effects on aggregate savings, investment and income, have been considered only for the mature capitalist economy. The direct effects of a monopolistic mode of rivalry have been viewed as a relatively secondary problem of misallocation of resources, and often as the necessary price of progress. Since diversification in the mature economy, with its large market and a productive structure in which domestic expenditure is not structurally prevented from creating domestic income, need not result in *technical* inefficiency, such a possibility has been completely overlooked.

In this light it becomes understandable that Stigler should ask, with respect to Gort's finding that American industry has been diversifying at an accelerating rate, how one can explain "this increasing and . . . even accelerating diversification, when one of the most famous theorems in economics says that the division of labour increases with the size of the market?"[27] He forgets that this theorem holds only in perfect competition, and that the division of labour is limited not only by the extent, but also *by the competitive structure* of the market—by the extent to which each firm is free to expand either within its original industry or to invest in any other it may choose.

The literature on economic development almost completely disregards the problem of monopoly, and the critique of the private-enterprise system that hinges on it is considered irrelevant for the underdeveloped economies. This is true even of the Marxist school, although Marxist theorists put the problem of monopoly in the centre of their economic and political analysis of capitalism. The prevalence of monopoly in the underdeveloped economies is sometimes recognized as an empirical fact, but it is then generally attributed to the persistence of quasi-feudal traditions and to an alliance of the new capitalist classes with the pre-capitalist ruling classes, or to the domination of foreign capital. In other words, it is seen as a sign of *immaturity*, as a symptom of a yet insufficient development of indigenous capitalism proper, rather than as one of its results. Even Marxists thus concede the possibility of growth under capitalism, at least up to the stage of maturity, and in this respect they do not challenge the view of their opponents.

If the underdeveloped countries display symptoms of relative stagnation, or develop in a pattern which is so distorted from a welfare point of view that it runs into ever-recurring bottlenecks and becomes socially and politically intolerable, this is ascribed mainly to their inability to develop a properly functioning capitalist system in opposition to inherited backwardness and repression from within, and to the overwhelming power of economic and political imperialism from without. Thus, for example, Paul A. Baran wrote that

> . . . a *complete* substitution of capitalist market rationality for the rigidities of semi-feudal servitude would have represented . . . an important step in the direction of progress. . . . While in the advanced countries, such as France or Great Britain, the economically ascending middle-classes developed at an early stage a new rational world outlook . . . the poor, fledgling bourgeoisie of the underdeveloped countries sought nothing but accommodation to the prevailing order. . . . It is quite conceivable that a "conservative" exit from this impasse might have succeeded in breaking the deadlock, in loosening the hide-bound social and political structure of their countries and in creating the institutional arrangements indispensable for a measure of social and economic progress.[28]

It would be foolish to deny that these institutional arrangements are a *necessary* condition of progress, or that they can lead to a substantial measure of progress. But aside from the question how they are to be brought about except through that same progress itself, one must ask: Are they also a *sufficient* condition? If monopoly is for all practical purposes inevitable in the conditions from which development must start in our times, will it not compound the difficulties of growth—and they are many and grave—that are independent of the particular characteristics of the social system?

Since 1952, when Baran wrote the essay quoted above, over forty new countries have achieved political independence, and of those which had been sovereign before, many have had to embark upon development policies as a result of mounting external and internal political pressures. Some of these countries, at least, still put their hope for development in some "Young Turk" movement striving to introduce the capitalist market rationality of which Baran spoke. Their aspirations can hardly be assumed to be limited to *some* measure of progress; the real question before them is whether long-run, continued advance is possible. The question is therefore whether the "conservative exit" from the impasse of underdevelopment is in fact an exit, or rather a *cul-de-sac*. The question is whether it may not lead, because of the objective conditions in which it must take place, to an early blocking of growth—even in the ideal case, where there is no foreign domination or other extraneous obstacles, where feudal backwardness is thrown off, and where a capitalist market rationality is fairly completely introduced.

The substitution of capitalism, however imperfect, for tribalism, primitive despotism, semi-feudalism, or a system of semi-capitalistic *latifundiae* is no doubt a step in the direction of progress. It may also readily be granted that the external factors which hold back development are in reality often much more important in the here-and-now of practical policy issues than any innate tendencies of a capitalist pattern of development to stifle its own growth. Yet, it is possible that the external obstacles will gradually be removed through international action, or that under the umbrella of political alignments around the great power blocks there will be considerable leeway for different routes of development in the domestic sphere of the underdeveloped countries. The question whether development along the lines of private enterprise will not remain a very small step towards progress, limited only to the threshold of growth, therefore remains very real.

If it is granted that the economic structure of the underdeveloped countries is most likely to assume monopolistic forms, the immediate question that needs to be answered is whether the defences of the viability and growth potential of the advanced monopolistic private enterprise system are equally applicable to the underdeveloped countries. These defences are mainly three: (a) the constant expansion of the market through diversification; (b) compensatory intervention by the government; and (c) expansion of the market through foreign trade. The last two will be dealt with in Chapters 4 and 5. What of diversification? Can it, by itself, assure sustained growth, as it seems to do in the advanced economies?

The answer must be in the negative. In the advanced economy, diversification and innovation stimulates the demand for capital goods, creates employment and widens the markets, and thus staves off stagnation. In the underdeveloped economy, however, where the import-coefficient of investment is high, the employment-creating effects of diversification-induced investment will be much smaller.

Furthermore, the income distribution in the underdeveloped countries is highly unequal to begin with. To the extent that the higher incomes originate in profits this inequality is a condition for the accumulation of capital, and can therefore only be eliminated by reducing the overall rate of accumulation. Greater equality would only dissipate savings into consumption. A widening of the market through the reduction of the savings ratio would only mean a lower rate of growth. But not only the relative income distribution is important, but also the *absolute* size of the shares of the different income groups, for these determine the absolute extent of the market for different categories of goods. The absolute size of demand represented by the upper-income groups remains small even if one includes the relatively privileged urban classes of workers, civil servants, and the members of the commercial classes.

If there are considerable disparities between the technically determined scales of production and market size with respect to the goods of mass consumption, then similar or even greater economies of large-scale production are likely to exist in those industries that cater to the demands of the wealthy few. Many of these industries, it must be remembered, are a late development even in the advanced economies, and are thus the product of a technical universe in which a high degree of specialization and large-scale production are the rule.

The diversifying monopolists are therefore likely to be forced, to an increasing degree, to instal sub-optimal plant, in which their profit rate can be maintained only through various forms of subsidization and by other means which ultimately fall upon the shoulders of the mass of the population. If there are sectors in the economy whose standards of consumption are compressible, this process can continue for a good while, but this manner of creating new investment outlets only diverts potential output and consumption away from the industries of mass consumption to those of relative luxury goods. The overall scope for the application of advanced techniques which depend on large scales of output is thereby reduced. The gains in productivity which can be achieved will be smaller as economies of large-scale production have to be foregone for lack of a sufficient market, and the rate of overall capital accumulation will therefore be less than its potential. In practice, the drying up of investment outlets will generally cause capital flight together with diversification of that capital which stays at home.*

The technological dependence which characterizes an underdeveloped economy and which, in combination with its initially small markets, creates the monopolistic structure, therefore also takes away the main defence that such a structure can be held to have against stagnation: diversification and its inherent widening of the market, even if the constant waste of productive resources which it entails in order to maintain the existing system is accepted as the necessary price for the residual progress that can be achieved.

One further point remains to be added. Where markets are small, monopolistic concentration may itself be highly concentrated, and may reduce the incentives and opportunities for diversification. Oligopoly, we have seen, retards process innovation because it leads to an expanded scale of output and therefore involves the encroachment upon the market shares of

* Many of the points made earlier have also been made in a study of Brazil by the United Nations Economic Commission for Latin America, under the direction of Maria Conceiçao Tavares. This study, which takes Brazil as the prototype for the process of growth and import substitution in Latin America, emphasizes—like most ECLA studies—the role of the external sector rather than the competitive structure. Nevertheless, the differences are more a matter of emphasis than contradiction, and most of the phenomena described here as accompanying the process of development are confirmed by that study. Particularly interesting is the analysis of the increasing orientation of Brazilian industry to the markets represented by the high-income sectors, which the study calls "vertical market growth", and which had its roots in the high level of imports of consumers' goods by the capitalist export sector before the Great Depression forced Brazil and other primary producers into import substitution. The market for luxury goods was in this case large, and yet it is exceedingly small in terms of optimum size of plant.[29]

rivals. Where the total market is small, there may develop an "oligopoly of oligopolies", in which firms will be reluctant to invade the sphere of interest of their rivals even by way of diversification, for fear that their entry into other industries will bring about reprisals in the form of an attack upon their market shares in their original industries. Such a situation can lead to a far-reaching trustification of entire sectors, and the oligopolists will then at best tend to go into so-called "joint ventures", or else stagnate completely.*

NOTES AND REFERENCES

1. JOAN ROBINSON, *Essays in the Theory of Economic Growth*, Macmillan & Co., London, 1963, p. 41.
2. JOSEPH A. SCHUMPETER, *Capitalism, Socialism and Democracy*, Harper & Bros., New York, 1942, pp. 82–84.
3. JOAN ROBINSON, *Economics of Imperfect Competition*, Macmillan & Co., London 1933. EDWARD HASTING CHAMBERLIN, *The Theory of Monopolistic Competition*, Harvard University Press, Cambridge (Mass.), 1933.
4. W. ARTHUR LEWIS, *Economic Development with Unlimited Supplies of Labour*, The Manchester School, May 1954, reprinted in A. N. AGARWALA and S. P. SINGH (eds.), *The Economics of Underdevelopment*, Oxford University Press, New York, 1963, p. 401.
5. JOAN ROBINSON, *Essays . . .*, pp. 25 and 34.
6. JOAN ROBINSON, *Economics . . .*, p. 5.
7. JOE S. BAIN, *Barriers to New Competition*, Harvard University Press, Cambridge (Mass.), 1956.
8. PAOLO SYLOS-LABINI, *Oligopoly and Technical Progress*, Harvard University Press, Cambridge (Mass.), 1962—first published in Italian in 1956.
9. FRANCO MODIGLIANI, New developments on the oligopoly front, *The Journal of Political Economy*, **66,** June 1958. See also the discussion in the same journal, **67,** August 1959.

---

* At a relatively advanced stage this may lead to the trustification of nearly the whole economy. Japan is an extreme example of such a process, where the same group of oligopolists appeared and reappeared together in a wide range of industries, without any one of them necessarily having a dominant share in any specific industry. This apparently peaceful sharing not only of the markets, but also of the investment outlets, can of course not be seen from a study of concentration ratios in specific markets—which may not increase at all. For a particularly interesting study of this interlocking chain of oligopolies see ELEANOR M. HADLEY, *Concentrated Business Power in Japan.*[30] For an example of the individual-market type of approach, see EUGENE ROTWEIN, *Economic Concentration and Monopoly in Japan.*[31]

10. PAOLO SYLOS LABINI, *op. cit.*, p. 34.
11. *Ibid.*, p. 33.
12. FRANCO MODIGLIANI, *op. cit.*, pp. 221–2.
13. JOAN ROBINSON, *Collected Economic Papers*, Vol. II, Basil Blackwell, Oxford, 1960, p. 8 and p. 244. See also her review of Galbraith's *American Capitalism* in the *Economic Journal*, December 1952.
14. EDITH TINTON PENROSE, *The Theory of the Growth of the Firm*, John Wiley & Sons, New York, 1959.
15. MICHAEL GORT, *Diversification and Integration in American Industry*, National Bureau of Economic Research, Princeton University Press, Princeton, 1962.
16. WILLARD L. THORP, *The Integration of Industrial Operations*, U.S. Bureau of the Census, Washington D.C., 1924.
17. WALTER F. CROWDER, *The Integration of Manufacturing Operations*, Temporary National Economic Committee, U.S. Senate, Monograph No. 27, Washington D.C., 1941.
18. M. A. ADELMAN, The measurement of industrial concentration, *The Review of Economics and Statistics*, **33**, November 1951, p. 278.
19. GORT, *op. cit.*, pp. 27–28.
20. PENROSE, *op. cit.*, pp. 11 and 14.
21. For one of many similar definitions, see JOAN ROBINSON, *Economics of Imperfect Competition*, p. 17: "A firm is a concern very similar to the firms of the real world, but which produces only one commodity." If our argument is correct, this slight difference makes the firm completely *dissimilar* to any firm in the real world.
22. In static, short-run theory, profits are obviously also assumed to be maximized only in the short run, the long run being disregarded. But short-run profit maximization may conflict with long-run profit maximization when there is imperfect competition. This has led various writers to introduce the concept of asset maximization in connection with monopoly and oligopoly. See, for example, WILLIAM FELLNER, *Competition Among the Few*, Alfred Knopf, New York, 1949, p. 162, and SCHUMPETER, *op. cit.*, p. 96. This is also implicit in JOAN ROBINSON'S *Essays in the Theory of Economic Growth*, Macmillan & Co., London, 1963, p. 45.
23. See also SYLOS-LABINI, *op. cit.*, p. 52. A similar distinction is made by many theorists who dealt with the monopoly problem, for example by FRITZ MACHLUP, *The Economics of Sellers Competition*, Johns Hopkins Press, Baltimore, 1952, and by J. M. CLARK, *Competition as a Dynamic Process*, The Brookings Institution, Washington, 1961, chapter 2.
24. PENROSE, *op. cit.*, pp. 99 ff.
25. Quoted in PENROSE, *op. cit.*, p. 69, from A. D. H. KAPLAN, *Big Enterprise in a Competitive System*, The Brookings Institution, Washington, 1954.
26. TIBOR SCITOVSKY, Economies of scale, competition, and European integration, *The American Economic Review*, March 1956, pp. 75 ff.
27. GORT, *op. cit.*, p. xx.

28. PAUL A. BARAN, *On the Political Economy of Backwardness*, The Manchester School, January 1952, reprinted in AGARWALA and SINGH, *op. cit.*, pp. 76–78.
29. United Nations, Economic Commission for Latin America, MARIA CONCEIÇAO TAVARES, The growth and decline of import substitution in Brazil, *Economic Bulletin for Latin America*, **9,** No. 1, March 1964.
30. ELEANOR M. HADLEY, *Concentrated Business Power in Japan*, unpublished doctoral dissertation, Radcliffe College, 1949. Dr. Hadley, who studied the concentration of economic power in Japan while serving on the staff of the Supreme Headquarters of the Allied Powers after World War II, goes so far as to consider Japan's economic structure as a gross deviation from the image of a "normal" capitalist system (cf. p. 372). Similar observations were made by other Western economists—for example, CORWIN D. EDWARDS, *Report of the Mission on Japanese Combines*, U.S. Department of State, Washington, 1946, p. vii. See also ROBERT A. BRADY, *Business as a System of Power*, Columbia University Press, New York, 1943, chapter III.
31. EUGENE ROTWEIN, Economic concentration and monopoly in Japan, *Journal of Political Economy*, **72,** No. 3, June 1964.

CHAPTER 3

GROWTH IN THE PSEUDO-CLOSED
ECONOMY: (I) THE CASE OF
LAISSEZ-FAIRE

THE INITIAL CONDITIONS

The analysis of growth usually starts with a model of a closed economy, but the assumption of technological dependence means that imports are required by definition. In order to avoid the complications introduced by the problems of foreign trade we shall assume, as a first approximation, that the level of exports is at all times sufficient for the necessary imports, or that the economy has other sources of foreign exchange to pay for them. We shall assume that the necessary adjustments to set free enough foreign exchange for the imports of capital goods have already been effected at the start of the process, through any one of the various mechanisms that may bring this about. We shall ignore all income effects that may arise through a changing volume of exports, and shall call this a pseudo-closed economy.

The first requirement for the description of the process of development is to specify the behaviour postulates of the model. In Chapter 1 we defined underdevelopment as including the existence of a politically determined goal of economic development. Strictly speaking, this means that the government cannot be excluded from the analysis, for the social objective of growth must be embodied in a set of policy measures designed to attain it, independently of the actions and motivations of individuals. But in order to maintain the usual device of first analysing a pure *laissez-faire* economy, we shall assume that the government entrusts development to the activity of individuals without active interference on its own part, and will refrain from inter-

intervention as long as actual growth achieves the desired rate, but that it stands ready to be the growth-promoter of last resort and to adopt a more active role in case its initial policy fails to achieve the objective.

For the sake of realism we may picture the government as representing some "Young Turk" movement which enjoys broad popular support. Economic growth is a prime national goal which takes precedence, as the process starts, over particular sectoral interests. At the same time, development is to take place exclusively through private enterprise, which alone is charged with carrying out the functions of investment and production for the market. Those areas of investment and production which are traditionally accepted as belonging in the domain of government, such as the provision of social and economic overheads, will be ignored for the time being.

Our imaginary government, intent on introducing a fully developed capitalist system, will do everything within its power to create the institutional arrangements and a general climate favourable to the promotion of private enterprise. The legal and institutional framework is set up so as to stimulate capitalist accumulation and to create confident expectations. There may be some system of economic planning and programming, but this is of a strictly indicative nature, and relies for its implementation on the voluntary activity of private entrepreneurs. Its main purpose is to create confident expectations by providing forecasts and projections, but the government neither intends to ensure their achievement through direct action, nor does it contemplate any coercive measures to make individual entrepreneurs adhere to them. It may use the carrot freely, but will not brandish any sticks.

This policy not only leaves private entrepreneurs as free as in the usual *laissez-faire* model to decide their own investment, price and output policies, but in addition creates a social climate in which "strong animal spirits" meet with general approbation, as an attitude which conforms to the national goals. Entrepreneurs whose investment policies work towards the national goal can expect favourable legislation and other support from the government, and will be given advantages over their more sluggish confrères. The general state of expectations in the economy is thus assumed to be favourable.

By contrast with the behaviour postulates of a similar type found in the literature on economic development, these assumptions are here taken only as *initial* conditions. They are not parameters, but variables which themselves depend upon the way the system will function in the course of time. Since we postulate that development, as a national goal, is to take place within the framework of a private enterprise system, the achievement of the goal devolves upon the emergent capitalist class. If the national goal is to be attained through the economic actions of individuals pursuing their own ends, the national policies must further those private ends. If a conflict develops, one or the other will have to give way to a greater or lesser extent.

We further assume, as has already been implicit in what was said before, that there is no lack of so-called entrepreneurship. The vaunted shortage of this "factor of production", to which so much of the observed backwardness is often attributed, may be no more as Paul Baran put it, than the tautological statement that "in the absence of industrial capitalism there are no industrial capitalists, and vice versa".[1] Once we postulate that the underdeveloped economy is bent on economic growth, we already imply that there is an adequate supply of men of talent and leadership who are capable and willing to put this development into effect. That they may lack in technical and economic sophistication is another matter; this, precisely, is why they so often look to some collective effort to support their individual endeavours, why they often regard the State as the repository and executor of the collective political will, whose task it is to supplement the deficient individual entrepreneurship.

Among the initial technical conditions which determine the process of growth in our model, the dependence on foreign technology has already been discussed at length, and little needs to be added here in regard to its objective aspects. There is, however, a connexion between this dependence and the behaviour postulates which deserves mention, although it carries us perhaps a little into the field of social psychology. Economic analysis usually postulates that individuals are motivated by the desire for material gain, but the rules of the game which circumscribe the *manner* in which this pursuit of gain may take place are generally left implicit. It is taken for granted that there is in society a generally accepted code of behaviour according to which some ways of profit-making conform to the accepted mores, while others are opprobrious. Such rules of the game cannot be simply transposed from one period to another or from one social framework to a different one without being made explicit. In an underdeveloped economy there are probably many of these unwritten rules of behaviour which differ significantly from those which are taken for granted in the advanced countries. Among them, we venture to suggest, is the rule that innovation must consist of an emulation of the techniques of the advanced countries.

Entrepreneurs in an underdeveloped country take the advanced countries for their model. It is reasonable to suppose that this relates not only to the goal, but also to the choice of means. Advanced technology is a visible symbol of progress for producers, managers, engineers and technicians, no less than the adoption of Western dress is such a symbol for the consumer. The motivation for accumulation and growth is no doubt bound up with the possibility of giving external expression to the urge to emulate the advanced countries, to disassociate oneself from backwardness. If "Indian businessmen, for example, . . . believe that the 'American way' of producing is the best and only way"[2] this is not necessarily an irrational attitude. The belief that the "American way" of doing things is the best and only way seems irrational only when technique is considered merely as a means to an end, as it is in the advanced countries (and one may suspect that even there it is not quite so), and has no intrinsic symbolic value attached to it. But if technique, besides being a means for maximizing profits, is also a symbol of the socially approved goals, if it is, in a sense, goal-setting for other members of the society, then the preference for the "American way" of doing things fulfils the function of reaffirming these goals. It is not only a part of the given situation, but must be considered rational on its own terms.

The desire to be "modern" and "advanced" is part and parcel of the urge to accumulate, quite apart from the objective factors that circumscribe the choice of techniques which we discussed earlier, and apart from the fact that entrepreneurs and technicians in the underdeveloped countries simply do not know any alternatives. One might even say that the ability to dispense with imitation is already a symptom of a relatively high degree of development. This does away, on the one hand, with the social pressure to emulate the advanced West, and on the other hand, it provides the knowledge, the skills, and the practice needed to evolve indigenous techniques.

We further assume that the underdeveloped economy possesses a certain economic surplus which is, or can be made, accessible to entrepreneurs for investment. The concept of the economic surplus is adopted from Paul A. Baran,[3] who distinguishes between *actual* and *potential* surplus. The former is similar to the usual concept of saving, i.e. the excess of actual output over consumption, but the latter is defined to include the consumption of durable goods. The potential surplus is "the difference between the output that *could* be produced in a given natural and technological environment with the help of employable productive resources, and what might be regarded as essential consumption."* The actual surplus determines the rate and path of growth, and with given techniques and resources, its size depends on the structure of the system and on its mode of operation.

Development must start from the existing actual surplus. Where this is small in relation to the development goals, an underdeveloped economy will usually have to take the first step in closing the difference between actual and potential surplus by eliminating part of its non-essential consumption. This may take the form of a general system of taxation, or that of a greater or lesser degree of expropriation of certain social classes, which need not be the traditional privileged classes. The addition to the economic surplus may also come from foreign aid or borrowing. In all cases it implies political action and, once such a surplus is realized, it involves the question who shall effectively control its use, for the manner in which the initial actual surplus

---

* There is a formal similarity between Baran's two concepts of actual and potential surplus and those of the actual and natural rate of growth in Harrod's terminology.[4] There is, however, the difference that Harrod, like all Keynesians, takes the savings ratio—and consequently its complement, consumption—as a psychological constant, determined by individual preferences, while Baran distinguishes between actual and *essential* consumption. The latter is, briefly, that level of consumption which is established by *social convention* as necessary to maintain production with full employment of the available resources.

is used will determine the extent to which the system will be able to realize its potential surplus. As already stated, we assume that the realization of the initial surplus is the first and last positive action taken by the government, and that it will put this surplus at the disposal of capitalist entrepreneurs. Henceforth all accumulation is supposed to come out of capitalist profits.

Among the initial conditions of the model we further assume that within the relevant range there is no bottleneck to growth as a result of a scarcity of natural resources. Since it is assumed that all the necessary foreign exchange for imports is available, all the technically required natural resources can be imported if they are not domestically available.

For the purpose of our analysis, it will be convenient to ignore population growth, since it does not affect the results; with a growing population, all the results obtained would merely be accentuated. With respect to labour, we might adopt W. Arthur Lewis' assumption, namely that unskilled labour is in perfectly elastic supply at a wage level determined by the average level of subsistence outside the capitalist sector, and that a lack of skilled labour will at most be a temporary bottleneck because it is possible to train labour during the gestation period of the investments that initiate the growth process.[5] For many underdeveloped countries this assumption is quite realistic, but it is not so for a number of other important cases. In addition, the assumption is necessary only for a particular pattern of growth.

The assumption of an elastic labour supply, fed from disguised unemployment outside the capitalist sector, is necessary only where (a) growth takes place only through capital-widening investments, and (b) where it involves no initial fall in domestic employment, as it well may if there is a rise in the savings ratio (voluntary or forced) coupled with a shift in the composition of imports towards investment goods. With a lower aggregate expenditure on consumption, the shift of imports towards investment goods may entail a shift of consumption towards import substitutes, at the expense of traditional goods and services. The latter are likely to have a higher labour content than the import substitutes which are produced by more capital-intensive methods. Employment can therefore fall in the consumers' goods sector and release labour for investment even if total domestic spending remains unchanged, and with balanced trade. If we admit the possibility that investment will be financed from foreign aid or borrowing, so that domestic consumption need not fall to make investment possible, and if the output produced by the new investments is a substitute for previous imports, it is necessary to assume an elastic labour supply if the wage level is not to rise.

When development takes place by way of displacing a pre-existing artisanate, however, it will sooner or later create its own labour supply. The developing capitalist sector has, by definition, a lower labour–output ratio than the traditional industries it displaces. It will therefore tend to throw out of employment at least some of the traditional producers—artisans and petty capitalists—and in the process of its own growth will thus create a pool of labour which, in addition, may often possess a considerable degree of skill. Where the initial surplus originates in domestic income, its appropriation and diversion from, say, conspicuous consumption to investment in modern industry will generate the initial supply of labour necessary to start development. Thus, whether this initial surplus comes from forced savings or from a voluntary increase in the savings ratio, it will reduce consumption demand and thereby set free labour. Some of this labour will previously have been engaged in commodity production (except where the surplus is directly extracted from the subsistence sector), i.e. mostly an urban artisanate and the petty bourgeoisie. These strata, one may plausibly assume, have a higher level of skills and a higher traditional level of living than that which prevails in the subsistence sector.

It seems that such a process, of modern industry invading the markets of a pre-existing artisanate and, by displacing part of its labour, may better account for the gap between rural subsistence levels and the industrial wage level than some of the explanations given by Lewis. Such an automatic creation of an elastic labour supply for the capitalist sector, as a by-product of the introduction of modern, more capital-intensive techniques, may be part of the explanation for the high rates of urban unemployment even in those underdeveloped countries which do not suffer from population pressure, and for the often surprisingly high degree of labour unionization, with a relatively high level of wages for the employed, despite an apparent overall excess of labour.*

As for the savings function of our model, we shall make the classical assumption that all savings come out of profits, and that all wage income is consumed (but not that there is no consumption out of profits). This must be qualified in regard to the initial conditions, since it is assumed that the original investible surplus may originate in forced savings. We may assume, for simplicity, that the source of this original surplus is outside the capitalist sector, and that it is a once-and-for-all saving of a stock of investible resources. As said before, all further investment is supposed to come out of capitalist accumulation.

Investment will be entirely governed by the decisions of capitalist entrepreneurs. In the initial state of our under-developed economy we assume that there is a high propensity to accumulate which, as Joan Robinson says, "depends on the historical, political and psychological characteristics of the economy".[6] But this high initial urge to accumulate which we may take as being satisfactory in terms of what society expects

---

* The displacement of traditional industries by modern capitalism is, of course, the classical process as known from history; in the underdeveloped countries this displacement was often originally carried out by imports. The emergence of a national capitalist sector which, in turn, displaces those imports, only represents, so to speak, a second stage in the original artisanate-destroying effect of modern industry.

An interesting case in which the expropriation of a social class simultaneously produced an increase in the economic surplus, and directly created a labour supply from among the members of that class, is represented by Japan in the early stages of her development. In the transformation that followed the Meiji Restoration in 1867, the lower nobility who, as retainers of the feudal lords, had traditionally lived on—albeit often very scanty—stipends paid out of the lords' feudal dues, were directly and indirectly expropriated by the commutation of the feudal dues in the 1870's. This very numerous class—the samurai class as a whole was estimated for 1870 at nearly 2 million people out of a total population of 34 million—was thereby rendered almost completely destitute. Having been divorced from the land for centuries, they were thereby converted into an urban proletariat. As a military caste, these samurai were in addition tied by the bonds of tradition to the upper nobility which had allied itself with the rising mercantile bourgeoisie, and they constituted the core of Japan's early industrial labour force, particularly in the heavy industries. This proletarization of the lower nobility, once it had set in, was clearly recognized by the ruling classes for the advantages it could bring to industrialization, and was consciously fostered.[7]

of its entrepreneurs can only be maintained if it also turns out to be satisfactory to the individual entrepreneurs. As Joan Robinson brings out clearly, there is a reciprocal relationship between the rate of accumulation and the level of profits: "The accumulation going on in a particular situation determines the level of profits obtainable in it, and thus . . . determines the rate of profit expected on investment. The rate of profit in turn influences the rate of accumulation. . . ."[8] The initial urge to accumulate is, so to speak, an *ex ante* concept, a propensity; to be maintained, it must be validated by subsequent results. This means that not only must profits be sufficient to provide the resources required for the intended rate of accumulation to go on, but if they are not, the rate of accumulation may fall off even if additional investible resources are made available to entrepreneurs, for example in the form of loans.*

In addition to the rate of profit, investment is also a function of technology, and this in turn is a function of the capacity to import. Again, as will be recalled from the analysis in Chapter 2, the rate of profit is a function of technology and the absolute size of the market. We thus have investment depending directly on technology (in the sense of accessibility of techniques with a competitive advantage over the traditional industries; within the relevant range, we take this supply of techniques to be practically unlimited), and on imports (by the assumption of technological dependence), and indirectly, via the rate of profit, on technology and market size.

To conclude the description and recapitulation of the initial conditions of the model, it remains to add that we shall disregard the problems that rise in connexion with the financial system. It will be assumed that there is no securities market and no direct lending and borrowing among firms. Gross investment

---

* This seems to be a rather roundabout way of saying that investment is a function of the rate of profit, but it points to the implications that frustrated expectations may have for the working of the system. If the privately desired rate of accumulation is high enough to conform to the political goal of growth, but the realized rate of profit is insufficient to maintain it, then as long as the economy remains committed to *laissez-faire*, policy will have to ensure that the rate of profit is what it was expected to be. It will not be enough to provide entrepreneurs with additional funds to make possible a rate of investment higher than that warranted by their rate of profit, for the profits are not only a means for accumulation, but also their end.

is supposed to be financed out of gross profits; accumulating depreciation funds are deposited with banks who use them as resources against which they may lend to borrowers at the ruling rate of interest. All firms are supposed to be closely held companies which do not sell shares to other firms. The central bank implements the government's development policy and allows the money supply to rise in step with the increase in the volume of transactions, at a constant rate of interest. The government may create credit through the central bank to provide finance for investment.

Finally, we make the heroic assumption—already mentioned before—that all development in our economy takes place in the complete absence of foreign interests of any kind, that is to say that the operations of all firms are solely guided by what happens in the developing economy. Even casual observation shows that this comes near to abstracting from one of the most important aspects of reality in the underdeveloped countries. The justification for ignoring what is surely one of the most decisive determinants of real-life development in many underdeveloped countries is that we wish to bring out those factors which affect the process of growth in the ideal case of the purely national, autonomous private enterprise system. In fact, it is this hypothetical situation which is usually discussed in the literature on development, which treats foreign enterprise—if it mentions it at all—exactly in the same terms as indigenous enterprise. The usual assumption is that foreign firms act only in response to the economic conditions in the economy where they happen to be located, and the only characteristic in which they differ from national firms is that they may have to transmit part of their profits abroad for the payment of dividends to foreign shareholders.

THE MECHANISM OF MONOPOLISTIC GROWTH

Much of the picture of the process of growth we have in mind has already been implicit in what was said in the preceding chapters; in drawing together the strands of the argument, some repetition will be unavoidable. Our discussion will mainly revolve around those factors which tend to inhibit the expansion of markets in conditions where the process of industrial development is accompanied by, and takes place through, the emergence of monopolistic structures.

Suppose that the government of our underdeveloped economy has obtained an initial fund of investible capital which it now puts at the disposal of entrepreneurs willing to invest in modern industry. Suppose also that all steps have been taken to ensure that potential investors can initially obtain all the foreign exchange they need to import the required producers' goods at a constant rate of exchange. We may imagine this to have come about through the imposition of a tariff on imports of consumers' goods, which raises their domestic price and thus creates an incentive for the production of domestic substitutes, while simultaneously releasing foreign exchange for imports of producers' goods.

Investment in new industries now begins in a number of fields in which an established demand already exists. In part, that demand has been mapped out by previous imports;[9] in part, entrepreneurs know it as a matter of common observation since it represents the basic necessities of life. Investors know that by introducing modern methods of production they will be able to produce the import substitutes at a competitive cost (at the price level established after the imposition of tariffs*) and, in particular, that they will be able to produce the commodities so far supplied by the traditional artisanate and petty capitalists and to displace them from their markets.

The degree of this competitive advantage depends on the choice of technique and consequently on the scale of output, and will lie between two extremes: at the upper end of the range, the scale will be limited by the size of the market (including increments expected during the lifetime of the investment) and by the size of the optimal plant, whichever is the smaller, by considerations of risk, by the entrepreneur's technical and organizational ability, and by the amount of capital available to the individual firm from all sources together—own

---

* We ignore here the widely observed fact that the chain of causation is in reality the other way round. Tariffs are imposed so as to raise import prices above the domestic cost level, and within fairly wide limits the choice of technique is therefore probably more determined by the elasticity of demand for the imports than by their price.

capital, bank credits, or government loans and grants. At the lower end the scale of production will be limited by the smallest economic size of plant which the technology available from the advanced countries can supply and which still provides an average cost advantage over the traditional techniques that is at least equal to the expected rate of profit.

Being rational capitalists, the investors have a propensity to monopolize and would, if they could, like to capture the whole of the prospective demand in their respective markets. The more advanced the technique they choose, the greater will be their cost advantage over the traditional producers and competitive imports, and the larger will be their scale of output. The closer will they thus come to the desired monopolistic position. If the entrepreneur can obtain that position, it will be possible for him to squeeze out the traditional producers by cutting prices. Once he has been successful, he can raise prices again to a level that will prevent re-entry but will still be sufficient to arrogate to himself the greater part of the real cost advantage he derives from his superior efficiency.

The potential monopolist is, of course, aware that the existing size of the market could probably be further increased by still lower prices, so that if additional economies of large-scale production exist, he might make still greater profits. But in a low-income market, most goods of mass consumption are likely to have a low price elasticity, so that the economies of larger scale would have to be very substantial to make such a price-reducing, output-expanding policy profitable. In any case, if the capital–output ratio rises with scale, limitations of finance are likely to arrest such a trend; indivisibility, limited technical and organizational ability, and uncertainty with respect to the price and income elasticity of demand beyond the experienced range will act in the same direction, and will restrain the entrepreneur from establishing plant on a scale that is significantly larger than the proven volume of demand at the ruling price.

It follows that it is most likely that plant will generally be established only on a scale which represents a fraction of the existing demand, albeit a significant fraction. This will particularly be so if the entrepreneur is uncertain with respect to his chances of driving out the traditional producers within the economic lifetime of the investment. The invasion of the market will take time, and the traditional producers will be eliminated only gradually, and possibly only partially—some of them perhaps taking a reduction of their income without going out of the market. During this interval between the investment in capacity of a given size and the displacement of those traditional producers which will make its full utilization possible, new entrants may appear, possibly operating on a smaller scale and a correspondingly higher cost level, but still able to get in under the umbrella of the monopolistic price set by the first producer. Alternatively, it is possible that if the first firm settles down to a more or less fixed level of output which accounts for only a part of the potential market, new producers—possibly with still more efficient techniques—will enter, partly at the expense of the first firm's market share, partly by making further inroads on the share of the traditional producers. In both alternatives, of which there could be many variants, there will be a tendency for oligopolies to arise in the course of time. For simplicity, let us nevertheless first consider the case of monopoly.

Let us assume that the first entrepreneur in a given industry is not limited by the size of his capital, and that the available technique permits or requires a scale of production that is sufficient to capture total industry demand, and that he can also successfully prevent entry. The establishment of the new monopolistic industry, whatever its factor proportions, will initially attract labour. We may suppose that the labour force hired to carry out the domestic component of the investment is later put to its current operation. Let us see first what happens to employment if the new industry invades a market previously supplied by the traditional artisanate. What follows owes much to W. Arthur Lewis' classic *Economic Growth with Unlimited Supplies of Labour*; the differences from his analysis will become apparent as we go along.

As the new industry's output comes on the market, the traditional producers will gradually be driven out. Productivity in the economy will rise and real national income will grow, but at the same time its distribution will change. The new industry will displace labour and reduce income in the artisan and petty-capitalist class; to some extent this will take the form of disguised unemployment. Some of the displaced labour will be reabsorbed in the expanding capitalist sector, but since this has a higher output–labour ratio than the traditional industries, there will be a net displacement of labour in the aggregate. As soon as the initial labour-attracting stage is over, this will assure the capitalist sector of an elastic labour supply which will persist so long as the invasion of the traditional markets is not complete. As mentioned before, it is likely that the displaced artisans will for the most part be an urban class, with a higher level of skills and education than the industrially unskilled agricultural labour force.

Following Lewis, we assume that the wage level in the capitalist sector is determined by the average level of subsistence outside it. We differ from him, however, in considering that it is not mainly the subsistence sector—which is mostly rural—that counts, but the average productivity and traditional standard of living of the artisan and petty-capitalist class. It is another matter that they may be impoverished in this process, and that an influx of rural surplus labour into the cities may further depress their standard of living and wages; but the very fact that there is such an influx from the countryside—even where land is available—and no return migration from the urban slums indicates that it is the traditionally higher urban wage level that serves as a benchmark.*

It is reasonable to assume that capitalists, particularly if they must adopt a relatively advanced technology, will prefer to recruit their labour force from among the comparatively skilled and more sophisticated urban strata, and will leave the labour reserve in the rural sector largely untouched. As the expansion of the capitalist sector reaches the limits of the markets of traditional industry that can profitably be occupied by modern methods of production, this labour supply may become inelastic. It is then by no means certain that further expansion, say into import substitution or into the production of intermediate goods required for modern production, will turn to the rural labour force for additional supplies of labour. If the gap in productivity levels is greater than the marginal reduction in the

---

* Lewis by no means equates the subsistence sector with agriculture; it includes all those occupations which are not carried out with the help of capital and wage labour. The latter is defined as the capitalist sector, which may include agriculture if it is capitalistically organized.

wage level that can be brought about by the induction of cheaper labour from the rural excess population, capitalists may find it more profitable to adopt more capital-intensive techniques rather than to employ more labour. This is particularly true if urban labour has become unionized. The redundant labour force of the rural sector and urban slums would then represent a non-competing group. Tendencies towards capital-intensification which arise because of the pressures of competition among firms, will then be reinforced by the growing effective scarcity of labour—of that kind of labour that really matters, namely the urban, more or less sophisticated strata of the working population, who can be trained and disciplined with relative ease.

Workers in the capitalist sector, which produces mainly manufactured goods, buy wage goods from the subsistence sector, which produces mainly food. If the total wage bill of the capitalist sector is greater than the demand for wage goods which had previously come from the artisan class that is now being displaced, and productivity in the subsistence sector remains constant, the price level of wage goods will rise. This will happen only if the growth of the capitalist sector has a net labour-absorbing effect. To the extent that growth takes place through the displacement of traditional industries, this rise in the prices of wage goods will be limited, since we have assumed that the industrial wage level will be equal to the average income of the artisan class. With a higher capital–output ratio the total share of wages, and the demand for wage goods, will tend to fall. The terms of trade of the capitalist versus the subsistence sector will either remain unchanged or, if the former exploits its monopolistic positions, will turn against the latter. The economy's gain in productivity will accrue mostly or entirely to the capitalists; an increasing share of aggregate income will go to profits.

To the extent that the development of the capitalist sector proceeds by way of import substitution, it will have a net labour-attracting effect, provided that total domestic spending rises in real terms. In this case the requisite labour force will either have to be bid away from the traditional urban occupations through higher wages, or will have to come from the rural subsistence sector. In either case the total wage bill will increase;

in the former because wages will be bid up, and in the latter because part of the former subsistence population will enter the exchange economy through having become wage labourers—possibly at a higher level of real income than before. Demand for wage goods will go up and will turn the terms of trade against the capitalist sector. In this case, some part of the economy's gain in productivity will be passed on to labour in the capitalist sector and to producers in the subsistence sector. In reality, both trends, of displacement of traditional producers and of imports, are likely to be present simultaneously, and the net effect depends upon the relative shares of imports and traditional domestic production in the total supply of capitalistically produced goods.

Suppose now that the growth of the capitalist sector has proceeded to the point where it has replaced all those imports whose substitution is technically and economically feasible in the first round, and that it has invaded all those industries in which primitive methods of production ruled formerly and the aggregate demand for which permitted the introduction of modern mass-production methods. Let us assume that the employment-creating effects of import substitution have outweighed the labour-displacing effects of squeezing out the traditional producers, and that part of the increment to national income has been passed on to the subsistence sector through improved terms of trade and to workers through a larger wage bill, although the bulk of the additional income has accrued to the capitalists. Some of the additional income will be spent on the products of the capitalist sector itself, thus widening its markets, some of it will create a demand for new services and goods, and some of it will increase the demand for imports. What, however, happens to the bulk of the accumulated profits?

In the classical model, it will be remembered, accumulated profits are supposed to be spent, after deduction of capitalists' consumption, on the wages of workers producing new capital goods. Thus, all income generated in the economy becomes new expenditure, and there can be no lack of effective demand for the output produced. The gain in productivity brought about by technical progress generates new demand, and the system is able to expand up to the limits given at any time by technique, supplies of natural resources, and labour.

On our assumptions, however, the investment expenditure of the capitalist sector, both in the initial stage and in the ongoing reinvestment of its gross profits (disregarding for the moment all factors that may reduce the rate of investment) will create domestic employment only to a fraction of its total volume. The rest will represent demand for imported plant and equipment. With exports or other sources of foreign exchange revenue unrelated to the level of domestic investment, the latter will not re-create the income withdrawn from domestic product in the form of gross profits. Moreover, where the growth of the modern capitalist sector displaces traditional industries, the change in techniques will also reduce the demand for the simple domestically produced tools and other producers' goods which were required for the old methods of production. In terms of Harrod's famous equation for equilibrium growth, if G, the rate of growth, is equal to the savings ratio S (= roughly, to the share of profits) times the reciprocal of the capital coefficient C,

$$G = S \cdot \frac{1}{C},$$

then, if the import component of investment is denoted by M,

$$G = S \cdot \frac{1 - M}{C},$$

so that if exports are independent of the domestic sector, the capitalist sector, and consequently savings and profits, must grow at an increasing rate to maintain full employment of its capacity.[10] If G in the above equation is taken to mean Harrod's warranted rate of growth G_w, that is, the expected rate of increase in domestic income and demand which will enable entrepreneurs in the capitalist sector to realize their expected profits, then the spread of the sector itself, and the shortfall in the creation of domestic income and employment caused by the import component of its investment, will produce an actual rate of growth G_a which is below G_w. Thus, entrepreneurs will find their expectations frustrated once the capitalist sector has usurped the field of expansion initially represented by the traditional sector and by imports. Any shortfall of G_a relative to G_w will tend to reinforce itself, and the capitalist sector will veer off its intended rate of accumulation.

This familiar Harrodian "knife-edge" problem will, in addition, be aggravated because under the conditions we have assumed there will be a tendency for an independent rise in C and, in all likelihood, an even greater increase in the import component M. For in an economy with "unlimited supplies of technical progress" the rivalry among firms, and to some extent among industries, creates strong incentives for an increase in the capital coefficient; and because the introduction of a more advanced technique—which by assumption must be imported —will generally raise the import component in total investment, M tends to rise faster than C. In fact, the rise in C and M will take place even if, at the limit, net investment falls to zero; for the introduction of improved techniques will continue, as long as rivalry is at all effective, even if there is only replacement-investment.

In addition to the "knife-edge" type of depression of the rate of accumulation, which is mainly brought about by the import-dependence of investment, there will also be a shrinking of the available investment opportunities as a result of the monopolistic structure. The cyclical and the structural effects are independent, but reinforce each other. The fall in the rate of investment as a result of monopoly may set in even before the capitalist sector has entirely occupied the markets of the traditional industries and imports.

Let us briefly recapitulate the process described in Chapter 2. As the monopolists' or oligopolists' profits accumulate, their search for investment outlets will probably first turn to their original industries. Expansion along the existing demand curve without technical progress is ruled out, for the increased output obtained by the additional investment can only be sold at a lower price, and the marginal profit rate will therefore fall.[11] Investment in the original industry can therefore only take the form of cost-reducing improvements. But these changes enlarge the scale of output, so that such investment will create excess capacity unless the elasticity of scale with respect to cost is lower than that of demand with respect to price.

If demand is expanding, the monopolist may invest in his original industry, but sooner or later the outlets afforded by it at the going rate of profit will become exhausted. It is, furthermore, plausible to assume that the monopolist will from the outset have established plant with some excess capacity, both as a means to prevent entry, and because indivisibilities may have forced him to build ahead of demand. An expansion of demand will therefore generally only take up some of this existing capacity. With indivisibilities of plant, the increment to demand that would be required to justify the establishment of additional optimum-sized plant is likely to be very considerable. As stated before, it is on empirical grounds most improbable that demand for a particular industry should expand at a rate anywhere near the rate of profit, except when the firm is still in the stage of occupying the economic space vacated by much less efficient producers or by imports which have been excluded by tariffs or other protectionist measures. Hence, sooner or later our representative monopolist will have to search for investment outlets outside his original industry. The oligopolistic firm, for reasons already explained, will have even stronger and earlier inducements to diversify.

The first step towards diversification will probably be through investment in products which have some technical or market propinquity to the original activity. It may involve—where products are related through process similarity—a better utilization of existing resources, including management and knowhow; or, in the case of market similarity or vertical integration, it may further strengthen the firm's monopolistic position in addition to providing it with new investment outlets.

Eventually, however, the expansion of the monopolistic firm will come up against increasingly severe limitations of market size. The first areas to which modern industry is likely to turn are those markets which are sufficiently large to permit the exploitation of the advantages of large-scale production. These will be industries producing goods of mass consumption, and some intermediate goods which serve as inputs to a large number of industries. Examples are the traditional "first" industries —textiles, beer, cigarettes, matches, soap, oil pressing and refining, grain milling, lumber mills, glass, cement and the like.

As the opportunities for expansion afforded by this base of the consumption basket become exhausted, the firm is forced, in its attempts to diversify, to move up a demand pyramid which tapers off rapidly, in terms of the absolute size of demand, relative to the technically determined scales of output. The disparity between market size and optimal plant size tends to increase, and all the adverse consequences described earlier become still more pronounced. Furthermore, as industry expands into the markets provided by the upper-income groups, it must increasingly compete against imported consumer goods. These represent mainly the demand of the wealthy—the capitalists themselves and other privileged strata in general—and are likely to have a low price elasticity. Import substitution on a scale of production that is at a marked cost disadvantage by comparison with similar goods produced in the advanced countries will therefore require very high protective tariffs or outright prohibitory import restrictions.

This protection, so frequently and so easily obtained, appears on the surface as being conducive to the country's economic development: it vacates additional economic living space for domestic industry, it improves the balance of payments through import substitution (or so it seems, at least in a short-run view), and it diverts scarce foreign exchange from the imports of luxuries to the apparently so essential imports of capital goods. On the surface—and on the principle of the consumer's sovereignty—all seems to be well. Industrial growth can go on, after a fashion, and even industrial employment may continue to rise. But the additional industrial production which moves into the economic space so vacated increasingly turns to the relatively small-scale, high-cost production of luxury goods, and the scarce foreign exchange is diverted from unessential imports of finished luxury goods only to be used for importing the capital goods needed to make the same unessential luxury goods at home. There is indeed some generation of domestic added value as a result of this substitution, so long as it is not spurious, but it may be bought at a high social opportunity cost. Expansion along such lines creates a productive structure which requires an increase in the consumption of capitalists and other high-income groups which, broadly speaking, is a drain on the aggregate accumulation of capital.*

* This qualitative change in the pattern of industrial development, as it turns away from mass-consumption goods to luxury goods produced behind high barriers of protection, may explain some of the dissatisfaction of the underdeveloped countries with their rates of industrial growth. Judging by

As the field of expansion of the capitalist sector narrows down, diversification leads progressively to the foregoing of the advantages of large-scale production. The process is likely to be gradual, and at each stage the diversifying firm will attempt to utilize more fully some of its existing resources by introducing products which have some affinity to its former lines of activity. Step by step, however, new indivisibilities create new partial—and seemingly temporary—excess capacities; the balancing of the productive set-up is in fact never achieved, and at the margin there will always seem to be some facilities which permit better utilization if some additional investment is made. Gradually, the degree of specialization is reduced, and except where technology confines the firm to a narrow range of products, a conglomerate of diverse small-scale activities tends to develop around the core activity of the firm. In time, the former may even come to overshadow the latter. As a result of the small scale of the market, much of this diversification will assume an intra-plant form, by contrast with the parallel phenomenon in the advanced countries, where it results in inter-industry and multi-plant links of ownership and control.

Since the upper-income groups are likely to have a high propensity to import, diversification through the substitution for these imports can be successful only if the new domestic production does not diverge too far from the previous imports in terms of quality, function, and appearance. For this to be possible, the new substitutes will generally have to contain a sizeable proportion of imported inputs; the import coefficient of current production is therefore likely to be rising at the margin. A good part of this type of production will often be no more than what is commonly called "last-touch import substitution", in which the domestic value added does not consist of much more—if that —than the profit margin provided by the tariffs.

This kind of expansion results in a paradox that illustrates a point made by Schumpeter, namely that "a system . . . that *every* given point of time fully utilizes its possibilities to the best

---

the statistics taken at their face value, these are often higher than those of the advanced countries. In part, of course, this reflects the low initial base, but in addition there is the awareness that the statistics also obscure the fact that much of this growth is bought at a very high social cost, and runs into growing difficulties.

advantage may yet in the long run be inferior to a system that does so at *no* given point of time, because the latter's failure to do so may be a condition for the level or speed of long-run performance".[12] For at any given point of time, the investment carried out is apparently efficient, since it always helps to absorb some excess capacity of the previously existing resources, so that the marginal capital–output ratio seems to fall. And yet, the rate of growth of productivity will decline because the advantages of large-scale production and of technical progress are increasingly given up. If the existing industrial structure is taken for granted, then the existence and continual re-creation of excess capacity seems natural, and diversification along such lines is rational. Moreover, it responds precisely to market demand, to the dictates of the sovereign consumer. But as Modigliani has pointed out in his analysis of Sylos-Labini's theory, the existing structure itself, and consequently the shifts and changes in the pattern of production which emerge in it, may be far from rational from the standpoint of the economy as a whole and its goal of economic growth.

We have already observed that the competitive structure in an underdeveloped economy is most likely to be oligopolistic rather than monopolistic, and that the tendency to diversify will therefore be more pronounced and will be more likely to lead to the fragmentation of markets and production. In addition, it can be seen that in certain conditions the necessity of diversification tends to transform an initially monopolistic industry into an oligopolistic one. For as a monopolist expands by way of diversification, he continually invests in new side-lines, and after a certain time these may come to account for the bulk of his revenue while the original activity has become subsidiary. Meanwhile, demand for his original product may have risen and techniques of production in that line may have changed. With much of his total resources committed to other lines of production, the monopolist may no longer be able to retain control of his original market and, since much of his revenue now originates elsewhere, he may also have less inducement to do so. This is particularly so if the new techniques for producing the original product have less affinity to his new activities than the former technique, so that their adoption would require a massive conversion of the whole plant. A new entrant may then have the advantage of the latecomer. Thus, oligopoly may develop because the older firm is driven to diversification in the search of investment outlets, while new entrants arrogate to themselves the accretion of demand in the original industry.

From the point of view of the social cost of diversification, the results under oligopoly will generally be more adverse than under monopoly. Like the monopolist, each oligopolist will try to expand into products that have some technical or market affinity to his original activity. But in spite of possible differences in size, all oligopolists in a given industry will tend to have similar techniques of production. Any new product that has a technical or market propinquity to the original activity of one firm will therefore have a similar affinity to that of another firm in that industry. Although at any given point of time each oligopolist will try to strike out in a different direction than his rivals, in time they will all tend to diversify into much the same group of new products, so that oligopoly in the original industry will, with variations of the respective market shares in the different fields, be repeated in the secondary industries. To be sure, there will be differences in the membership of each such oligopoly; there will be outsiders and there will be varying degrees of market concentration. But this differentiated oligopoly will have its roots in undifferentiated oligopoly, and its core will represent a group of closely linked and interdependent interests. In terms of the economic behaviour that counts for our analysis here, namely the mode of investment, there is little reason to believe that differentiated oligopoly will differ in any important respect from undifferentiated oligopoly.

By distinction from the situation under monopoly, the oligopolists will have to share among themselves any new, progressively smaller increments to demand which the income distribution and the demand elasticities allow. The effects on the economies of large-scale production will therefore be even more pronounced. At the extreme, the limits to the scale of production which is profitable for any single firm may be such that firms which in their original industry are oligopolistic, come closer to a state of Chamberlinian monopolistic competition in their secondary industries. But since the constraints of technology and market size are present as before, this is far from being a blessing, for it means that industrial expansion can no longer take advantage of large scale and technical progress. Such a nearly competitive market structure is merely a reflection of inefficiency.

In the factor markets, diversification will work in the same direction: retarding a rise in efficiency and market size. If industry tends, at any given point of time, to expand into relatively small scales of production, the lumps of capital needed for each such venture will not be large, and the required capital may be available to firms from internal accumulation, particularly if in each new line of production they go from big to small. Diversification may therefore also be a deterrent to the development of a capital market; the absence of the latter will, in turn, impede the concentration of finance for large-scale undertakings. On the other hand, it may happen that the push towards diversification, into markets which are too small to sustain an optimal scale of output, will lead to the establishment of considerable excess capacity, thereby pushing up the investment–output ratio, and in particular the import coefficient in the new industries.

More important still is the effect of diversification on the labour market. The move away from mass-production goods, which are typically manufactured by relatively highly mechanized methods, will tend to increase the demand for skilled labour. The smaller the scale of production, the more it involves commodities of a relatively high degree of fabrication and technical sophistication, the higher will be the demand for skilled labour. And the greater the rivalry for the marginal markets among the oligopolists, the more they must share them with each other in ever new oligopoly-bred oligopolies, the likelier are they to compete against each other in the labour market. The wages of skilled and semi-skilled labour, as well as of those occupations which are called into being by the requirements of an oligopolistic structure, will tend to rise and to eat into profits. The fragmentation of the market will reduce the opportunities to counter this by skill-displacing technical improvements (which would raise the scale of output), thus further diminishing the profitably of investment and decelerating the rate of growth. As the process works itself out, the capitalist sector will paradoxically come to face an effectively inelastic labour supply, within an economy which in the aggregate may have "un-limited supplies of labour". The capitalist sector then comes to display, in a perverted fashion, many of the characteristics of the advanced economy, and particularly its labour scarcity—without, however, possessing the technical progressiveness of the latter.

What is involved here is not merely the shortage of skilled labour that any underdeveloped economy is likely to face as soon as new techniques are introduced. This is a familiar pheno-menon, but it would be no more than a temporary bottleneck unless the nature of the growth process under oligopoly always re-created the shortage and aggravated it. This may explain why an underdeveloped economy may, beyond a certain level of industrial development, come to be plagued both by a scar-city of labour and rising wages and prices, and by massive un-employment of unskilled labour and disguised unemployment in the traditional sector, just as it has both an overall scarcity of capital and an excess of savings. The so-called "structural un-employment" of the underdeveloped countries thus obtains an additional meaning: it is not only the result of technical im-balances, but is caused by the pattern of growth that evolves in a non-competitive structure.

In reality the shift from the production of mass-consumption goods, using a relatively mechanized and generally labour-displacing technique of production, to skill-attracting diversifi-cation, will of course not take place in neatly separate stages, but both trends will operate simultaneously. Some industries will still be in the first stage when others have already reached the limits of expansion their original markets could afford. At the same time, some additional opportunities for expansion will emerge as the industrial sector as a whole grows, particularly in the production of intermediate goods used by a wide range of industries.

If the expansion of the capitalist sector begins with import substitution, as was generally the case, most typically so in Latin America, the initial net effect may, as already noted, be labour-attracting. Where the original level of imports was high, as was the case in some of the wealthier Latin American coun-tries, the sequence seems in fact to have been the reverse of that described above. Massive industrialization began with the goods that were previously imported and much of which catered to the demand of the upper-income groups, while the so-called "sedentary" industries that produced mainly manufactured wage goods remained technically and economically stagnant, and represented, for a good part, the domain of a petty, relatively backward capitalist sector. This difference in sequence does not affect the basic conclusions of our analysis with respect to the direction of development, but as far as can be judged from the evidence it seems to have produced more violent fluctuations in the process of growth—waves of rapid development alternating with periods of relative stagnation—instead of the gradual exhaustion of the investment outlets described above.[13]

But even if the process is initially labour-attracting, rivalry among firms will, up to a point, lead to increased mechanization, and this will narrow its own markets by displacing some of the labour that was originally absorbed, particularly in the lower skill levels.[14] At the same time, diversification will begin to raise the demand for labour of medium and upper skill levels, and will create a stratum of privileged labour.* In the given structure of the economy this scarcity of labour is real and provides the economic basis for a high degree of unionization, which further reduces the elasticity of the labour supply. This tendency may be reinforced by various institutional factors, but it could probably not be maintained in the long run in the face of massive unemployment unless the unemployed were to a large extent a non-competing group.

The trend towards diversification does not leave the political and social framework unaffected. Producers will begin to develop a pronounced interest in the categories of upper-income demand. As they come to be forced to look for investment outlets in the more sophisticated commodity groups, and

* The shift away from the mechanized mass-production industries and the falling relative scale of output (which, incidentally, may not be discernible in the statistics because it may take the form of intraplant diversification, so that census data may continue to list an establishment by its main activity although it may in fact produce a variety of only remotely related products) may also diminish the employment opportunities for the highest ranks of professional skills, such as engineers, scientists, highly trained technicians, managers, and administrators, and lead to a "brain-drain" to the advanced countries.

as they begin to emulate their bigger counterparts in the advanced countries (as a matter of fact, often in partnership with them) by attempting to stimulate the demand for their product through artificial differentiation, they also become increasingly interested in the pattern of income distribution in the economy. Politically, they will tend to favour an increasingly unequal income distribution not only by reason of their immediate interests as recipients of profits and payers of wages, but also because it is more and more the upper income classes who provide their marginal markets, more the relatively advanced urban areas and industrialized regions in the country that are the main source of their revenue, and not the more backward rural areas. If they are confronted with a shortage of labour in that segment of the labour supply that really matters for them, they may acquiesce relatively easily in wage rises, particularly since an oligopolistic structure makes it easy to use a wage increase as the occasion and signal for an all-round increase of prices and profit margins.

This attitude towards the income distribution rarely expresses itself in forms which clearly reveal its real foundation—a productive structure which has become oriented towards the consumption pattern of the relatively privileged classes—but assumes various ideological guises. The original push for increased inequality naturally comes from the group that stands to gain immediately, but the other relatively privileged strata, and particularly the producers, tend to acquiesce in such trends. In general, they create a public climate in favour of rising income disparities in which all the relatively favoured strata of the population, including much of the privileged urban labour, share in some degree. Ostensibly, the advocacy of increased income inequality will often go under the name of providing greater incentives for higher productivity and greater efficiency, or that it will increase the overall savings ratio on account of the higher propensity to save of the higher income recipients. In practice, however, it is rarely the incentives of productive workers that are increased most, but rather the salaries of civil servants or of the professional and labour *élite*, together with the incomes of a host of functionaries and intermediaries, and most of all—the incomes which derive from property. The coalition of these interests, which may include the organized labour *élite*, will gradually become politically irresistible if it has not indeed held sway from the outset, and will crystallize in corresponding wage policies, tax systems, and the whole array of policy variables that affect the distribution of income directly and indirectly.

Whatever the particular pattern of development followed by such a system, if left to its own devices it will yield a falling rate of accumulation as a result of the declining gains in productivity that the existing competitive structure permits in terms of its own rationale. Monopoly and oligopoly will have a two-fold effect: on the one hand, they will prevent capital from outside each industry from encroaching upon the fields they have arrogated to themselves, and on the other hand they tend, in Baran's graphic expression, to become "suffocated in their own profits". At the same time, an increasing share of the economic surplus that this structure creates is diverted into the consumption of those strata which live off the same surplus, but do not participate in its production. In part, this takes the form of increasing income disparities, as explained in the preceding paragraph. In part, and perhaps more importantly from a quantitative point of view, it takes the form of swelling the size of those economic occupations that in one way or another make their living out of the existing surplus.

The savings ratio of these strata may be high, but this does not affect the decline in the overall rate of accumulation, for what is at the root of the problem is a fundamental misallocation of resources, the building of a productive structure and its corresponding occupational structure which retards growth, and increases the gap between the actual economic surplus and the potential surplus. Generally, however, average income in these social groups which, as Baran describes them so ably, dwell predominantly in the sphere of circulation rather than production, will be low, for their occupations are wholly open to entry and thus exposed to fierce competition. But poor as these petty traders, intermediaries and purveyors of a variety of services that crowd the bazaars and sidewalks of the cities may individually be, their aggregate drain on overall accumulation may be very considerable.[15]

It may be objected that even if monopolistic structures cannot be avoided in the given conditions, there is no reason why the process of import substitution should not go on, from final products to intermediate goods, and from there to capital goods, thus eliminating in the first instance the income- and employment-depressing effects of the import-dependence, and ultimately also removing the technological dependence? Would not such a continuous import substitution widen the field of expansion of the capitalist sector even under a *laissez-faire* system?

The answer lies partly in the characteristics of the competitive structure and partly in the *laissez-faire* system's inherent contradiction between the private and the social interest. It can, of course, not be denied that as the growth of industry spans a wider spectrum of goods, opportunities arise for the production of intermediate goods which serve as inputs for various industries. But from the point of view of the disparities between the technically given scales of output and the size of the available markets these are, in principle, no different from the final goods; if anything, the disparities may be greater because the production of intermediate goods going into many different industries is more frequently based on continuous-flow processes and geared to large scales of output. If the markets for final goods are small in relation to the available technology, the same will be true, with few exceptions, with respect to intermediate goods.

Before a sufficiently large market for such intermediate goods has been created by the initial growth of industry, it will often be the case that the fragmentation of industrial production, as a result of diversification, will have built up a productive system in which the total amount of producers' goods may be considerable (and involve a high import component which, taken in the aggregate, seems to present a large field for further import substitution), but which in its own turn is fragmented into a multitude of specific types of materials and equipment. The diseconomies of scale for each of these are likely to be large, and with respect to capital goods this is made worse by the fact that in the underdeveloped economy with its small stock of capital goods there is relatively little replacement demand. The extent of the market will therefore provide little incentive for entrepreneurs to embark upon the production of capital goods, even if the requisite skills were available.[16]

In addition, the producers of the end goods will strongly resist import substitution for their inputs in general, and particularly in the case of capital goods. They know from their own experience, being themselves import substituters, that this will raise their costs; but even if these additional costs could be fully passed on to consumers, they are very reluctant to serve as guinea-pigs for untried domestic equipment, the purchase of which is a long-run commitment of resources. Any defect in the equipment or in a critical raw material may endanger the business of the producer of the end goods out of proportion to the actual difference in its cost. In other words, the elasticity of demand for imported capital goods and for many intermediates is likely to be very low. Drastic policy measures would be needed to overcome this, but under *laissez-faire*, in any case, there is no automatic mechanism whereby import substitution can be kept up continuously. On the contrary, there are strong forces at work to prevent this, and many underdeveloped countries have become aware of the increasing difficulties of further import substitution. Even substantial government intervention is often unable to combat this "decline of import substitution", as it is called in the study of Brazil cited earlier.[17]

It is therefore probable that under a *laissez-faire* system the country that is more developed will indeed show to the less developed the image of its own future. But this will happen in a way not foreseen by Marx or by those who quote his prediction. The difference is that the future to which he referred is, under contemporary conditions, drastically foreshortened; the level of development at which stagnation tendencies become a danger is much lower than in the older, advanced countries, who began their growth in a different age. The latter have means to offset these tendencies in one way or another; the underdeveloped countries have no similar remedies. In a *laissez-faire* system there seems to be no mechanism by which this barrier to sustained growth can be broken. There remain two apparent exits from the impasse: government intervention and foreign trade. To these we turn in the next two chapters.

NOTES AND REFERENCES

1. PAUL A. BARAN, *The Political Economy of Growth*, p. 235.
2. RICHARD S. ECKAUS, *The Factor-Proportions Problem in Underdeveloped Countries*, in AGARWALA and SINGH, *op. cit.*, p. 353.

3. BARAN, *op. cit.*, pp. 22–43.

4. ROY F. HARROD, *Towards a Dynamic Economics*, Macmillan & Co., New York, 1948.

5. See W. ARTHUR LEWIS, *Economic Development with Unlimited Supplies of Labour*, in AGARWALA and SINGH, *op. cit.*, pp. 401–2.

6. JOAN ROBINSON, *Essays in the Theory of Economic Growth*, p. 37.

7. The role of the lower nobility in providing both the bulk of the initial surplus and the core of a disciplined industrial labour force is stressed in many analyses of Japan's early development. See, for example, E. HERBERT NORMAN, *Japan's Emergence as a Modern State*, Institute of Pacific Relations, New York, 1940, pp. 81 ff., and particularly pp. 157–9; also, G. C. ALLEN, *A Short Economic History of Modern Japan, 1867–1937*, F. A. PRAEGER, New York, 1963, p. 15 and elsewhere, and THOMAS C. SMITH, *Political Change and Industrial Development in Japan; Government Enterprise, 1868–1880*, Stanford University Press, Stanford, 1955.

8. JOAN ROBINSON, *op. cit.*, p. 47.

9. ALBERT O. HIRSCHMAN, *The Strategy of Economic Development*, Yale University Press, New Haven, 1958, p. 83.

10. See HARRY G. JOHNSON, *International Trade and Economic Growth*, George Allen & Unwin, London, 1958, chapter v.

11. See PAUL M. SWEEZY, *The Theory of Capitalist Development*, Oxford University Press, New York, 1942, pp. 275 ff.

12. JOSEPH SCHUMPETER, *Capitalism, Socialism and Democracy*, Harper & Bros., New York, 1942, p. 83.

13. See MARIA CONCEIÇÀO TAVARES, The growth and decline of import substitution in Brazil, *Economic Bulletin for Latin America*, **9**, No. 1, March 1964, where the development of Brazilian industry is described as having followed the pattern of import substitution for the upper-income categories of demand.

14. For a discussion of the effects of mechanization on the various skill categories of labour which, although written twenty-five years ago, is still very much to the point, see JOHN M. BLAIR, *Technology in Our Economy*, T.N.E.C. monograph No. 22, Part II, Washington, 1941, particularly pp. 143 ff.

15. BARAN, *op. cit.*, pp. 171–3.

16. See NATHAN ROSENBERG, Capital goods, technology and economic growth, *Oxford Economic Papers*, New Series, **15**, 1963, p. 219.

17. See MARIA CONCEIÇÀO TAVARES, *op. cit.* This study of Brazil, a relatively wealthy and large underdeveloped country, clearly recognizes that for an underdeveloped economy the choice often lies between oligopoly and monopoly, and that the alternative of a competitive structure does not exist. Thus, the author says: "Paradoxical as it may seem, it can reasonably be argued that, in view of the economies of scale that could be effected in certain sectors, a greater degree of concentration is needed, or even monopoly", adding that although the motor-vehicle industry in Brazil, for example, is made up of seventeen firms, this mere

number does not ensure competition, for "their joint action on the market is actually para-monopolistic in terms of prices, without any of the advantages of a monopoly in terms of costs". See pp. 9–10, and footnote there. See also DUDLEY SEERS and others, *Cuba: The Economic and Social Revolution*, University of North Carolina Press, Chapel Hill, 1964, p. 53.

CHAPTER 4

GROWTH IN THE PSEUDO-CLOSED ECONOMY: (II) THE CASE OF A MIXED-ENTERPRISE SYSTEM

THE LIMITS TO GOVERNMENT INTERVENTION

Our discussion now turns to the question to what extent it is possible for government intervention to counteract the tendencies described so far. But in order to examine what possibilities for sustained growth such a modification of the *laissez-faire* system holds out, we must be clear about the nature of the government intervention we have in mind, and about the limits it can reasonably be assumed to have in the general case.

Clearly, since we are discussing growth in a private-enterprise system, and not *in vacuo*, in abstraction from the nature of the socio-economic system, it would carry us outside the frame of our analysis to contemplate a kind and degree of government intervention that would amount to the transformation of the fundamental characteristics of a capitalist system. The very term "private-enterprise system" implies that its basic feature is the maintenance of private property in the means of production, and this sets the limits to the type and extent of government intervention and public enterprise that can meaningfully be discussed in this context: it can never be carried so far as to reduce private enterprise in the long run from the position of the dominant feature of the system to a subordinate factor in the economy's structure and performance.

It must be emphasized that what is important here is not only the long-run property relations, but also the mode of performance. The very meaning of the term "mixed-enterprise system" implies that the mere facts of formal control or even ownership

137

at any given point of time are not sufficient to draw a hard and fast line between an economy that is "predominantly" of a private enterprise type and one that is not. There is, in this respect as well as in others, a very high degree of variety between economies, and the classification of concrete cases as belonging to one or the other category requires more than the application of mechanical criteria.

It is certainly clear that it is not the quantitative weight of the public sector as such that is decisive for the distinction, but rather the role it fulfils in the economic process, and particularly what function it performs with respect to the creation and control of the economic surplus. It is the rules of the game appropriate to a given property system that define the characteristics of an economy. In this sense an economy may be of a private enterprise type even though its public sector is large or even growing, if the mode of operation of its public sector follows the rules established by the private sector. The crucial distinction, it seems, is what guides the accumulation of capital. If it is the pursuit of private profit—private here in the sense of the particularistic interest of each enterprise, whoever its stock holders may happen to be—then the economy is a private-enterprise system.

The government intervention and public enterprise that will be discussed in this chapter is therefore of a kind that is limited to the support of private enterprise and to the mitigation of any adverse effects that may result from its untrammelled operation, but is not intended to compete with private enterprise or to supersede it. In other words, government activity will be limited in such a manner as to involve no basic interference with the private-property system viewed as a whole, and with its basic motivating force, the accumulation of private profit. This does not, of course, exclude the possibility that in specific cases the government may restrain the pursuit of private profit or interfere in other ways to regulate particular economic activities, but these are to be seen as exceptions to the rule.

In addition to these limits to government conduct, which follow by definition from the restriction of our analysis to the possibilities of growth in a private-enterprise system, it is necessary to see what changes in the nature of the political framework, as originally assumed, are likely to occur as a result of the development process itself. By contrast with the behaviour postulates of a similar type found in the literature on economic development, these assumptions are here taken only as *initial* conditions. They are not parameters, but variables which themselves depend upon the way the system will function in the course of time. It is probably hardly necessary to justify the view that, at least in problems of development, the political elements are inextricably intertwined with the purely economic; but if government intervention is to be discussed it is certainly impossible to do otherwise, for government action is nothing but political action. Let us then look at the policies we have assumed initially, and see what can reasonably be said about their possible directions of change.

The initial role of government, it will be recalled, was supposed to be strictly permissive. Suppose, as we have done before, that the expected results have at first materialized: enterprising investors have come forward and, possibly taking advantage of the opportunities opened up by the newly won national sovereignty and various direct and indirect incentives provided by the government, they have begun to develop a modern sector along the lines indicated in the preceding chapter. The initial stage of expansion raises national income and produces the socially expected growth. The capitalists' own expectations, too, are satisfied, and for a while the actual rate of accumulation equals the desired rate of accumulation. The reliance on private enterprise appears to have been justified; nothing is as successful as success.

The shift to profits which this development produces is not only not unforeseen, but is a necessary condition for further growth: if accumulation is to proceed, the share of profits must be large, and consumption must be kept low. To the extent that traditional producers are displaced by the development of the modern capitalist sector, there may be a loss in terms of welfare, but this is considered an inevitable short-run sacrifice for the sake of progress and the welfare gains that are ultimately supposed to come forth. If growth has taken place mainly through import substitution, there may be an immediate gain in welfare for the economy as a whole: The displacement of imports is regarded as a sign of the development of the national economy, and its protection against the supposedly unfair advantages that foreigners have is almost self-evidently justified. So far, then, all seems to be well: national income is growing, accumulation is going on, employment may also be rising, and under favourable conditions even the traditional sector may share in some of the gains. The initial policy of the government has paid off handsomely, the trust placed in private enterprise has proved well founded, and meanwhile a capitalist class has emerged and is growing in proportion to the expansion of the sector it has created.

As the capitalist sector of the economy grows, its political importance also rises, for it is in a real sense the social and economic carrier of the political aims of the country. It is the emergent class of private entrepreneurs which palpably is responsible for the achievement of the goals embodied in the government's initial policy. By the same token, the other social and political groups formerly represented in the government partly decline in relative importance, and partly come to identify themselves more closely with the viewpoint of the capitalist class and its interests. The initial success of the latter seems to prove that the pattern of economic development which it is able to produce is, if not the only conceivable pattern, certainly the most feasible one, the one that is most immediately at hand. Alternative paths not only seem increasingly utopian, but they soon cease to be a real choice.

For with the rise of that class whose self-interest was the moving force on which the initial policy relied in order to achieve the desired development, further decisions can no longer be made *in vacuo*. Even if one assumes some idealized version of a government which stands outside and above the interests of the politically and economically dominant forces in the social system, it would be only in a very early stage of development that such a government would be able to disburse privileges and inducements to a passive and submissive class of private entrepreneurs, on conditions decided on the political level and guided by the "general good of the people". The further progress of development will soon require the active cooperation of the class that the initial policy helped to create, and the government will increasingly have to pay heed to the conditions which that class believes are necessary so that accumulation can be maintained or increased.

Generally, such a change is not likely to be a sharply defined break with the past; more often than not, it will take place imperceptibly and unconsciously. Slogans and formulae, as well as the outward form of the system, may remain unaltered while the substantive content is transformed. An underdeveloped country is particularly prone to changes of this kind, for on the one hand the general low level of development largely precludes the emergence of "countervailing" forces of sufficient strength, cohesion, and articulateness to hold in check the particular interests of that class which by virtue of its growth-creating role has attained dominance, and on the other hand, the narrow base of the intellectual and professional strata forces the government to recruit its administrators to a large extent from among groups which readily identify with the outlook of the intrepreneurial class, if they do not actually belong to it. The administration itself is therefore likely to become imbued with the viewpoint and attitudes of that class, and the more successful the latter is initially, the more unreservedly is the government likely to accept the framework which it lays down for further development. If our previous analysis of the economic process is correct, then the conditions which seem best suited to promote further growth will be those which appear, no doubt in the form of sincerely held and well-meant conviction, from the perspective of a largely oligopolistic structure. One would have to assume a peculiar kind of universal harmony to think that these conditions are compatible with the general interest.

Where growth is foreshortened, and is not accompanied by the parallel development of that great diversity of articulate socio-economic groups and strata, and of long-established institutions, that hold each other in check and to some extent neutralize each other's particular interests, as it has emerged in the long evolution of the advanced countries, but where, by contrast, oligopolies are brought into the world full-blown through the implantation of modern technology and represent the greater part of that class which is initially responsible for all the growth there is, the scope for government action which is independent of that class is in the nature of things much narrower than in the advanced countries.

COUNTER-CYCLICAL POLICIES
AND GROWTH

Let us now turn from the discussion of the limits to the scope of government action to that of its direction, beginning with what it can do to counteract the insufficient expansion of markets.

As the capitalist sector expands, the tendencies described in the preceding chapter begin to set in: the expansion of income falls behind the intended rate of investment, and investment opportunities begin to diminish. The producers, resting on the laurels of their past successes, are unable to see or accept the fact that the causes of their falling marginal rate of profit are inherent in the working of the system; nor is the government much more likely to adopt a critical attitude towards the economic and social order it has helped to bring into being. The difficulties which the process of development begins to encounter are therefore ascribed to objective factors which are beyond the control of individual entrepreneurs, beyond the power of the government—in short, factors which are entirely outside the system. The ascription of the difficulties that begin to be encountered to external obstacles is all the easier because these do, in fact, exist, and it is merely a matter of shifting the emphasis to come to the sincerely held conviction that these factors alone are responsible for all the woes that may beset the underdeveloped economy in the course of its growth.*

The entrepreneurial class does not see that the diminishing expansion of income is due to the high import-dependence of its investments, and that the lack of investment outlets is the result of the monopolistic structure and the fragmentation of production which it causes; they only see that if further imports could be replaced by domestic production, more domestic expenditure could be shifted homeward and new investment outlets would thus be provided. Alternatively, they consider that if only their costs—the high level of which they take as

* This may be at the root of the tendency of many underdeveloped countries to "externalize" most of their economic problems and to insist on support by other countries (to which they are no doubt entitled not only as a matter of equity but also as a matter of enlightened self-interest by the donor countries) without showing any signs of being able to put their own house in order.

given, as far as their choice of technique and scale at any given time is concerned—could be reduced in one way or another, further industries would become commercially profitable at the anticipated rate of profit. Being used to rely on far-reaching government support, and appealing to the goal of economic development, they expect the government to rally to their support in these areas, hoping that thereby they may restore their former profit rate and maintain their rate of accumulation. Sooner or later, however, mere permissive forms of government support, such as additional protectionist measures, will run into diminishing returns, and government intervention will have to take more direct forms if the political goal of economic growth is not to be scaled down progressively to that level which the system can sustain of its own accord at any given time.

What kind of action can the government take? Let us first deal with the fall in the rate of investment that comes from actual growth falling below the warranted rate of growth, and the consequent under-employment of productive capacity and labour. The return of the capitalist sector to a normal rate of capacity utilization is a necessary condition for any further expansion of capacity; it is therefore necessary first to achieve that increase of demand which entrepreneurs expected when they made their investments, if growth is to continue. The government may therefore resort to conventional policy measures to increase domestic expenditure through deficit spending. But whereas in a highly developed economy the deficit-financed expenditure will work its way through the economy and expand demand all round, the effects in an underdeveloped economy, where the capitalist sector produces only a relatively small proportion of wage goods, will be highly different, and will vary in accordance with the specific nature of the spending undertaken by the government. Such counter-cyclical government action is important not because it contributes to growth directly, but because entrepreneurs' expectations cannot be left frustrated, and the system must first be pulled up to what, on its own terms, is a normal level of output, before further growth can be expected to come forth.

But being "development-oriented", the government of our underdeveloped country will be reluctant to incur expenditure which does not result in the creation of some productive, or at least useful facilities, even when the immediate purpose of the expenditure is to increase overall domestic demand, no matter how. Leaf-raking or pyramid-building, not to speak of direct-income subsidies, will generally be anathema. The government will therefore most probably undertake public works to increase the economic or, at least, the social infrastructure.

These public works will tend to be labour-intensive, which is what is intended, unless they are undertaken for their own sake, that is to say, with a view to increasing the productive system of the economy. If the spending is carried out in areas remote from the urban centres of the capitalist industries, their effect in raising the demand for the products of that industry may be negligible, for the labour force will mostly be recruited from the rural sector's excess population. Both for reasons of location and because of imperfect mobility of commodities, and because of differences in the structure of demand of different segments of the populace, the better part of the income so created will be spent on the output of the subsistence sector, i.e. agriculture and some of the traditional artisanate. The proportion of expenditure that will trickle back to the capitalist sector will have less impact, the more that sector has already diversified and become geared to the production of high-income commodities. The building of an irrigation dam in an agricultural area, mainly with the help of locally recruited labour, is unlikely to augment to any appreciable extent the demand for wireless receivers, television sets, electric refrigerators, cosmetics or nylon stockings, or even for modern-style shoes, dress or canned foods. If the output of the agricultural sector is not elastic, and if public spending is sizeable, the price of food will rise, and will to that extent affect the capitalist sector adversely by worsening its terms of trade against the subsistence sector. Public spending will in this case not only fail to benefit the capitalist sector, but by sending up the price of food it may reduce the demand of the urban working class and of other low-income strata for manufactured goods.

If public spending is directed to projects within the industrialized, mainly urban areas, the effects may be similar in kind, although they will probably be more favourable to the capitalist sector. Again, the major proportion of the additional income will be spent on the products of the sector that provides the bulk of the wage goods—agriculture; the price level of the latter, and consequently the real wage level of the industrial labour force and the residual demand for manufactured goods, will depend on the supply elasticity of food and on the cross-elasticity of demand for industrial products with respect to the price of food. The lower the former, and the higher the latter (which we take to be negative), the less efficacious will public spending be in expanding the demand for the output of the capitalist sector. It is reasonable to assume that both elasticities vary with the level of economic development in the directions indicated. The higher the overall level of development, the more elastic will be the supply of food, and the less will a rise in the price of food tend to reduce the demand for manufactured goods. Where the absolute level of development is low, deficit spending will therefore tend to have little effect on pulling up a capitalist sector to its normal capacity level of output.

To put the matter in the more usual Keynesian terminology, the expenditure out of additional income on products of the traditional (mainly agricultural) sector is, from the point of view of the capitalist sector, analogous to an import leakage. The demand for its output which is generated by public spending is (disregarding saving) equivalent to the reciprocal of the marginal propensity to consume traditional products. This "capitalist-sector-multiplier", as it might be called, is likely to be low—the lower, the more labour-intensive the public expenditure, and the less it attracts labour in the areas in which the capitalist sector is concentrated. And the lower this multiplier, the greater, of course, is the volume of expenditure needed to generate a sufficient increase in demand for the output of the capitalist sector to provide for the full employment of its capacity.*

Although the availability of idle resources is a *prima facie* justification for deficit spending, this remedy may, in the

---

* This does not contradict the empirically observed high income-elasticity of demand for manufactured goods, as obtained either implicitly, by correlating the growth of average or aggregate income with the consumption of different categories of goods, or from family-expenditure studies. The latter are, for one thing, usually based on data collected for urban families, and for another thing, they are generally cross-section analyses which cannot be expected to reveal the trends described above. The results obtained from aggregate correlations simply reflect the fact that whatever growth there is comes from the capitalist (industrial) sector.

conditions of an underdeveloped economy, create inflationary pressures even when the expenditure does not exceed the limits given by the existing excess capacity of capital and labour. This is a manifestation of the so-called dualism that is characteristic of underdeveloped economies, where it is not the capitalist sector which suffers from a deficiency of effective demand that produces the bulk of wage goods, but the subsistence sector, which generally has a low elasticity of supply. Public spending then often injects additional demand into the sector where its main effect is to create demand inflation, while the sector which has idle capacity benefits little, if at all. At the same time, the rise of the price level in the former sector presses on the general wage level, and tends to cause a cost push in the capitalist sector. If prices in the capitalist sector remain stable, the cost rise eats into profits and reduces accumulation; if the cost rise is passed on to the consumer, this further narrows the markets.

In conditions of poverty the rise in the price of food and other basic wage goods may reduce the demand for most manu-factured goods. Public spending may simply have the effect of widening the area of the exchange economy by drawing into the ranks of wage labour part of the underemployed rural popula-tion; it will, however, have little effect as a cure for a deficiency of effective demand in the capitalist sector, even when the price level of wage goods remains constant. Where this is not so because the supply of these goods is inelastic, the income effect will be aggravated by a price effect, and the cure of public spending may be worse than the disease.

In reality the two sectors are, of course, not so sharply demarcated, and public expenditure is rarely overwhelmingly directed at one sector's output to the exclusion of the other. Some spillover will always occur. When this happens, and when public expenditure pushes demand against an inelastic supply for the better part of aggregate expenditure while achieving only a partial effect in the sector whose demand it was meant to expand, the inflationary pressures so created will not easily come to an end. For the capitalist sector, having seen that public spending helps to *some* extent, and yet continuing to suffer from deficient demand, is likely to attribute the inadequacy of the effect to an insufficiency of the cause. It may therefore easily call for more of the same. Even where the government invests

in productive facilities, the inflation generated by the investment will not necessarily be self-liquidating once these investments bear fruit. For if they are such as to increase the
productivity of the agricultural sector—for instance, irrigation
works, land reclamation and the like—consumption in that
sector may simply go up. The price of the marketed agricultural
surplus, that is, the wage goods supplied to the capitalist sector,
will then either remain at the level attained at the end of the
inflationary process caused by the investment expenditure, or
even rise.

This may explain to some extent why an underdeveloped
economy may have a deficiency of demand together with continuous inflation. Even when allowance is made for all kinds of
other factors, which no doubt contribute to such developments,
it seems difficult to explain on other grounds the persistence of
substantial excess capacity despite almost permanent inflation
which seems to have been typical of the development of many
underdeveloped countries—notably Latin America—throughout a long period. We shall presently revert to this point for, as
will be seen, a monopolistic structure augments such tendencies.
First, however, some points must be made regarding the effects
on wage costs and demand in the capitalist sector.

The capitalist sector will for obvious reasons be vitally
interested in shifting the consumption function for the traditional products, both as a result of the possible adverse changes
described above, and as a matter of long-run policy. Such a
shift can be achieved in various ways: capitalists are likely to
demand, and frequently to obtain, government control over the
prices and output of the traditional sector, particularly agriculture, or to bring about a heavier taxation of the peasants.
This will produce a two-fold result: first, it will lower the price
of the main component of wage labour's consumption, and thus
relieve the pressure on money wages which forces the capitalists
to pay out a larger part of their output in the form of wages.
This pressure may be strong even if there is substantial unemployment in the industrial labour force, as long as the going
wage rate represents the conventional subsistence level; it will
naturally be stronger where the industrial labour supply has at
some stage in the growth of the capitalist sector become scarce,
as previously described, and if it is unionized. Secondly, since

the output of the two sectors is largely complementary in demand, the holding down of the price of agricultural goods will not only maintain the level of money wages in the capitalist sector, but will also tend to shift expenditure to the output of the industrial sector.* In considering the relationships between the two sectors, W. Arthur Lewis' observation is very much to the point, namely that "the fact that the wage level in the capitalist sector depends upon earnings in the subsistence sector is sometimes of immense political importance, since its effect is that capitalists have a direct interest in holding down the productivity of the subsistence workers".[1]

We conclude, then, that deficit spending, unless planned and directed to specific objectives with a degree of precision and care that is altogether implausible for an underdeveloped country, will have only an insignificant effect in raising demand for the output of the capitalist sector to its normal capacity level. Underutilization of capacity will become a more or less permanent feature, and the rate of profit will tend to fall at the margin. The existence of excess capacity will induce further concentration within the existing industries, and will deter entry by outside firms, thus increasing the rigidity of the monopolistic structure and barring its transformation through the introduction of more efficient techniques. To some extent, the capitalists will attempt to restore their former profit level through their own action—partly by raising their prices, and partly by introducing cost-reducing innovations which will drive out some of the firms, but will not raise total output and reduce prices. For the reasons stated earlier, their scope for such autonomous action will be limited and self-defeating, and sooner or later they will turn to the government to assist them in regaining their expected rate of profit.

DIRECT AND INDIRECT SUBSIDIES
TO THE RATE OF PROFIT

One way of restoring the anticipated rate of profit is to induce the government to direct its public spending to projects which

* We continue to use the terms "subsistence sector" and "agricultural sector" interchangeably simply because in reality the two are largely overlapping. Analytically, they are, of course, quite distinct.

will reduce the capitalists' cost of production. Ignoring various direct and indirect subsidies, which are the obvious form of cost-reducing public expenditure, this means, where public works are concerned, to channel them into economic overheads which serve mainly the capitalist sector: roads and harbours, transportation and communication systems, water and power facilities, and the like. Evidently these are real additions to the productive capacity of the economy and raise its overall productivity. But by themselves they will not restore normal capacity utilization in the capitalist sector. To have a significant effect in this respect, the public investment would have to be very large.

The volume of expenditure on such works is in practice likely to be heavy in relation to total investment and aggregate expenditure. This type of expenditure may therefore easily run the economy into the inflationary barrier, particularly since the lumpiness which generally characterizes such works makes it necessary to build ahead of demand. Nor is it to be expected that because such investments are directed to productive facilities, this will liquidate the inflationary pressures they generate once their output and services come on the market. For in a monopolistic structure the new facilities will serve to reduce the costs of production of their users, and thus raise profits to some anticipated level, but not necessarily to expand output and lower prices. The rigidity of the monopolistic structure will therefore cause inflation to have a ratchet effect once it has set in: rises in costs will tend to be passed on to consumers, but reductions in costs will not.

In reality the underdeveloped economies do not, of course, have the foreign-exchange revenues that adjust automatically to import requirements, as we assume for the time being throughout. Investments in economic overheads, which are often highly import-intensive, will thus also aggravate the balance-of-payments difficulties which are typical of most underdeveloped economies. On balance, therefore, the adverse effects of such infrastructural investment will probably outweigh any cost-reducing, profit-increasing, or market-expanding results for the capitalist sector. Needless to say, this does not deny the need for the building of such economic overhead facilities in their own right; we are for the moment merely considering their effects as a measure to counteract stagnation tendencies, and in this respect they are not likely to take up much of the slack in the capitalist sector.

Having said all this, let us nevertheless assume that the government's deficit spending has been planned and executed in such a way as to be successful at least in restoring the rate of profit which entrepreneurs expected. Let us also assume that the excess capacity that has developed in the capitalist sector has become accepted as part of the "natural state of affairs", particularly because it is outwardly undistinguishable from the technically unavoidable excess capacity that always accompanies growth. At the new level of "normal" capacity utilization, and with newly validated profit expectations, accumulation will go on at the socially and privately desired level, and all will seem to be well. But the continuous pressure of excess capacity, which is now only in part a voluntarily held reserve against future increases of demand, as would be normal in any growing economy, but is rather due to a chronic deficiency of effective demand, will cause firms to seek alternative employment for the idle resources. There will therefore be a strong pressure to accelerate diversification, and the attempt to escape a falling marginal rate of profit because of deficient demand will push the capitalist sector all the more rapidly towards a falling rate of profit because of contracting economies of large-scale production and declining investment opportunities.

Where government spending is financed through taxation rather than deficits, a similar argument holds. In regard to the stimulation of demand in the capitalist sector the effect will indeed be worse, for public spending can have a demand-stimulating effect only if it does not contract private spending. Taxation-financed expenditure is obviously offset by a reduction of spending elsewhere in the economy, and the net effect of such a redistribution of expenditure, say from the traditional to the capitalist sector, depends on the compressibility of income and its accessibility to taxation in the former, and on the marginal propensity to consume the products of the latter, as well as on the specific nature of the public spending so carried out, as discussed before. If consumption in the non-capitalist sector can be squeezed, and if the income extracted from it is spent in ways that will maximize the generation of demand for the output of the capitalist sector, the slack in the latter may be taken up to that extent.

Where the existing social and economic structure is such that a surplus can be extracted from the non-capitalist sector and channelled into expenditure on the products of the capitalist sector, for example through the taxation of a landowning class or of the peasantry, this will, of course, not only take up any existing slack in demand for the output of the capitalist sector, but will also promote growth in general by providing a surplus for productive investment, and by broadening the markets for the capitalist sector. This, in fact, is the classic manner of financing the initial accumulation in the capitalist sector, and has often been the historical pattern of growth. But by the same token it is reasonable to assume that the margin of *additional* income transfers is narrow.

Where the possibilities for additional income transfers from the non-capitalist to the capitalist sector are limited, the taxation of the capitalist sector itself will be ineffective; for if the taxes are absorbed, they will reduce the net rate of profit and thus depress investment, and if they are shifted on to consumers through higher prices, as is possible in a monopolistic structure, they will contract demand and thus diminish investment opportunities.

Sooner or later, however, the incompressibility of income in the subsistence sector, and the reluctance to depress investment through the taxation of capitalists' profits, coupled with the political resistance that is likely to be put up against the latter course in an economy bent on promoting a "favourable investment climate", will put a limit to the redistribution of expenditure that can be effected through taxation. The government will then be under strong temptation to resort to inflationary spending. This will in the short run augment profits, but with rigid wages the volume of real demand for the output of the capitalist sector will fall off, and with it the rate of capacity utilization, thus pushing up the cost level. With rising wages, the level of capacity utilization may be maintained, but costs will be pushed up directly after a greater or lesser time lag. With a monopolistic structure, the capitalist sector will then be sent into a wage-price spiral. Rising domestic prices will lower the relative price of imports, increase the demand for them, and press on the balance of payments from the expenditure side, while rising costs will reduce the profitability of exports and press on the balance of payments from the revenue side. The effects of inflation on development have been extensively discussed in the literature and need not be recapitulated here, except to add that in an underdeveloped economy, the ailments of which are due to technical and structural rigidities, the standard remedies for inflation may have very doubtful results.

GOVERNMENT PROCUREMENT AND DIRECT INVESTMENT IN COMMODITY PRODUCTION

We have seen that the traditional types of public spending are very unlikely to achieve more than, at best, an expansion of demand to the normal capacity level of the capitalist sector. In general, they must be expected to fall short even of that target, and to succeed mainly in raising the rate of profit to the level originally expected by entrepreneurs, but at a reduced level of output and employment. There is, however, within the traditional domain of government action a possibility that public spending may be directed so as to affect directly the level of demand for the output of the capitalist sector, namely through direct government purchases of its goods.

In the developed countries this usually takes the form of defence expenditures which, in addition to creating income and demand, have the "convenient" property that they involve no subsidization of consumption as other types of government procurement might have. In the underdeveloped economy, however, defence expenditure is the most import-intensive of all expenditures, and unless the imports of armaments are financed through foreign aid earmarked for this purpose, they will be a severe drain on the economy's resources.* In any case, this type of spending will have a negligible effect on the level of

---

* Regrettably, the well-meant advice frequently given to underdeveloped countries to adopt more labour-intensive techniques and to forego the superior efficiency of techniques which are ill adapted to their factor endowments, has but rarely been extended to the area of defence, where a much lower level of efficiency than that which is usually taken for granted might be a good thing all round.

output in the capitalist sector, and the less so the more the productive system is geared to the supply of consumers' goods.
Government purchases of commodities for purposes other than
defence will not only have limited scope in an underdeveloped
economy, but if they are intended as income transfers in kind,
they can be expected to be resisted by the capitalist class for the
reasons succinctly described by Paul A. Baran: "They would
not only raise the floor under the wage level, but would also
contradict the fundamental principle of a capitalist system that
income, whether in cash or in kind, can only be earned through
work—unless it comes from property."[2]

Government procurement has indeed played an important
role in the past development of some countries, sometimes to the
extent of laying the foundations for the development of the
whole capitalist sector. Japan's early development is perhaps the
outstanding example of a case where entire industrial complexes
were created on the basis of government purchases of the goods
necessary to build up a large military establishment, together
with the military and civilian infrastructure to support it.[3] To
a lesser extent, the same is true of Czarist Russia in the late
nineteenth and early twentieth century. This type of development, however, not only required a particular class structure in
which feudal-military elements were prominent, a relatively
large pre-existing surplus which could be shifted from private
to public consumption and investment, a considerable export
surplus—in good part extracted from the meagre living standards of the mass of the population through very oppressive
measures—and a specific concatenation of external and internal
historical conditions; more importantly from the point of this
study, it was possible only in a period in which the technological
gap between the developed and the underdeveloped countries
was incomparably smaller than it is today, and when the
building up of an effective military machine, capable of international "competition" on more or less equal terms with more
advanced countries, was still within the range of the technical
capability of less advanced countries. Under modern conditions
the type of autonomous development of which Japan is practically the only example is no longer conceivable. In the field of
defence as in the field of civilian production, it is necessary to
avoid the fallacy of thinking that development is merely a stage

by stage progress from poverty to wealth which can be repeated in much the same fashion by different countries, irrespective of the stage of history at which they start. To repeat a point already made earlier: development has an historical dimension, in the sense that its pattern must differ according to the external circumstances, and particularly the technical conditions, which each country finds when it begins its process of growth.

It may still be objected that government intervention may not be restricted to the mere support of the capitalist sector and to the promotion of its growth, strictly on the terms set by the latter. It can, one may think, also complement that sector without thereby exceeding the limits postulated earlier in this chapter. To be the growth-promoter of the last resort, the government may, for example, invest in productive facilities without thereby necessarily superseding the capitalist sector in its own domain.

At first glance the argument seems entirely plausible: if private investment lags because the investment outlets open to private entrepreneurs involve a falling marginal rate of profit, or because a deficiency of effective demand has saddled the capitalist sector with unintended excess capacity, while at the same time the economy suffers from an insufficient overall rate of capital formation, there is obviously a case for "peaceful coexistence" between private and public enterprise, and the latter can and ought to enter those fields which the former finds unattractive. Moreover, this mixed enterprise system is not a mere theoretical possibility, but is a fair description of what governments in underdeveloped countries often actually do.

Governments indeed often invest in directly productive capacity, either on their own or in partnership with private capital. In the case of such joint ventures, however, the government is often expected to pay the piper but not to call the tune; its participation is a more or less disguised subsidy to private investment in commercially unprofitable areas where the government is expected to assume the risks and losses so as to assure private capital of its anticipated profit rate. This is essentially no different from any other kind of subsidization, and need not detain us further. It is obvious that the *modus operandi* of such mixed enterprises will be determined essentially by the same considerations that apply to purely private enterprise.

This means that their policies in regard to output, prices and investment will be guided just as much by the dictates of the market and of *private* profitability as if there were no government participation.

Much the same is true of many pure government enterprises. The scale of government investment in enterprises which do not directly serve the capitalist sector, and the extent of subsidization of individual enterprises it can undertake, are subject to severe restrictions. The stronger the capitalist class, both politically and economically, and the narrower the tax base, the more is it likely to maintain a close watch over government expenditure and to insist that government enterprise, when it cannot be avoided, should conform to the rules of the game of a capitalist order. Government undertakings are expected to "pay for themselves" not in terms of their social benefits, but exactly as if they were private enterprises pursuing a "sound" business policy. This means that they will adopt the same monopolistic practices with respect to output, prices and investment, as private enterprises, and will involve the same waste of resources, with only minor modifications. Among these differences, the most important one may be that the government may be content with a lower rate of profit than would be acceptable to a private entrepreneur; but once such a floor has been determined, profit maximization will often be the guideline for economic activity, just as it is in the private sector.

These rules will normally only be relaxed when the output of such government enterprises serves to subsidize costs in the private sector. Otherwise, for instance if the government were to invest in a new industry, it would be expected to adopt a "conservative" approach in determining its scale of output, and its current production would have to be guided by the principle of profit maximization, so that its prices would be set where profits, rather than output, are highest. Least of all might such an enterprise compete against private firms, and whenever they operate in the same market, it will be private enterprise that sets the pace, except when private firms are altogether weak and inefficient.

The areas which government enterprise in directly productive facilities can enter—on the assumption that the fundamentally private-enterprise character of the economy is not to be attacked

—are in the long run in any case severely limited; the initial shouldering of development risks by government may be acceptable or even welcomed, just as it often is in an advanced economy, but it cannot invade the field of commodity production to any substantial extent. For although such investments will often widen the real margin of growth, they must soon reach a boundary beyond which they begin to compete with private enterprise. The degree to which the government can continue to open up new frontiers of investment outlets for private enterprise depends on the resources it can mobilize for this purpose, that is to say ultimately on the level of productivity and on the pattern of development that a private enterprise system can achieve on the basis of *its own rationale*, and on the degree of compressibility of income in the non-capitalist sector from which the resources for such investment must come in the absence of massive foreign aid.

In a monopolistic structure, which at best expands into additional areas opened up by public investment, the social benefits so created will mostly be privately appropriated, and in the new fields the monopolistic rules of the game will be applied as soon as they are taken over. The gains in productivity will not be passed on to consumers in the form of lower prices; the narrow markets which gave rise to monopoly will be prevented from expanding by the rationale that dictates their behaviour; and by the same token any new investment outlets will, after sporadic bursts of renewed growth, again depend upon subsidization from the public purse. The size of that purse depends in the last resort upon how much can be extracted from the non-capitalist sector. The higher the initial level of development achieved, and the greater the potential economic space which private enterprise has not yet found it profitable to exploit, the greater is the scope for such government intervention, and the further can it postpone a fall in the rate of growth.

The introduction of new, more advanced techniques can give the monopolistic structure a new lease on life just as major innovations do in the advanced countries. The scope of government intervention in the underdeveloped countries, where private enterprise may be too timid to avail itself of all the opportunities of technical progress that can be adopted, often at no additional cost, from the advanced countries, may in practice be very substantial. Furthermore, there is much scope for government action in the field of reducing the under-developed economy's technological dependence, that is, in the production of producers' goods. There is, however, one thing that the government cannot do so long as it is unable to super-sede private enterprise: it cannot prevent the emergence of irrational productive structures, because of the interaction be-tween the technical and structural constraints with the logic of a capitalist market rationality. It can therefore, in Baran's terminology, increase the actual surplus of the economy, but can not achieve the realization of its potential surplus.

The promotion of sustained growth would require measures to remove the constraints that necessarily appear in a private-enterprise system to the full extent allowed by objective tech-nical conditions; they would require that investment, output and price policies, the composition of output and the distribu-tion of income, be dictated by a rationality which is totally alien to a private enterprise system. To be effective, such measures would have to be of a scope that would be wholly incompatible with the long-run coexistence of private with public enterprise. One or the other would have to win out, and as Joan Robinson has aptly said, ". . . any government which had both the power and the will to remedy the major defects of the capitalist system would have the will and the power to abolish it altogether, while governments which have the power to retain the system lack the will to remedy its defects".[4]

In fact, even that limited degree of government intervention and productive enterprise that would seem to be possible with-out serious infringement of the capitalist sector is not likely to be undertaken. An underdeveloped economy, if it has become committed to a private enterprise system, is likely to adopt an attitude to the relationship between public and private enter-prise and to the role of government in the economic sphere in general which, by comparison with the advanced countries, is even "more catholic than the Pope". Forms of government intervention and control, and areas of public enterprise which in many developed capitalist countries are considered fully compatible with the retention of the private enterprise character of the system, are often quite unthinkable in underdeveloped countries. Anyone who has followed the relationships between public and private enterprise in those underdeveloped countries where the former has significant weight will be aware of the narrow limits for effective government action outside the limits indicated in this chapter. In reality, the government we pictured in the beginning will in the course of time tend to redefine its development goals in accordance with the rationality of the private property system and with the rate of growth it can sustain. Since the political and economic changes in the early stages of growth take place in an environment which is still shot through with backwardness in all areas, retrogression may easily set in.

The capitalist class, facing shrinking investment opportunities, may have recourse to capital flight, and may settle down to a low-level equilibrium. It may fall back into an economic and political alliance with the pre-capitalist landed interests and mercantile classes, and—perhaps more frequently—may assume the role of *comprador* in relation to foreign capital. This will happen all the more easily the more severe the social and political strains to which the relinquishment of its progressive role gives rise. Economic stagnation will then be paralleled by social and political atrophy, and the inability to provide for economic progress will make it necessary to maintain the system through political repression. The government, either helpless in the face of what seems to be the "objective" incapacity of the system which it has created to provide for growth, or having succumbed to the outlook of that system, will increasingly try to rely on foreign aid. To pacify domestic discontent, it will often assume an overtly militant anti-colonialist, anti-imperialist stance, and tend to externalize its problems by laying the blame for all its woes exclusively at the door of the foreign powers or foreign private interests; at the same time, it will more or less covertly ally itself with these forces in an effort to obtain aid, possibly trade concessions, and external support for its régime.

We have throughout ignored the overwhelmingly important problem of foreign influence and intervention, and we do not propose to discuss it in detail, except to point briefly to one of its aspects. Foreign aid, whatever its source, is primarily granted because of considerations arising out of the political rivalry among the Great Powers. It will therefore always include at least implicit political conditions. One of the first conditions that are attached to aid is the maintenance of internal political stability, for it is on the basis of the policies expected from the government of the day that the aid is given. Any change of government in the recipient country thus carries the danger, from the viewpoint of the donor country, that the policies which are relevant for the latter will also change. Therefore, both the donor countries and the recipient governments will be prone to regard *any* demand for social, economic or political change as at least potentially subversive, as endangering the existing régime in its entirety.

From without, there will thus be pressure to maintain the stability of the prevailing system, even if the donor countries are not in sympathy with some of its manifestations, and even if they consider that it may in the long run produce internal explosive stresses. Any departure from the existing system is a leap into the political dark. From within, the stunted capitalist class, together with its pre-capitalist and other social, political and economic allies, will increasingly erode the development policy and bend it to its own ends, lowering its targets and trimming them to what it believes is in its own interest to carry out.

All these are tendencies; to state them thus starkly is to overstate them by comparison with concrete countries and specific periods. There may, in certain circumstances, be counter tendencies and offsetting factors that will allow a capitalist system to achieve a higher initial rate of growth or a longer span of sustained development, leading to a higher absolute level of affluence, before the system becomes ossified. An underdeveloped country having rich and easily opened up natural resources may do very well for a very long time under a capitalist system, provided it can retain control over its resources and reap their benefits; the same will be true of a country which is able to obtain large capital transfers from abroad. But where resources are bountiful, the economic problem disappears; with no scarcity, any economic system can work well. Most underdeveloped countries, needless to say, are very far from that fortunate position.

But there seems to be yet another way out of the impasse. There is, in principle, no need for a country to be limited to its domestic markets and their constraints, as we have assumed so far, and hence no disparity between technology and market size need result. With free trade, our whole problem would seem to disappear. The question whether this is in fact so will occupy us in the next and last chapter, where we turn from the "pseudo-closed" to the open economy.

NOTES AND REFERENCES

1. W. Arthur Lewis, *Economic Development with Unlimited Supplies of Labour*, A. N. Agarwala and S. P. Singh (eds.), *The Economics of Underdevelopment*, pp. 409–10.

2. See Paul A. Baran, *The Political Economy of Growth*, p. 106.

3. Scholarly opinion is agreed, with minor differences of emphasis, on the overwhelmingly important role of government investment and procurement in Japan's early development. This government intervention —more properly said, initiative—was not restricted to direct military procurement, although it was no doubt motivated to a large extent by strategic considerations. The developmental role of the military industries in Japan is stressed by the Japanese historian Ushisaburo Kobayashi, *Military Industries of Japan*, Oxford University Press, New York, 1922, but he emphasizes that the importance of strategic considerations did not remain confined to industries producing war matériel, but extended even to such essentially civilian industries as wool weaving and spinning or food processing. Smith, in the work cited earlier, also says that ". . . the Meiji leaders were quite aware that economic strength was an element of military power, but this awareness did not dominate their thinking on industrial policy" (Survey of the empirical evidence on economics of scale, *Business Concentration and Price Policy*, National Bureau of Economic Research, Princeton, 1955, p. 35) so that they devoted considerable resources to the development of civilian industries. One of the most authoritative statistical studies of Japan's economic development, by Henry Rosovsky, *Capital Formation in Japan 1868–1940*, The Free Press of Glencoe, 1961, shows that about half of all government investment was in military industries and expenditures throughout the period from 1887 to 1940, and Rosovsky adds that "throughout Japanese industrialization, the government was ready to buy and produce vast quantities of military equipment. It is, of course, impossible to say precisely what effects this policy had on private heavy industry, but it must have been a tremendous stimulus" (*op. cit.*, pp. 24–25 and 27). Another well-known scholar, William W. Lockwood, states that ". . . Particularly before 1910, and again after 1937, Army and Navy orders for munitions and other war equipment . . . were the props upon which many of Japan's heavy industries were built and upon which they depended largely for their profits" (Lockwood, *The Economic Development of Japan*, Princeton, 1954, pp. 415–16). See also E. H. Norman, *Japan's Emergence as a Modern State*, and Smith, *op. cit.*

4. Joan Robinson, *Economic Journal*, December 1936, quoted in Baran, *op. cit.*, p. 133.

CHAPTER 5

GROWTH IN THE OPEN ECONOMY: (III) THE FOREIGN-TRADE ESCAPE FROM STAGNATION

IN THE real world the underdeveloped countries come up against a severe external obstacle to growth: their capacity to import lags behind their needs, for economic development brings in its wake a rise in import requirements. These, however, cannot be met adequately because revenues from exports of traditional goods can, at best, be expanded only slowly, and at the same time there seem to be serious difficulties in developing new exports. Demand as well as supply factors are responsible for this external constraint on development, which we have so far ignored.

The long-deferred question that must now be asked is not only whether it is practically possible to lift this restriction sufficiently for growth not to be retarded, but furthermore, whether an expansion of exports, if it can be achieved, will not at the same time eliminate the internal obstacles which have occupied us until now. Is it not precisely foreign trade through which the barriers of small domestic markets can be broken, so that the gap between the latter and the technically determined scales of production will be bridged, and most of the difficulties which we have ascribed to this factor will thus disappear at a stroke? The argument seems eminently plausible, yet this chapter will try to show that the difficulties of increasing exports in line with the import needs created by the process of growth are, on the supply side, rooted in the same conditions which make for the crystallization of monopolistic structures at an early stage of industrial growth, and which in the last analysis cause the stagnation tendencies we have discussed earlier.

The balance-of-payments restrictions on growth are generally so severe that they have tended to overshadow many other growth-inhibiting factors. They have been the central issue in the international arena since the end of World War II, if not already since the Great Depression. In 1964 this problem was the focus of the largest international conference on economic affairs ever to be held—the United Nations Conference on Trade and Development. On the political level, this conference represented, in one aspect, the culmination of the tendency of the underdeveloped countries to "externalize" their growth problems, and to regard the prevailing pattern of international trade as the chief culprit for their unsatisfactory rate of progress. This pattern of trade reflects an international division of labour which evolved under colonialism, is dominated by the advanced countries, and works in their favour even where trade is free, and all the more so where it is subject to artificial barriers.

The inequities wrought by this structure of international trade are no doubt real enough, and it is anything but our purpose to minimize them. It is none the less necessary to emphasize that the insufficient capacity to import which thwarts the growth of the underdeveloped countries is as much the result of the maladaptation of their productive structure—the modern sectors of which are almost exclusively oriented towards the domestic market—to production for the foreign market, as it is due to the adversities which they face in the markets of their prospective trading partners. But before going into the determinants of this "inward-directed" pattern of growth, it will be helpful to look briefly at the structural relationship between exports and growth in an underdeveloped economy.

EXPORTS AS A SUBSTITUTE FOR A DOMESTIC PRODUCERS' GOODS SECTOR

Where exports have virtually no domestic market, and the existing producers' goods sector is negligible, the sectorization of the economy into a consumers' goods and a producers' goods sector is coterminous with its partition into a domestic and an export sector. The latter "produces" the economy's capital goods via the imports it makes possible, and the domestic sector supplies the consumption goods needed for both sectors.*

* Imports of consumers' goods are neglected for simplicity.

For the clarification of the relationship between these two sectors, it will be convenient to use the Marxian model, which distinguishes between sectors by their different technical and functional characteristics in the circular flow. The static, closed-economy model is familiar:[1]

(I)   Producers' Goods Sector: $O_1 = K_1 + W_1 + P_1$

(II)   Consumers' Goods Sector: $O_2 = K_2 + W_2 + P_2$

where O is output, K is constant capital (for simplicity, fixed capital costs), W is the wage bill, and P is the capitalists' surplus, or profits, all per period of time. In the stationary state there is no net investment, so that all profits are consumed. The equilibrium condition is that the supply of producers' goods must equal the demand for them that comes from the replacement of the capital goods used up in both sectors in the process of production. Similarly, the supply of consumers' goods must equal the demand arising from the income of workers and capitalists in both sectors:

$$\begin{array}{cc} \text{Supply} & \text{Demand} \\ K_1 + W_1 + P_1 = & K_1 + K_2 \\ K_2 + W_2 + P_2 = & W_1 + P_1 + W_2 + P_2. \end{array}$$

Each of these equations reduces to

$$K_2 = W_1 + P_1.$$

The model of equilibrium growth (or, in Marx' terminology, the schema of expanded reproduction) has the same form, only that now savings and investment are introduced. Since we assume that all capital accumulation comes out of profits, the difference by comparison with the stationary model is that the capitalists' surplus is now broken down into its constituent parts, according to the purposes to which they are applied. The model then looks as follows:

(I) $O_1' = K_1 + W_1 + Pc_1 + \Delta Pk_1 + \Delta Pw_1 + \Delta Pc_1$

(II) $O_2' = K_2 + W_2 + Pc_2 + \Delta Pk_2 + \Delta Pw_2 + \Delta Pc_2$

where the total profits P of the stationary model or now divided into Pc, the stationary amount of capitalists' consumption, ΔPk, the increment to constant capital, ΔPw, the increase in the wage bill, and ΔPc, the addition to the capitalists' own consumption. The equilibrium condition is as before. By equating the supply of Sector I with the demand for its output that arises in both sectors from replacement and from net investment, and the supply of Sector II with the demand for consumers' goods that comes from the income going into consumption in both sectors, we obtain the equilibrium equation

$$[K_2] + Pk_2 = [W_1 + Pc_1] + \Delta Pw_1 + \Delta Pc_1,$$

in which the stationary terms have been put in brackets.

This model brings out an important aspect of the process of circulation which we have already mentioned earlier: each sector is dependent on the other for part of its requirements, but produces more than it needs of its own output. Only these surpluses enter into the exchange relationships between them. The two sectors must therefore stand in a specific quantitative relationship to each other. In the stationary state this proportionality depends only on the capital–output ratios, that is to say on technology, and in the dynamic model also on the capital-intensity and on the savings ratio. On our present assumptions, the latter two are roughly given by the relative shares of profits and wages.

It is immediately obvious that this proportionality between the two sectors holds only when they are in the same market for their entire "surplus" output; otherwise there is no more reason why they should be proportional to each other than there is for the product of two different countries to stand in a fixed ratio to one another. For if in a closed economy one of the two sectors should expand more than is warranted by the demand created by the other, its prices and profits would fall, and in the long run capital and labour would migrate to the other sector until the proportionality between them was restored.

If instead of a domestic producers' goods sector, however, there is an export sector, no such proportionality need exist. The expansion of the export sector depends on foreign demand and on its own accumulation. The latter is the strategic variable with respect to the sector's impact on domestic growth, for the profitability of expansion in the export sector is affected only indirectly and partially by the domestic sector. The export sector depends on the domestic sector only for the supply of wage goods. This can be seen clearly if we deduct from the last equilibrium equation the terms that represent the stationary flows, and obtain the incremental equilibrium equation

$$\Delta Pk_2 = \Delta Pw_1 + \Delta Pc_1,$$

which shows that investment in the domestic sector depends entirely on the increase in the demand for consumers' goods generated by the growth of the export sector.

Assuming that foreign demand is perfectly elastic, the export sector will expand until the supply schedule of its domestic factors rises against it, and attains some equilibrium level. Beyond that level, the accumulating profits will not necessarily migrate into investment in the domestic sector because in conditions of technological dependence this investment will not create its own demand. If technology permits the substitution of capital for the factors that tend to become scarce (either directly, or indirectly, by displacing labour and thus offsetting the rising costs of other factors, such as might result from diminishing returns of natural resources), the equilibrium size of the export sector may be shifted further upwards. Such a substitution of capital for other factors will raise the import coefficient of the export sector, and the volume of domestic demand will at best grow more slowly. Where the supply of factors, for instance natural resources and labour, is elastic, and the export sector operates in competitive conditions abroad, it may easily overexpand and, at the limit, reduce rather than increase the capacity to import.

Even an expanding export sector does not necessarily induce growth in the domestic sector; there are, in fact, strong forces working against such an outcome. We are not speaking here of the widely observed fact that such export sectors are often outposts of other economies in the countries where the exports are produced, so that accumulating profits are repatriated and reinvested wherever the anticipated return is highest—which may or may not be the place where these profits originated. Even in the ideal case where the export sector is indigenous, it is, on the demand side, completely independent of the domestic economy, and substitutability of factors may also make it independent to some extent with respect to the supply of labour: it is often in the economy, but not of it.

Such an export sector provides the economy with a given capacity to import, and to that extent removes the technical bottleneck that results from the absence of a domestic producers' goods sector. It will not, however, substitute for the latter in terms of automatically widening the domestic market through the investment outlays that expand the export sector. On the contrary, the larger the volume of the imports it permits, the more will the import-competing industries at home be depressed unless they are protected by a conscious development policy. In the absence of such a prior policy it is only under the impact of a violent shock that resources will be shifted to the domestic sector. This occurred in Latin America in the 1930's, when falling exports no longer made it possible to satisfy the demand for manufactured goods by imports and necessitated substitution, and at the same time declining prices of capital goods and shrinking investment opportunities abroad made domestic investment relatively more profitable.

The size and the rate of expansion of the export sector determines, through the volume of the imports it makes possible, the limits within which the domestic sector can expand. It provides, on the one hand, the capital goods needed, and on the other hand, the greater the volume of these equivalent imports, the wider is the field of expansion for domestic investment. If there were no constraints on the growth of the export sector, we would, of course, have the trivial case of the economy that has all the markets and investment opportunities there is any use for, and our problem would have vanished.

The problem of the underdeveloped countries, however, arises precisely because their exports fail to expand sufficiently, both in terms of the import capacity they provide, and in terms of the markets they create by generating income and employment. Wherever a process of growth starts, import requirements rise more rapidly than income. An initial high level of exports, such as some countries have had for a long time by virtue of the accident of possessing rich natural resources or as the heritage of the international specialization left behind by a colonial economy, may make it easier, once development is initiated as a social goal, to effect the necessary changes so that domestic savings can be converted into foreign exchange for imports of capital goods. The general case, however, is that the level of exports is neither enough to satisfy the import requirements created by domestic development, nor to raise income and employment sufficiently to compensate for a slow rate of growth in the domestic sector.

What, then, are the factors that retard the expansion of exports from the underdeveloped countries, apart from artificial barriers to trade? For an economically meaningful answer, we must consider the concrete nature of the commodities involved and the factors that affect their expansion on the demand as well as on the supply side, and in particular, we must go back to the rules of behaviour that govern the system and to its structural characteristics.

GAINS FROM TRADE AND COMPARATIVE ADVANTAGE

An underdeveloped country will export primary products or semi-manufactures of a low degree of fabrication. Were it otherwise, the country would hardly be defined as underdeveloped, because the lack of manufacturing industry is so closely associated with the poverty and the backwardness in applying known techniques by which we define underdevelopment. Whatever the historical origins of this specialization, the present international division of labour and the level of exports attained under it are necessarily the point of departure for any process of development. The question before the underdeveloped countries is therefore three-fold: (a) can they, as a matter of practice, expand their traditional exports sufficiently to accommodate their growth requirements; (b) if they can—does this represent the optimal gains from growth; and finally, (c) if they cannot expand along these lines, what are the obstacles, on the supply as well as on the demand side, that stand in the way of diversifying their foreign trade in the direction of manufactured goods?

On the principle that specialization raises efficiency, the theory of international trade tells us that a country will be better off with trade than without it; the opening up of trade between two countries will result in gains for both, or at least one will gain while the other will be no worse off than before. Differences in factor endowments will cause each country to specialize in the production of those commodities which require relatively much of the factors of which it has an abundance and which are therefore cheap. Foreign demand will flow towards those commodities in which each country specializes, and trade will tend to equalize factor prices and will to some extent be a substitute for the movement of factors.

If there is agreement among economists of all persuasions, whether they are protectionists or free traders, it is that trade will, in principle, result in gains. The controversy is about the conditions under which these gains can be realized, and about who will gain more and who less. The conflict of opinions reflects a fundamental difference of orientation, on two levels: on the one hand, views differ according to whether the problem is approached from the viewpoint of static trade theory, which speaks of welfare gains, or from that of the theory of growth, which speaks of gains from growth, for the two rest on contradictory sets of assumptions;[2] on the other hand, the advocates of free trade often represent a Harmonistic point of view, in which the benefits of trade are considered from a "cosmopolitan" perspective, while their adversaries take the individual nation as their unit of reference.[3]

The logic of international trade theory as such is unassailable, and as always, the source of the divergences of opinion about its results must be sought in the different underlying assumptions which the protagonists make. Out of many similar formulations of the basic postulates of current trade theory, that of Harry G. Johnson may be quoted.[4]

> ... it is assumed, on the consumption side, that tastes and the distribution of the means of satisfying wants (property ownership, or claims on the social dividend) are given; and that, on the production side, technology and the supply of factors of production are given (the latter implying that factors are immobile between countries). Production functions and factors are assumed to be identical in all countries; the outputs of goods are assumed to depend only on inputs of factors into the production processes for those goods, and factors are assumed to be indifferent between uses. Further, production is assumed to be subject to constant returns to scale, so that the marginal productivities of factors depend only on the ratios in which they are used. Finally, perfect competition and the absence of trade barriers (tariffs and transport costs) are assumed.

This is obviously a very formidable array of assumptions, scarcely one of which can claim the status of a valid empirical generalization or even of a condition that can be established through policy manipulation, least of all in a context of growth. The logical truth of the theorems built on these foundations may be incontestable, but as Hicks has said in a related context, the question is how much bearing they can have on what goes on in the real world.[5] It is not the task of this study to go into the subtleties of international trade theory, but its theorems and the policy conclusions drawn from them are so firmly established that at least a few observations must be made on the subject before we can take up the causal link between the impediments to trade expansion and the structural factors discussed earlier, which are the main interest of this essay.

This leads us directly to the controversy associated with the theory of Raúl Prebisch, formerly the Executive Secretary of the Economic Commission for Latin America and now the Secretary-General of the United Nations Conference on Trade and Development. Prebisch's theory is mainly expounded in two essays, *The Economic Development of Latin America and its Principal Problems*,[6] and *Commercial Policy in the Underdeveloped Countries*,[7] but many of his ideas are shared by a number of prominent development economists, and have had a deep influence on the literature on development, particularly in Latin America and in the publications of ECLA.[8]

Prebisch attacks the "gains-from-trade" conclusion of classical trade theory both on the analytical level and on empirical grounds. In his view, the assumptions underlying the theory are largely invalid, and the historical record does not support its explanations or predictions, but on the contrary, tends to refute them. He divides the world into two groups of countries, those which represent the "centre" and those which are at the "periphery".* The periphery has historically supplied the centre with foodstuffs and raw materials, buying manufactured goods in return. This trade, however, has not resulted in rising real incomes in the peripheral countries, in contradiction to what should have happened according to theory.

There are two chief causes for this failure of the underdeveloped countries to gain from trade.† The first is due to the

---

* The choice of terms implies the dependence of the growth of the peripheral countries upon the processes taking place in the centre.

† This argument does not deny that the opening of that trade may initially have raised income.

fact that the countries at the centre are their own largest customers for their products, so that cost and price movements emanating from their internal markets become transmitted to their external markets. This would remain true even if there was price discrimination between the two markets. Since the countries at the centre have a scarcity of labour, and wages are inflexible downwards, the wage increases which occur during the upward turn of the business cycle have a ratchet effect, and there is therefore a secular trend for the prices of export goods from the centre to rise. This argument of Prebisch's could be extended to saying that the internal markets of the centre countries are largely monopolistic, so that even if their export markets are competitive there is a tendency for the price level of their goods to rise over time, either directly, or indirectly, through the effects of monopolistic prices on the cost level of competitive industries. The gains in productivity which the advanced countries have achieved have, in other words, been distributed in the form of higher incomes and prices rather than through stable money incomes and falling prices.

The peripheral countries, by contrast, have no significant home markets for their export products, and they operate under conditions close to atomistic competition in their export markets. In addition, they usually have an elastic labour supply. This keeps the costs of labour constant, particularly in their export industries which are mainly specialized to primary products and use unskilled, chiefly rural labour. The result is not only that the centre fails to pass on to the periphery the gains from its own productivity increases, in so far as they are expressed in prices, but the periphery is unable to retain the benefits of its own rises in productivity.* These are passed on to their customers in the centre in the form of lower prices. Therefore, Prebisch argues, there is a long-run trend for the net barter terms of trade of the peripheral countries to fall.

The second reason for the peripheral countries' inability to expand their import capacity through greater exports results

---

* The productivity gains of the centre are in any event likely to be higher, because they depend on the existence of a highly developed manufacturing industry.

from the divergent income elasticities of demand for primary products and for manufactured goods. While the former is low, the latter is high, by an extension of Engel's law to aggregate consumption. With the beginning of growth in the under-developed countries, the income elasticity of their demand for manufactured goods, that is to say in the first instance for imports, rises, while incomes in the advanced countries already are at a level where further increases produce a falling income elasticity of demand for primary goods. Part of this decline is due to Engel's law, and part to technical progress in the advanced countries, which substitutes man-made for natural products and reduces the materials coefficient in production.[9] The combined effect of these trends, coupled with adverse price elasticities, is to worsen the income terms of trade, the capacity to import.

The stagnation of export revenue which results from these factors holds down incomes in the peripheral countries, and for lack of a sizeable domestic sector they cannot compensate for this at home, nor can they obtain the means whereby they might reduce their dependence on imports or which would enable them to develop alternative export industries. To this must be added the deleterious effect of the cyclical instability of their exports, which drop sharply in periods of recession in the centre, and thus place their growth at the mercy of the ups and downs of business cycles in the advanced economies.

Prebisch's arguments have been violently criticized on a variety of grounds and on different levels; some have contested his theoretical argument, others the relevance of movements in the commodity terms of trade, while others again have questioned the validity of the empirical substantiation of his analysis. Much of the critique of Prebisch's arguments is no doubt valid within its own limits. Thus, for example, it has rightly been pointed out that he has failed to take into account the quality improvements in manufactured goods, which cannot be reflected in their price changes, but which have been passed on to the underdeveloped countries. Aside from the welfare gains derived from improvements of consumers' goods, there can be little doubt that the greater productivity of imported machines, for example, is an important offset to the deterioration of the terms of trade which may appear from the statistics. Although it would be difficult to measure this gain, it has no doubt made growth "cheaper" in terms of exports of primary goods.*

Another objection to Prebisch's thesis of deteriorating terms of trade is that he has neglected the fall in transportation costs, which benefits mainly the exporters of bulky goods in which freight accounts for a large proportion of final value.[10] This objection rests mainly on the data given by Kindleberger,[11] which show that freight costs fell steadily, by about two-thirds, between 1870 and the eve of World War I. This argument meets Prebisch on his own empirical ground, for he sought factual support for his thesis in data for the same period. We cannot here go into the details of this controversy, but it must be questioned whether the cost changes that occurred during a period in which a major technical revolution took place in ocean transportation still have much practical relevance for contemporary conditions.† The index of ocean freight rates used by Kindleberger for 1948–52, if carried forward to 1966, shows no trend in either direction, and in this period, at least, the effect of freight costs on the terms of trade must be taken to have been neutral.

The Prebisch controversy relates mainly to the secular trend, and data for a relatively short span of time cannot, therefore, prove much either way. Despite this reservation, it is of interest to examine the data for the period 1950–65 which have been published by the United Nations, if only for the important practical reason that the development problem assumed major political importance mainly in this period.[12] As can be seen from Table V.1, the net barter terms of trade, for all trade between the underdeveloped and the developed countries, have shown a slight downward trend, of about 1·5 per cent per annum, during this period. When exports of fuels are excluded, the rate increases to nearly 1·8 per cent. When the price indices of exports less fuels are compared with the price indices of

---

* These improvements in the quality of equipment, however, usually take the form of a higher scale of output to which each unit is adapted, so that while growth in general indeed becomes cheaper in terms of exports of primary goods, it is also true that the establishment of monopolistic structures becomes cheaper.

† It will be remembered that the conversion of ocean shipping from sailers to steamships took place mainly in the last quarter of the nineteenth century.

TABLE V.1. *Indices of Terms of Trade, Import Capacity, and Export Quantum, 1950–65 (1958 = 100)*

Year	F	T_1	T_2	T_3	C_1	C_2	C_3	Q_1	Q_2
1950	113	112	114	136	85	99	118	76	87
1951	233	124	133	165	94	111	138	76	84
1952	148	94	115	139	80	92	111	74	80
1953	115	105	108	121	87	99	111	83	92
1954	128	112	116	124	96	106	114	86	92
1955	190	111	114	121	100	109	117	91	96
1956	233	108	111	119	105	113	121	98	102
1957	167	103	105	110	101	105	111	98	101
1958	100	100	100	100	100	100	100	100	100
1959	107	97	98	97	105	106	105	108	108
1960	111	97	100	98	109	111	109	113	111
1961	118	93	96	94	108	107	105	117	111
1962	98	91	93	89	115	111	105	126	119
1963	120	93	96	93	126	120	115	135	124
1964	124	94	100	97	136	127	123	143	127
1965	140	94	102	98	140	131	126	150	129
Coefficient of regression*	(3·40)	−1·52	−1·77	−3·89	3·32	1·63	(−0·36)	5·00	3·15
Standard error	108·8	5·8	5·8	10·8	6·2	6·5	10·9	4·1	3·2
R^2	0·146	0·588	0·656	0·773	0·858	0·603	0·024	0·961	0·981

Notation: F   U.K. Chamber of Shipping index for general trip charter rates, as used also by Kindleberger. The index for 1948 and 1949 is 197 and 150, and for the first 10 months of 1966, 127.

T_1 net barter terms of trade, all commodities. T_2 net barter terms of trade, excluding exports of fuels.
T_3 net barter terms of trade, exports less fuels vs. machinery.

C_1, C_2, C_3 import capacity, defined to correspond to T_1, T_2, T_3.

Q_1, Q_2 quantum indices of exports from underdeveloped countries, all exports and exports less fuels.

* Significant except where put in parentheses, at better than the 1 per cent level.
Source: United Nations *Monthly Bulletins of Statistics*, December 1955, 1960 and 1966, and January 1964 and November 1966.

machinery, the crucial growth-determining class of imports, the deterioration of the terms of trade in this period seems to have been about 3·9 per cent per annum.*

Of even greater interest are the indices of import capacity. For all trade, the annual rate of increase during this sixteen-year period seems to have been 3·3 per cent, but when fuels are excluded from the calculation, this rate of growth declines to 1·6 per cent. The capacity to import machinery, finally, shows no significant trend whatsoever. In other words, despite an annual increase of 5 per cent in the quantity of their total exports, and of 3·2 per cent in exports without fuels, adverse price trends have made it impossible for the underdeveloped countries to increase, in this period, their capacity to import.

Although trend lines fitted to such a short period must, as indicated before, be treated with reservations, it seems that the historical record, even if it provides no support for Prebisch's arguments, also does not support his opponents. The nagging question that must be answered by the adherents of orthodox doctrine is, as one of them, Gerald M. Meier, has recognized clearly, why it is that "the historical experience in numerous poor countries reveals considerable growth in their foreign trade, but only a slow rate of domestic development"?[13] The point of the question is hardly blunted by the examples which Meier cites to support the statement that "the optimism of the classicists has been vindicated in many cases", for the cases are in fact few, and some of his examples, notably those of Great Britain and Japan, show the opposite for their early development, while others are inconclusive.

On the theoretical level, the arguments against Prebisch are not convincing because they apply an allocative principle that holds under static conditions or for continuous change to a problem of growth, which is essentially discontinuous, and furthermore often rest on a widely prevalent confusion between the use of theory as a tool of prediction and as a planning criterion. It is no answer to Prebisch, to argue a case which at best makes sense only in the framework of a planned system, in

* In view of the large standard errors, not much significance can be attached to the absolute values of these coefficients; all we are interested in is their relative magnitudes and the directions of change over the entire sixteen-year period.

which the conditions that must be fulfilled to make the theory produce its predicted results are subject to conscious control. One may surmise that Prebisch, who has inspired much of the planning activities in Latin America, would have no bone to pick with such an approach. But in the absence of means for effective manipulation of the conditions, where they cannot be taken to represent empirically valid generalizations, we obtain a set of analytical statements that cannot be falsified, or, if presented in normative terms, an utopia, rather than a theory.

One example of this confusion between a positive and a normative approach is Gerald M. Meier's defence of the factor–price equalization theorem, which is worth quoting at some length: [14]

> The expositors of the factor–price equalization theorem were careful to indicate the limits of the theorem's applicability by emphasizing its dependence on a very special set of assumptions—namely, the existence of perfect competition in all markets, constant returns to scale in the production of each commodity, identical production functions in all countries, and incomplete specialization in all countries (each commodity is produced in all countries). It need not then come with any surprise that factor returns have failed to reach equality between rich and poor countries when factor endowments have been so different that complete specialization has occurred, or economies of scale have led to complete specialization, or production functions have been dissimilar in different countries because of differences in technical knowledge and in the quality of factors, or impediments to trade have existed—when, in short, the restrictive conditions of the theorem have been so clearly violated in reality. . . . Finally, the failure to have even a tendency towards factor price equality, let alone full equality, does not mean that *measures which bring the economy closer to a fulfilment of the assumptions underlying the theorem might not be effective in diminishing the inequalities*, or that trade might not still contribute to a poor country's development. [Emphasis added.]

Meier's list of the violations of the conditions that are necessary for the factor–price equalization theorem to hold, even in a qualified form, amount to its clear indictment as a theory in the sense used above, however elaborate and refined its analytical apparatus may be. The clause we have emphasized brings us close to the heart of the problem. First, Meier implies that if a country would take the appropriate measures to fulfil the assumptions of the theorem, even acting on its own, it will thereby also come closer to achieving the results predicted by the theorem. This may be true for some of these conditions, but others are either not modifiable by policy or would merely make the situation worse. For example, should a country counter monopolies facing it from without by attempting to enforce a competitive structure within? Or should it, in the face of external barriers to trade, lower its own tariffs unilaterally?

It is very true, as Meier states, that when a country faces, in addition to restrictions on the supply side, also unfavourable demand conditions, "it becomes all the more necessary to strengthen (its) export position . . . in order that the response to even a weak external stimulus may be as extensive as possible."[15] But in order to do this, he recommends that the country should accomplish, *inter alia*, such things as "diminishing the prevalence of semimonopolistic and monopolistic practices", "widening of the capital market", "investment in transportation, communication, education, and manpower training", "increasing productivity", and "a capacity to reallocate resources". The sum total of these recommendations amounts to saying that an underdeveloped country will be able to export to the extent that it ceases to be underdeveloped—which leaves us exactly where we were before.

But secondly, and more importantly, one must ask how an underdeveloped economy can, without doing violence to the principle of comparative advantage, go from near-complete specialization to diversification by altering its factor endowments, or how it can, on the same condition, bring about the necessary similarity of production functions. An underdeveloped country, to repeat, will almost by definition have only primary goods to export. It will usually also have an elastic labour supply, and often also land and reserves of natural resources. According to traditional teaching, such a country should continue to export primary goods (or, in terms of a positive rather than a normative approach, this is what it *would* do if market imperfections were removed) since the production of these commodities is supposed to make intensive use of the abundant factors—labour and natural resources. This will and should go on until the supply schedules of these factors begin to rise or the demand schedules begin to turn against them, and then a new set of comparative advantages will appear on the margin.

Such an application of the law of comparative advantages may mislead not only because it is often held in average rather than marginal terms, but also because in growth we hardly ever deal with a continuous expansion path where the next set of comparative advantages is discernible on the margin of the existing productive structure. We are, on the contrary, usually involved in a problem of discontinuous shifts of production functions, of basic changes in the existing productive structure. Theory has not so far developed a way of indicating the direction of such changes as a linear development of the existing structure.

Even so, the use of the law of comparative advantages is all too often based on an empirically invalid assumption—namely, that primary products are labour-intensive or, because their *current* production is in many cases labour-intensive, so is the *expansion* of capacity in these industries. In the extractive industries, for example, not only the expansion, but even the current production is often highly capital-intensive. The major problem of the underdeveloped countries in this field is not the increase of their exports from existing capacity, but the creation of that capacity itself. And in this respect, there is often a tendency to overlook the problem of the investment requirements, which was formulated by Romney Robinson as follows:[16]

> Natural resources are *not* factors—not in the sense in which the term . . . is generally used. A natural resource becomes a factor only after some measure of preliminary investment work has been done upon it. Investment is the prerequisite to creation of any factor supply. . . . Some part of the investment may well be of a once-and-for-all character. A necessary part of investment in a mineral deposit is to remove the overburden or to dig a shaft. Similarly, if land is to function as a service-yielding factor, it must first be cleared of trees. So long as it is in use, it need never be recleared. It is typical of such once-and-for-all investment that no artifact, no capital good results. Yet the cleared field is as much the result of past investment activity as is a machine tool.

The building up of additional export capacity of primary goods thus requires prior investment, except where the domestic consumption of the existing output can be reduced and the surplus so freed can be diverted to exports. It is immaterial whether such prior investment has an infinite economic lifetime or not, and whether it is, in its current production, capital- or labour-intensive. In order to expand its output and exports of primary commodities the underdeveloped, capital-poor economy will therefore first have to accumulate domestic savings.

Empirically, the investment–output ratio for primary products is among the highest, even where fixed capital alone is considered. In the case of mineral resources, the investment is usually also highly import-intensive. In the case of plantations, such as coffee, cocoa, rubber and other tree crops, the maturation period is generally lengthy, of the order of magnitude of five to seven years, not counting the time needed for clearing the land. In other words, even in the favourable case, where land or mineral resources in the unexploited state are available and where the necessary investment has a low import coefficient, the saving of several years' labour may be required to build up an increment of capacity. To this one must add the working capital that has to be built up *after* the investment in fixed capital has been made. This "output-in-the-pipeline" will be the greater the more complex the process of production, and—what is in practice even more important for the category of goods we are considering here—the lower the concentration of exports in terms of markets.

The use of the law of comparative costs may indeed point to the desirability of investment in activities with a high capital–output ratio, particularly if it is of the non-depreciable kind described by Robinson so that current production will be labour-intensive. The high capital–output ratio implies that the returns to capital will be high relative to those of labour. Assuming that accumulation comes out of profits, this means that the rate of growth will be maximized so long as these investment opportunities do not diminish.

But to explain what has happened in reality, or to predict what is likely to happen in the future, we must take into account the actual behaviour pattern of private entrepreneurs in such an economy. In view of the long time horizons involved, private entrepreneurs will undertake such investment only if the rate of profit is high enough to offset the heavy time discount and the risk of selling in distant markets, or if the latter is somehow reduced. One way of reducing that risk is to diversify in terms of markets, but this increases the amount of working capital that has to be built up, so that it only means that investors will have to carry the costs of the risk, and that the absolute size of the investment needed will be larger. Another way of reducing the risk is through being closely tied to markets in which the seller, because of familiarity or preferential access, has an advantage.

If these factors are taken into account, it is not surprising that most investments of this kind have been undertaken by foreigners, from capital-rich economies, who had easier access to the large amounts of finance required and, in addition, were exposed to lower market risks because the exports were intended for their own home markets. In these, they usually had great familiarity with market conditions and often also assured sales outlets. To this they often added monopolistic and monopsonistic positions in the underdeveloped countries.

In a study of concentration in tropical trade, P. T. Bauer notes that "there is a fairly high degree of concentration in the external trade of many even of the larger and more populous of the so-called underdeveloped countries", the principal reason of which is "the advantages offered by the possession of large capital which appear to be very marked in foreign trade with tropical or sub-tropical countries exporting primary products. . . . Firms short of liquid resources may be unable to weather temporary adversity. . . . Unless reserves are ample wide fluctuations in the prices of export produce may also result in losses on stocks. . . ." Bauer's article deals with merchant firms engaged both in the export and in the import trade of the underdeveloped countries, with particular reference to West Africa, but his conclusions have more general applicability.[17]

If this is so, then those industries which from a planning point of view (and ignoring the demand side for the present) have a comparative advantage are in reality often out of reach of private entrepreneurs in underdeveloped countries. Potentially, they may have a comparative advantage in primary products because the untapped reserves of natural resources are abundant; but they cannot realize their advantage because they are unable to tap them. To develop these natural resources and reap the benefit of the potential advantage, they must concentrate large amounts of capital and carry out heavy investments; being capital-poor, they cannot do so and therefore fail to exploit their apparent comparative advantage; being unable to exploit their comparative advantage, they remain poor. The picture of the vicious circle of poverty is familiar.

But even if one were to make the far-reaching assumption that the indigenous entrepreneurs could somehow overcome the disadvantages they face on the supply side, by comparison with foreign investors, they would still be at a disadvantage in terms of demand conditions. Two factors have to be considered in this connexion. The first is the disadvantage of indigenous entrepreneurs compared with foreigners; the risk and uncertainty confronting the former are higher than those facing the latter, who can trade more easily within their metropolitan markets and in markets of other advanced countries. In addition, the underdeveloped economy will generally have a high concentration of exports in terms of commodities. Michael Michaely found this to be the chief factor responsible for the large amplitude of the fluctuations of their export prices.[18] This increases the degree of uncertainty, particularly for the indigenous entrepreneur who, unlike his counterpart from the advanced country, cannot hedge by diversifying his activities, and has no alternative investment outlets to fall back upon.

The second factor has already been mentioned in connexion with the Prebisch theory, namely that the income elasticity of demand for primary products is generally low, and the price elasticity is apparently also low in the downward direction. In rebuttal of this thesis, which ascribes the limited demand for primary products to strong objective factors, it has been argued (a) that Engel's law, to which Prebisch attributes the low income elasticity of demand, is applicable only to foodstuffs, not to industrial raw materials; and (b) that total world demand is irrelevant for an individual country, which may outproduce its competitors.[19]

As for the first argument, the estimates of the United Nations put the income elasticity of demand, for the period 1953–60, at 0·76 for foodstuffs, 0·60 for agricultural raw materials and ores, and 1·40 for fuels.[20] These estimates are no doubt imperfect and cover only a short time span, but they are nonetheless indicative. Prebisch's critics have mostly cast doubt on them on *a priori* grounds, and have adduced little positive evidence to the contrary. The applicability of Engel's law with respect to foodstuffs, and presumably also to some agricultural raw materials, seems to be generally accepted; [21] as for industrial raw materials, the evidence for a declining trend of their share in output because of substitution by artificial materials, and because of a falling materials coefficient, is very substantial. [22]

The second argument is an inappropriate application of short-run reasoning to a problem of the long run, and comes close to committing the fallacy of composition. It is true that an individual country may for a time outproduce and outsell its competitors, but if total demand is relatively inelastic with respect to income or price, or both, all countries will experience a secular decline in their export prices as they try to outproduce each other. It is, in fact, this competition among countries and among individual producers within each country that causes the gains from rises in productivity to be passed on to consumers. And it is this, no less than the large fluctuations that characterize the trade in primary products, that has led to the establishment of marketing boards and other attempts to set up monopolistic arrangements so that prices may be upheld and fluctuations counteracted.

In summary—if entrepreneurs in the underdeveloped countries were to do as conventional theory bids them do, the underdeveloped, capital-poor economies would often find themselves developing highly capital-absorbing export industries, in direct contradiction to what the principle of comparative advantage, as so frequently understood and applied, purports to say in their case. This is indeed what has often happened in the colonial-type economy, the profitability of which came from a large rent element involved in the monopolistic control of natural resources by a traditional landowning class or by foreign interests, which in the case of the latter was often also coupled with preferential access to the metropolitan markets and with monopolistic conditions there. Indigenous entrepreneurs are at a disadvantage on all these counts. Even if they can mobilize the necessary capital and are otherwise able and willing to invest in the primary goods industries, they will find that their market disadvantages will cause much of the expected profits to be passed on to their customers in the advanced countries.

Finally, even if the balance of payments aspects were ignored, the income effects of such investment would in any case be slight. Primary production is by definition an activity that has few backward linkages, i.e. it requires but few inputs from other industries. If the economy were based on individual holdings by peasants, the advantages of large scale which according to Bauer are essential in the foreign trade in primary goods would be lost, and in addition, competition would bid down prices until no more than the usual subsistence income was left. If production is organized along capitalistic lines, as is more usual, its higher capital-intensity will yield low returns to labour. The addition to the total wage bill will be the smaller the more primary and capital-intensive the increment to output and exports; and the capitalists' own consumption either has no significance in terms of its market-widening effects, or else means that savings and accumulation are low. From all points of view considered together, exports of primary products tend to become stagnant enclaves, with little impact on the domestic economy even when they expand.

EXPORTS OF MANUFACTURED GOODS

If what was said so far about primary goods is accepted, then by the same reasoning it must surely be the case that, with a lower capital–output ratio, generally lower concentrations of capital, greater backward linkages, a lesser necessity to concentrate in terms of goods, a higher income elasticity of demand and possibly also a higher price elasticity, exports should be expansible in the direction of manufactures?

Let us assume that the foreign trade of the underdeveloped economy is "more than free", meaning that it faces no tariff barriers or other restrictions against its own exports, but it may (but need not) still protect its own home industries against competitive imports. Its exports must, however, meet the competition of other exporters as well as that of producers in the importing countries. This, roughly, is trade on the basis of non-reciprocity which has been accepted, at least in principle, by the advanced countries and by GATT for trade with the underdeveloped countries. We shall later look briefly at the probable benefits that might be gained from a more far-reaching condition: tariff preferences for the underdeveloped countries, which are intended to put their exports at an advantage in the competition with producers in the developed countries (but not in relation to other underdeveloped countries).

When a country possesses some outstanding comparative advantage in a specific industry, that industry will evidently expand up to the limits of factor supply and demand elasticity. Such cases do exist, but they are hardly typical, and, moreover, they will generally have reached some equilibrium level before the development process starts. Persian carpets or Japanese lacquers, African wood sculptures or Chinese ivory carvings are certainly not representative examples of manufacturing industry. Industry is based on the transformation of natural materials by man-made factors, capital and skills. Both of these are notably short in an underdeveloped economy. An exceptional comparative advantage must be sufficiently great to offset the greater risk that is always involved in concentrating heavily on production for the foreign market. In the usual case, such comparative advantages are not pre-existing and readily recognizable, but must be created.

It is intuitively obvious that risk and uncertainty increase with distance and strangeness, since they are a function of knowledge and the possibility of exercising control over the external environment. The more an entrepreneur orients himself towards the domestic market, the greater his knowledge of demand and supply conditions, and the greater also the degree to which he can exert control over them. The inward-directedness of development is thus no accident or merely a distortion of the "normal" direction in response to external or internal market imperfections. These may emphasize such tendencies, but the observed pattern is essentially the rational path of growth in a private enterprise economy. Given the basic behaviour postulates of the latter, an inward-directed productive structure is all but unavoidable. This has led some writers to state that exports must as a rule be based upon a substantial home market.[23] Whatever the proportion between exports and domestic sales may ultimately turn out to become, and with the exception of those few cases where an industry is based upon the exploitation of some particularly rare resource or skill, the starting-point for a new industry will almost always be the domestic market.

The argument of our earlier chapters was that a growth pattern that is almost wholly oriented towards the domestic market will, given the technical conditions and the size of the markets of the underdeveloped countries, lead to monopolistic structures, and hence, that stagnation tendencies will set in at a relatively low level of economic development. But what is there to prevent a firm that begins by catering to domestic demand from breaking out of the limits on size and costs of production imposed by the smallness of the domestic market, by extending its operations to the foreign market? It may, in the light of what was said in the preceding paragraph, be unrealistic to assume that this would happen all at once, but such an expansion could, it seems, be gradual, so that uncertainty could be reduced by degrees? Surely this would break the entire vicious circle?

The answer is, first, that the greater risks of exportation imply that the expansion into foreign trade involves a falling marginal rate of profit, unless it is offset by corresponding gains from economies of large-scale production, made possible by over-stepping the bounds of the domestic market. For a monopolist this might be conceivable, if discontinuities of production functions are ignored. But as we have seen, the most probable market structure is that of oligopoly. This means that the scale of output is not only small because the total domestic market is narrow, but also because this market is further fragmented among a number of firms. Real costs of production are therefore high by comparison with those in the advanced countries, even in the more efficient firms. The lower wage level, and possibly other cost advantages, are rarely enough to offset the competitive disadvantages which result from smaller scale and lower productivity.

We come back here to the observation we made in an earlier chapter—that the modern establishments in the under-developed countries may be giants in their home markets, but pygmies in the world market. This, in fact, is one of the main reasons why these industries are as a rule not viable even in their home market without high rates of tariff protection, let alone competitive in export markets. Import duties are of course often set at prohibitive levels which have no direct relation to costs of production; they cannot therefore be taken as a direct reflection of the real cost differences. None the less, it is reasonable to assume that the level of import duties in different countries is not totally unrelated to the weight of the underlying economic and technical factors that determine these cost differences. Thus, for example, the average import duties applicable in 1960 in Argentina, Brazil, Chile and France were 151, 60, 93 and 18 per cent of the c.i.f. value, respectively; an inspection of the tariff rates for particular commodity groups shows that they were high even for industries in which economies of scale are presumably of no great importance.[24]

The domestic market is, as we observed before, the prime concern for the private entrepreneur, and the framework which guides his choice of technique and scale. If technology permits some latitude with respect to scale of production, and high costs can be shielded by tariffs, then the various factors discussed in Chapter 2 will push the scale of production downwards, by comparison with the typical size of plant in the advanced countries. Again, high concentration in the domestic market is not prevented thereby, but international competitiveness is. Only where technology enforces the similarity of production functions and, other things being equal, there is an advantage of factor costs, will the difference between an orientation towards the domestic and the foreign market become reduced, and a smooth expansion from the home market into sales abroad become possible.

In practice there are few instances in which the gap between the cost level that can be maintained in the home market and the internationally competitive price level can be bridged gradually, by way of a step by step expansion. Each individual plant must, in order to attain the competitive level of costs, shift to a new production function. This means not merely expansion of capacity at the margin, but a complete revamping of the entire production setup. The justification for that must come from conditions in the domestic market, to which the bulk of the firm's operations are geared. And what is true for expansion of capacity by existing firms is also true for new firms proposing to enter the market—they will as a rule optimize their scale of output and cost level by consideration of the domestic market. An existing structure is, for technical reasons, usually quite rigid and only large changes in the parameters can be expected to modify it significantly. This underlying technical inflexibility is further strengthened by the rigidities of an oligopolistic structure, for as we shall see in a moment, any change leads to repercussions in the domestic market structure and is resisted by its stability.

The United Nations has devoted considerable study to the possibilities of alternative techniques and to the effects of economies of scale. The findings of these studies generally lend support to the argument that the lower wage levels of the underdeveloped countries compensate only partially for the loss of economies of scale. Mainly as a result of the higher costs of capital, but also because of higher raw material costs and a lower efficiency of labour, the absolute cost difference may easily exceed the total labour cost in the underdeveloped countries even where similar scales of output are compared. In practice, however, the competition in export markets will be between *smaller* plants in the underdeveloped countries against *larger* plants in the developed countries, so that disadvantages of small scale will be added to the intrinsic lower efficiency due to other factors.[25]

Most of the policy recommendations that are made with a view to expanding the exports of manufactures from underdeveloped countries are borrowed from the reality of the developed countries, and rest on the expectation that marginal adjustments, induced by appropriate manipulations of the price system, will lead to a socially optimal allocation of resources. Among these policy instruments, devaluation holds pride of place, and some space must be devoted to a discussion of its probable effects. The presumption is of course not that devaluation will by itself promote growth, nor that it is a cure that can be applied recurrently, but that the economy is basically flexible enough to adjust its productive structure to the new set of relative prices established by the depreciation. If this were true, it might lead the economy over the threshold of continuous expansion, so that once it had been pulled into a competitive position *vis-à-vis* the world market, it would from that point on continue by its own momentum.

The real cost differences, however, are often so large that a one-time adjustment such as devaluation, within the range that is feasible, is hardly able to reduce them to a competitive level, even when the usual conditions for an improvement in the balance of payments are fulfilled, i.e. the sum of the demand elasticities for imports and exports exceeds unity, the supply elasticities are large, and the balance of payments is initially in a position where devaluation can restore it to equilibrium. If the underlying structural conditions are such that devaluation within the feasible range would still not make exports competitive, or if there are forces at work that tend to recreate the disequilibrium, the balance of payments may indeed be improved on the *import* side if the elasticity of demand for imports exceeds unity. But this improvement will only be gained at the expense of depressing investment through raising the costs of imported equipment. True, the domestic market will at the same time be widened by opening up further opportunities for import substitution and by inducing shifts in demand in favour of domestic goods. But at the same time the higher costs of capital will tend to reduce the scale of production, so that the direct rise in costs due to higher costs of imports will be reinforced by the loss of economies of scale. The outcome depends on the specific conditions, but it may make the productive structure even more inward-directed, and lead it away from a competitive position in exports.

When the domestic market structure is monopolistic, devaluation will have special repercussions. Let us assume that the money supply remains constant, and consider first the short-run effects. In any monopolistic or oligopolistic structure there will be a certain amount of physical excess capacity. At a given exchange rate, monopolists or oligopolists will therefore find it profitable to export this excess capacity if the unit price of exports in domestic currency is higher than their marginal costs. The larger the oligopolistic firm, the more likely is it to have excess capacity, for the less efficient firms will generally be able to stay in the industry at the price determined by the leading firm if they operate more closely at their capacity level. The larger firms will usually also have a greater difference between their average and marginal costs than the smaller firms, because their fixed costs are higher. Whatever exports there are out of excess capacity are likely to be concentrated in the large firms, quite apart from other factors that make for the concentration of exports in their hands.[26]

Devaluation will raise the domestic price of exports, and if it exceeds marginal costs, exports should be forthcoming. At the same time, costs will rise, and since capital goods are imported, the rise will be greatest where the cost of capital per unit of output is highest. With higher costs, the former level of output for the domestic market will not be enough to maintain the previous level of profits if the domestic price level remains unchanged. If the large firm had excess capacity, it will therefore be under pressure to increase its market share at the expense of its rivals. Although the rise in the cost of capital, and the greater pressure for increasing the operating rate, does not affect the short-run cost structure, the firm must, in its short-run policy, take into account its long-run position in the domestic market. It will therefore have to respond to the changed cost structure by setting its operating rate in the doemstic market, i.e. its market share, where it will maintain the former rate of profit. The greater the depreciation, the stronger will be the pressure to increase the operating rate and change the existing distribution of market shares. .

If larger scale involves relatively greater economies in capital per unit of output than in labour, the large firm will also gain a competitive advantage over the smaller firms in terms of relative cost increases. If economies of scale are pronounced with respect to labour, or if raw materials (which are generally constant with scale) are imported, the smaller firms will gain a competitive advantage over the larger. This will make it more difficult for the larger firm to drive out its smaller rivals. Since the large firm is the price leader, it will raise the domestic price if it cannot increase its rate of utilization to compensate for the new, higher cost level. With a constant money supply, real demand will shrink and, according to the analysis in Chapter 2, this will lead to a higher degree of concentration in the industry.

It is conceivable that the smaller firms, finding themselves pushed out of the domestic market, will shift their output to the export market. But even if the export price exceeds their variable costs they are unlikely, because of their small scale, to have the resources and the ability to engage in foreign trade. This possibility is therefore not very plausible.

Under oligopoly, then, devaluation may in the short run not

only fail to produce the anticipated increase in exports, but if the new cost structure sets in train changes in the internal structure of the industry, it may even result in a diversion of exportables to the domestic market, and in extreme cases, even in a fall of income as the smaller firms are driven out. The net effect cannot be predicted, for it depends on the pre-devaluation structure of the industry, the disparities in size and costs between different firms, the degree of capacity utilization, the extent of the devaluation, and many other factors. It is, however, safe to assume that a drastic shock to the existing cost, price, and market structure, such as will result from depreciation, cannot leave an oligopolistic structure unaffected. The odds are that it will bring about a higher degree of concentration, and thus make the larger firms, which in terms of efficiency and cost level are closer to their competitors abroad, more rather than less oriented towards the domestic market.

It must be emphasized that this analysis applies only to the conditions of underdevelopment, where *both oligopoly and import dependence* are present. For a competitive industry or for the case of pure monopoly, the results may be as predicted by traditional analysis, and the same is true if devaluation causes no appreciable rise in costs, even if the structure is oligopolistic. This will be the case in an advanced economy, where most inputs are produced domestically or where the supply elasticities of domestic substitutes for previously imported inputs is high and "beggar-thy-neighbour" policies can therefore be effective as long as there is no retaliation. The point is that the transplantation of remedies for disequilibrium which may be appropriate to the advanced economies may produce results opposite to those desired in the underdeveloped economies, and at best their effects are unpredictable.

What of the long-run effects of depreciation? Let it be assumed that the devaluation is substantial enough to raise the domestic price of exports to a level which yields the expected rate of profit, after allowing for all cost increases which it induces simultaneously and for the greater risks of exportation. New capacity should then be established to take advantage of the now profitable foreign market. In the case of pure monopoly or an oligopoly with tight collusion this may in fact happen. The monopolist is assured of his domestic market, and the establishment of additional capacity, if profitable in its own right, will at the same time provide him with an additional reserve to forestall a possible danger of entry. Also, in the long-run his entire production set-up may become adapted to the scale made possible by the addition of foreign to his domestic sales, so that economies of scale will be obtained and either domestic prices will be reduced or accumulation will rise, or a combination of both. From a social point of view, this will then be a favourable development.

Under oligopoly, however, the picture may be different. The establishment of new capacity in response to the apparent profitability of the export market is likely to be undertaken mainly by the leading firms who are capable of engaging in foreign trade, but it will always tend to destabilize the industry structure. If the new capacity is of the same efficiency as the old, any chance fluctuation in exports will cause output to be thrown on to the domestic market. Market shares thus obtained are unlikely to be given up again, and the leading firms will therefore gradually increase their shares at the expense of the smaller firms. Thus, capacity originally built for exports may in time become diverted to the domestic market, while the capacity of the smaller firms which are displaced will be rendered valueless.

If the new capacity is more efficient than the old—as may happen when the sales expected in the foreign and the domestic market together permit the exploitation of additional economies of scale—the pre-existing industry structure will be upset even more rapidly. The profitability of exports brought about by devaluation may provide the leading firms with the necessary leverage to strengthen their position in the domestic market, for at the new and lower cost level they will be tempted to use their advantage to drive out their rivals. Part of the new capacity will then again be diverted to the domestic market, in which concentration will increase although efficiency will rise at the same time. Some of the capacity displaced from the domestic market may be diverted to exports, but to what extent this will happen, and what part of the capacity of the leading firms will be available for exports after their domestic market shares have increased, depends on specific circumstances. Once again it must be remembered that despite the emphasis given in this study to the role of large scale production in the formation of oligopolistic structures, scale is relative, and even the larger firms in an underdeveloped economy are likely to be small compared with their foreign competitors. Their financial, organizational, commercial and technical abilities are not likely to be such as to make them enter foreign trade easily, and this is all the more so in the case of the smaller firms.

Even under favourable circumstances, the changes brought about by devaluation are of a once-and-for-all character. If the devaluation has brought about a reshuffling of the industry structure, with higher concentration in the domestic market, further investment for the export market may be impossible unless investors can capture at least some share of the domestic market. In addition to the factors discussed earlier, there is in practice always need for some base in the domestic market, for technical and economic reasons. Not only is the home market needed to absorb excess supplies which may result from chance fluctuations in foreign demand, but few manufacturing industries produce a homogenous quality of product. There is always a certain proportion of sub-standard products, of grades and types, or of by-products, for which domestic outlets must be found because the foreign market will not absorb them. The higher the degree of concentration in the domestic market, the more stable will the distribution of market shares be, and the fewer openings will exist for the absorption of such excess supplies or by-products.

The industry structure typical of an underdeveloped economy thus tends to counteract, to a greater or lesser extent, the results of devaluation. The market-expanding effects are not likely to be very substantial, and the tendency towards greater concentration in the domestic market—unless strong enough to produce monopoly or near-monopoly—will prevent the changes from going much beyond a once-over increase of exports. There is thus little likelihood that a continuous expansion of capacity and a rise of efficiency will be set in motion. This shows once more that the choice of an underdeveloped economy lies not between competition and monopoly in its various forms, but between oligopoly and monopoly. The latter is unquestionably the better choice both in terms of efficiency in the domestic market, and in terms of the capability to expand into foreign markets.

We have so far ignored any limitations on the demand side. Although the income and price elasticities for manufactured goods in general are higher than those for primary goods, the adverse factors stemming from the industry structure in the underdeveloped countries tend to reduce the possibilities for taking advantage of these seemingly more favourable demand conditions. Let us assume that cost differences due to smaller scale and lower productivity have been fully offset through devaluation. For those industries which produce mass consumption goods the income elasticity of demand in the markets of the advanced countries will generally be low, and so may be the price elasticity. For each individual country or producer, demand will, of course, in the short view be highly elastic, but in the longer view producers will run into the limits of their industry demand functions, just as in the case of primary products. Export prices will tend to decline, and will tend to throw the exchange rate out of equilibrium if wages are inflexible downward.

Nevertheless, if there were no trade barriers, as we have assumed, the possibilities of expanding exports from these industries—of which textiles are the classic example—would in practice be very considerable if they were allowed to displace domestic producers in the importing countries and competitors from advanced countries. But because of the same low income and price elasticities, these industries are generally stagnant also in the advanced countries, and are subject to high degrees of protection. This is the main area in which tariff preferences, such as demanded by the underdeveloped countries at the Geneva Conference on Trade and Development of the United Nations, could be effective—but this is also the area in which such preferences are least likely to be granted because of the massive displacement of labour and firms involved.

The realities of international trade are such that those industries in which the underdeveloped countries are competitive under conditions of free trade will not be allowed to become subject to free trade, while only those will be freed from trade restrictions in which they can hardly hope to attain a competitive position. The "voluntary" export restrictions on textiles which the United States, the chief protagonist of freer trade at the present time, has requested of the exporting countries in recent years, are a case in point. In the more sophisticated categories of manufactured goods, the underdeveloped economies will generally be at a greater competitive disadvantage, for obvious reasons, and the more so the more they allow their industry structures to develop in the way described in this study.

What of direct government intervention in the promotion of exports? There is probably a wider field for government intervention here than in any other area, although it is subject to the same constraints of resource availability that were discussed in Chapter 4. Apart from monetary and fiscal measures which have the end result of subsidizing exports, the government can promote exports directly by measures designed to reduce the risks and uncertainties of foreign trade, and through the provision of external economies. The specific measures falling into this category need not be described here, since most of them are well known as a matter of common practice. They include services of various kinds, such as market intelligence, advertising and commercial propaganda, technical assistance, export insurance, as well as a variety of direct and indirect subsidies such as preferential rates for government-controlled services, and finally, its activities in the field of commercial diplomacy.

All these measures, which have been widely resorted to in practice, can none the less be effective only within the limits set by the productive structure of the economy. Of all the possible instruments of government intervention in foreign trade, it is interesting to note that there is one—already discussed in Chapter 4 in relation to the domestic market—which could probably be effective, but has hardly ever been undertaken—namely, the direct procurement of goods by the government. In exports this would hardly infringe upon the private enterprise character of the economy. The reason for the failure of governments to resort to this instrument, say through State trading agencies, except in isolated cases where special reasons existed, is not only fiscal or administrative. Governments have undertaken expenditures much larger and riskier than those that would be required for a substantial scale of commercial operations. Nor can the failure be attributed to the inability of governments to engage in such activities for lack of the necessary know-how and skills. In underdeveloped countries, the government often represents the greatest concentration of skill and initiative in all fields, including that of production. The real cause for the reluctance of governments to resort to this kind of intervention must be sought in the fundamental rules of the game of a private enterprise economy, which reserve the functions of production and commerce to private entrepreneurs, except where they serve to support private producers. It seems that any socio-economic system requires that its basic rules be consistent in all fields, so that a different standard cannot easily be established for the case of exports or any other field of economic activity.

We must therefore conclude that even foreign trade, which would seem to provide the main avenue by which an under-developed country might escape the constraints imposed upon its growth by the initial small size of the market and the dependence on imported technology, holds out little promise of extricating the underdeveloped private-enterprise system from its predicaments—with or without government intervention, with or without favourable trade conditions. Under the most favourable circumstances, foreign trade may extend the field of expansion to some degree; in actual practice, the under-developed countries cannot expect to meet with favourable trade conditions in the foreseeable future. We may sum up by quoting an evaluation of the prospects given by Bela Balassa:[27]

> . . . under present-day conditions, less developed countries face also certain handicaps in attempting to accelerate their economic growth. The possibilities for expanding their exports of primary products and manufactures are often limited, and they encounter barriers in the process of import substitution, too. While import substitution has been an important factor contributing to economic growth in many of the developing countries in the last decade, this has often necessitated a high degree of protection, and protection entails an economic cost. On the one hand, it leads to the establishment of inefficient firms and monopolistic market structures; on the other, in narrow national markets, large scale economies are foregone or excess capacity generated. At the same time, import substitution becomes increasingly difficult and costly after imports of simple manufactures have been replaced by home products.

We have tried to expose the causes of these difficulties of growth. They are mainly the result of the interaction of objective technical and economic factors with the rules of behaviour appropriate to a private enterprise system. Together, they produce a socio-economic structure which is unable to provide for continuous growth. The absolute level of economic development that an underdeveloped country may reach in such a system depends on its specific circumstances, chiefly on its initial level of income and its size, and on the degree to which the balance struck by the different social forces and interests in the system is such as to permit the government to assume an independent role and to allow it to intervene, on the one hand, directly in production, and on the other hand, to exert enough influence to shape the economic structure of the system.

ECONOMIC INTEGRATION

We must still touch briefly upon the possibility of extending the boundaries of expansion through the economic integration of underdeveloped countries. It is beyond the scope of our discussion to discuss this complex problem in detail, and at the level of abstraction of this study only a few observations need be made.

There is no doubt that, since the size of the market is a crucial determinant of the productive structure and its growth potential, the integration of several countries into one market will to that extent lift the constraints. But the tendencies described in this study exist even in the larger and relatively more prosperous of the underdeveloped countries, so that the differences would at best be only relative. The median size of underdeveloped country, in terms of population, is under five million, and thirty countries out of eighty-five have less than three million inhabitants. The joining together of countries of this size would not yield markets large enough to counteract the tendencies described earlier to a significant extent. Furthermore, integration creates larger markets only to the extent that transport facilities exist or can be built, otherwise local monopolies will be shielded by distance from their potential rivals.

Where integration is supposed to be put into effect after an industry has already developed into the forms discussed previously in each of the constituent countries, there will be powerful resistance to the unification of the market except on terms which are favourable for the existing oligopolies. The oligopolists and monopolists in each national market will not easily give in to the breaking down of the barriers which shield them from the harsh winds of competition and the vicissitudes of wider markets. As Sidney Dell has pointed out, this resistance by the vested interests in each country affects also the chances for the establishment of new industries: "As in the developed countries, the import-competing industries tend to shout for help before they are hurt while the exporters are much less articulate; moreover, in the very nature of the case, the potential new industries that a broader market would encourage have no spokesmen at the outset of any integration programme."[28] And in addition, there are considerable political obstacles to economic integration even where there are no pre-existing vested interests to put up resistance, for "the self-same forces that make for political nationalism in the underdeveloped countries tend to encourage economic nationalism as well".

Just as the private-enterprise system narrows its own markets within the national framework, so it engenders forces that will prevent the widening of the field of expansion through breaking out of the national framework. Just as it is powerless to overcome the irrationalities of its own operation, so is it incapable of doing away with the irrational national boundaries left as a heritage from the arbitrary carving out of possessions by the colonial powers in past centuries. Thus, even under favourable conditions growth is likely to level off long before the level of affluence of the more developed economies even begins to be approached.

NOTES AND REFERENCES

1. What follows borrows heavily from PAUL M. SWEEZY's exposition of the Marxian model, in *The Theory of Capitalist Development*, Oxford University Press, New York 1942, chapter x.
2. See the survey by HOLLIS B. CHENERY, Comparative advantage and development policy, *American Economic Review*, **51,** March 1961, p. 19.
3. See, for example, PETER B. KENEN, *International Economics*, Prentice-Hall, Englewood Cliffs, N.J., 1964, p. 5.
4. HARRY G. JOHNSON, *International Trade and Economic Growth*, George Allen & Unwin, London 1958, p. 18.
5. J. R. HICKS, *Essays in World Economics*, Oxford University Press, Oxford, 1959, p. 260.
6. RAÚL PREBISCH, *The Economic Development of Latin America and its Principal Problems*, Economic Commission for Latin America, United Nations, New York, 1950.

7. RAÚL PREBISCH, Commercial policy in the underdeveloped countries *American Economic Review, Papers and Proceedings*, May 1959.

8. See, for example, HANS SINGER, The distribution of gains between investing and borrowing countries, *American Economic Review, Papers and Proceedings*, May 1950; GUNNAR MYRDAL, *Economic Theory and Under-Developed Regions*, Gerald Duckworth & Co., London, 1957, *An International Economy*, Harper & Bros., New York, 1956, particularly pp. 222 ff., and also *Rich Lands and Poor*, Harper & Bros., New York, 1957; CELSO FURTADO, *Development and Underdevelopment*, University of California Press, 1964.

9. See, for example, THEODORE W. SCHULTZ, Economic prospects of primary products, in HOWARD S. ELLIS and HENRY C. WALLICH (eds.), in *Economic Development for Latin America*, Macmillan & Co., New York, 1961, pp. 308–31, and especially Appendix table 4, pp. 326–8.

10. See HERMAN F. KARREMAN, *Methods for Improving World Transportation Accounts, Applied to 1950–1953*, Technical Paper 15, National Bureau of Economic Research, New York, 1961, particularly table 5, pp. 14–15.

11. CHARLES P. KINDLEBERGER, *The Terms of Trade, A European Case Study*, The Technology Press of the Massachusetts Institute of Technology and John Wiley & Sons, Inc., New York, 1956, p. 19 and Appendix A, pp. 336–40.

12. United Nations, *Monthly Bulletin of Statistics*, January 1964, Special Table B, and November 1966, Special Table C.

13. GERALD M. MEIER, *International Trade and Development*, Harper & Row, New York, 1963, p. 159.

14. *Ibid.*, pp. 164–5.

15. *Ibid.*, p. 187.

16. ROMNEY ROBINSON, Factor proportions and comparative advantage, Parts I and II, *Quarterly Journal of Economics*, **70,** May 1956 and August 1956; see Part II, p. 348.

17. P. T. BAUER, Concentration in tropical trade; some aspects and implications of oligopoly, *Economica*, **20,** November 1953.

18. MICHAEL MICHAELY, *Concentration in International Trade*, North-Holland Publishing Co., Amsterdam, 1962.

19. See MEIER, *op. cit.*, p. 62 and CHARLES P. KINDLEBERGER, *Economic Development*, McGraw Hill Book Co., New York, 1958, pp. 306–7.

20. United Nations, *World Economic Survey, 1962*, New York, 1963, p. 6.

21. See M. JUNE FLANDERS, Prebisch on protectionism: an evaluation, *Economic Journal*, June 1964, p. 324.

22. See note 9 above.

23. See KINDLEBERGER, *Foreign Trade and the National Economy*, p. 58, and the references quoted there.

24. SANTIAGO MACARIO, Protectionism and industrialization in Latin America, United Nations, *Economic Bulletin for Latin America*, **9,** No. 1, March 1964, Annex II, table B, p. 93.

25. For some of the relevant studies, see United Nations, *Industrialization and Productivity*, Bulletins 1 and 2; for a review of the available studies

and data, see BELA BALASSA, *The Theory of Economic Integration*, Richard D. Irwin, Homewood (Ill.), 1961, chapters 6 and 7, and *Economic Development and Integration*, Centro de Estudios Monetarios Latino-americanos, Mexico, 1965, chapter iv.

26. For a study of concentration in exports of Israel, see Bank of Israel, *Annual Report 1962*, Jerusalem, 1963, pp. 229–34.

27. B. BALASSA, *Economic Development and Integration*, pp. 81–82.

28. SIDNEY DELL, *Trade Blocs and Common Markets*, Constable & Co., London, 1963, p. 273.

EPILOGUE

THE outlook for the growth of the underdeveloped countries that emerges from this book is not very promising. It seems that even under favourable conditions any tangible lifting of the dull weight of poverty which crushes most of mankind, and against which it strains with rising rebelliousness, impatient hope, and bleak frustration, is a process not to be measured in the span of years over which hope can be kept alive without the sustenance of present achievement, but in generations, and possibly centuries.

The concrete historical conditions of our time open vast opportunities for progress; but the difficulties are commensurate with the potentialities, and they are not lessening. Technology has put the stars within reach of man, has freed him increasingly from the bondage to nature's niggardly provision, has lengthened his normal life-span, and has shrunk a world once measured in distances of months and years to the dimensions of hours and seconds.

But while technology has spread the awareness of these opportunities throughout a world which has become one, and has made people everywhere impatient to grasp them within their own lifetime, history has bequeathed a division of this one world into separate nations, each for itself and unto itself, and access to the marvellous achievements of science and technics is in practice barred to all but a few of them. The world has become smaller in physical distance, but socially it has become more fragmented. Contemporaneous contact between peoples has become almost instantaneous, but their historical distance, in terms of their various levels of achievement, has grown to millenia. Medicine has prolonged life—but only to drag out, for most, a misery made many times worse for having become aware of itself because of modern communications. Medicine has conquered disease—but only to swell the millions who press upon the meagre resources now available, and from which any start towards a better future must be made.

The initial poverty of most of the world, its social and political organization, the disparities and conflicts between nations and the cleavages within them, and the technical conditions—these are concrete realities that cannot be wished away by theorizing. These objective starting conditions raise obstacles to growth so formidable that it would be painfully slow even if it were to take place within a rational social order which is able to utilize the given technical opportunities to their fullest extent.

These opportunities are today such that for most nations, given their small economic size, technology decrees not only that a fully socialized mode of production is within reach, but that, by the same token, its private organization will hold back the attainment even of that relatively slow rate of growth which is feasible under the best of circumstances.

The only way in which the underdeveloped countries can escape their poverty is by availing themselves of the best that modern science and technology can offer. But we have seen that if they do so within the framework of a private property system, the creation of monopolistic structures is well-nigh inescapable. By virtue of its own rationale such a social order tends to erect ever-increasing obstacles to continued growth, and to arrest it at a relatively low level. The possibilities for successfully counteracting these tendencies from within such a social order are few and limited in their effects.

The choice of a particular social order—if the term "choice" is at all meaningful in the context of an historical process—is evidently no mere matter of economic organization. It involves all aspects of social life, and permeates the lives of individuals down to the deepest layers of their being. A social order, once established, produces from within itself forces that will perpetuate it, and only violent internal stresses and contradictions, or powerful external shocks, are capable of transforming it to a greater or lesser extent; even then, much of the old may linger on beside the new for many generations. The path chosen by the underdeveloped countries in their initial period of transformation therefore predetermines the direction of future progress, and the further they go along the chosen path, the less will they be able to deviate from it along the way—even if it seems to lead to a dead end.

But what the underdeveloped countries will achieve, and how soon, is not only their concern, but that of the world as a whole. Their poverty and discontent is the danger and fear of all, for the world has become a unity also in another, frightful, sense—that a conflagration anywhere may envelop it in a global nuclear holocaust. The conclusions to which this study points are difficult to accept not only because it is hard to acquiesce in hopelessness, not only because the misery and backwardness of three-quarters of the human race are no longer a fate accepted stolidly, as for thousands of years past, but also because the failure to solve this problem—beside which the problems of stability and growth in the advanced countries seem puny— carries the danger of engulfing the entire world in cataclysmic disaster.

The manner in which the underdeveloped countries go about achieving growth, and the success which they can hope to attain by choosing one or the other alternative, are therefore a matter of vital concern for all. That past success has been minimal is obvious for all to see; however great it may appear to be relatively, by this or that measure, there can be little doubt that world-wide discontent, nourished by bitter reality, is constantly with us, and may even be increasing. That there are objective possibilities for achieving more is equally indubitable. The growth rates of the socialist countries are higher than those of all others, with possibly two or three exceptions, and among the private-enterprise economies those that have had an effective measure of planning and government enterprise have progressed more than others.

For many, including people in the underdeveloped countries, these achievements of capitalism's rival social order seem to have been bought at a terrific human cost, and some believe that the price will never be paid in full. Only the future can prove the rights and wrongs of this matter, yet it must also be asked whether a continuation of the present hopeless suffering, such as we witness all over the world, is not an equally fearful human cost, and all too often borne in vain.

In reality, we see that many underdeveloped countries have chosen the private enterprise path for their development. Some, who had a measure of choice, have shied away from the price it seemed necessary to pay for adopting an alternative system; others have been led by natural historical continuation from a pre-existing, backward private property system into the more progressive one of capitalism; others again seem to have drifted into it imperceptibly, as it were, although they first intended differently. And most continue to be urged to work towards the fuller completion of the transition to capitalism, to the establishment of what for hundreds of years has been the only social order that provided for self-sustained economic progress.

This essay has stressed the growth-retarding forces in an underdeveloped private enterprise system, but nowhere has it denied the initial progress that capitalism will bring about when it supplants a backward social and economic order. Furthermore, we have dealt with tendencies of the long run, and there is no way of dating the long run and predicting when it will begin. It is in the nature of historical processes that only seldom will there be sharp points of inflection in the course of events, and only rarely will the forces at work in a system lead it into a complete impasse and thus become revealed with clarity and in isolation. Their influence, disclosed by analysis, is none the less real and at work all the time. Therefore, and because many of the underdeveloped countries who have already passed the initial stage of their growth already face stagnation tendencies, or see them looming on the horizon, there is little assurance in the Keynesian dictum that "in the long run we are all dead". The long run is with us all the time.

The reality being that most underdeveloped countries have opted for the capitalist way of developing, it is important to inquire what measure of success may yet be possible in such a system, what absolute level of development can be attained, and for how long it can continue before it begins to arrest itself. Success, if it can be discovered, must be viewed with hope by anyone concerned with the potential danger for the world at large that is inherent in the plight of the underdeveloped countries. It must be welcomed by all who, from a humanitarian standpoint, are not indifferent to the hunger and degradation of hundreds of millions of human beings.

Economic growth is always subject to initial constraints which are independent of the social order. But the social order, and the rules of behaviour and motives of men that guide economic activity within it, in turn determine to what degree and how quickly these constraints can be lifted. If this book has made a contribution to the isolation of the forces at work in this process, its purpose has been achieved, and the forging of instruments that may counteract their adverse effects for concrete cases is then no insuperable task.

The broad implications of our analysis for the direction that remedial action can take are clear. Much can be done, under favourable circumstances, even within the framework of a system that retains the essential characteristics of private enterprise. It is possible to prevent the excessive fragmentation of markets and to guide development towards higher efficiency and greater concentration. It is possible to raise the degree of specialization and to influence the distribution of income in such a way as to broaden the market base without necessarily reducing accumulation. It is possible, where the goal of development has broad popular support, to widen the area of public enterprise, particularly with regard to foreign trade and to the creation of a capital goods sector, so that the crucial technological dependence of the economy may be reduced. There is no law that says that the building of highways and power stations is an economic activity that is appropriate for government in a private-enterprise system, but the making of lathes and drop forges is not. It is also possible to reduce private risk and uncertainty through planning, and thus increase the opportunities for investment, provided that planning is backed up by the readiness of government to step in as the investor of last resort.

To what extent this, and more, can be done depends upon the balance struck between the different social forces that uphold and maintain the goal of economic growth, and to what extent the general welfare can be prevented from becoming interpreted as a function of the welfare and growth of a particular class. Ultimately, I believe that any system based on private enterprise will fall short of what can be achieved through the full utilization of the objectively given conditions, and I am sceptical of its chances to escape virtual standstill. The answer to the question what can be achieved can only come from the empirical study of concrete cases, and the aim of this study has been to analyse, not to present alternatives. The delineation of alternatives in the abstract is, in any case, a futile endeavour; in a meaningful shape they can only emerge from the analysis of concrete historical circumstances, as they exist in specific times and places. The universality of generalizations that go beyond indicating the broad nature of the forces at work is spurious.

APPENDIX TABLES

APPENDIX TABLE I/A. *Average Quinquennial Growth Rates of Physical Output per Establishment, U.S. Manufacturing Industry, 1904–47*

Industry	Growth rate	Industry		Growth rate
1904–47:		Gloves, leather		2·0
Total U.S. manufacturing industry	15·4	Meat packing		1·2
		Buttons		1·1
Cigarettes	88·0	Cordage and twine		−3·0
Carbon black	41·5			
Chemicals	33·8	*Other Time Spans*		
Coke-oven products	33·1	Automobiles	1904–37	134·6
Glass	32·9	Motorcycles and bicycles	1904–29	52·1
Flour	28·4	Tires and tubes	1921–47	51·1
Corn products	28·4	Oleomargarine	1925–47	43·0
Cigars	25·2	Chocolate	1921–47	37·6
Blast-furnace products	25·1	Liquors, distilled	1904–39	36·3
Fruits and vegetables, canned	24·7	Hats, wool-felt	1904–39	30·4
Petroleum refining	24·0	Wood distillation products	1904–37	28·0
Copper	23·4	Butter	1904–39	26·1
Cane sugar	22·3	Linoleum	1919–47	25·9
Salt	21·7	Carpets and rugs, wool	1904–39	23·0
Zinc	20·2	Silk and rayon goods	1904–39	19·1
Pianos	20·0	Malt	1925–47	17·8
Liquors, malt	18·9	Oilcloth	1904–37	17·1
Soap	18·4	Confectionery	1925–47	17·0
Steelmill products	17·8	Wool shoddy	1904–29	16·5
Beet sugar	16·7	Collapsible tubes	1925–39	16·2
Lime	16·5	Cheese	1904–39	15·0
Explosives	15·7	Ice cream	1923–39	11·8
Carriages and wagons	15·6	Lumber-mill products	1904–37	9·7
Paper and pulp	13·7	Cotton goods	1904–39	9·2
Leather	13·5	Milk, canned	1904–39	8·9
Rice	12·9	Firearms	1921–47	8·7
Knit goods	11·8	Bakery products	1923–39	7·5
Paints and varnishes	10·7			
Cement	10·4			
Cotton seed products	9·5	Tanning and dye products	1904–39	6·6
Shoes, rubber	8·9	Ships and boats	1904–39	5·4
Fuel briquettes	8·7	Secondary metals, non-		
Woollen and worsted goods	8·7	precious	1925–39	4·9
Clay products	8·1	Linseed products	1923–47	3·7
Lead	7·8	Turpentine and rosin	1904–39	2·6
Fertilizers	7·7	Lace goods	1914–47	2·3
Fish, canned	7·2	Wire	1904–39	0·7
Shoes, leather	6·6	Non-ferrous metal		
Chewing and smoking tobacco	4·9	products	1925–39	0·6
Ice, manufactured	3·7	Sand lime brick	1914–47	−1·4
Hats, fur-felt	3·1	Jute goods	1904–39	−1·8
Cane sugar refining	2·4	Linen goods	1904–39	−11·1

Source: SAUL S. SANDS, Changes in scale of production in United States manufacturing industry 1904–1947, *Review of Economics and Statistics*, **43**, November 1961, pp. 365–8.

Industry	

6. BENZOLE[b]
 Capacity, metric tons per day
 Cost of equipment, yen/ton
 Labour cost, yen/ton
     Cost–capacity ratio, capital
     Cost–capacity ratio, labour	

7. CEMENT[c]
 Capacity, 1000 metric tons/year
 Capital cost, dollars/ton
 Labour cost, dollars/ton
     Cost–capacity ratio, capital
     Cost–capacity ratio, labour	

8. FINISHED STEEL[d]
 Capacity, 1000 metric tons/year
 Capital cost, dollars/ton
 Labour cost, dollars/ton
     Cost–capacity ratio, capital
     Cost–capacity ratio, labour	

9. ALUMINIUM PLATE[e]
 Capacity, metric tons per year
 Depreciation cost, yen/ton
 Labour cost, yen/ton
     Cost–capacity ratio, capital
     Cost–capacity ratio, labour
	2

10. FOOD CANNING[f]
 Capacity, cans per hour
 Capital cost, total, dollars
 Labour cost, men/year
     Cost–capacity ratio, capital
     Cost–capacity ratio, labour
	&

Sources:
United Nations, *Industrialization and Productivity*, Bullet
Japan Productivity Center, *A Study on Size of Firms*, 1
NORMAN H. ISHLER, *Pre-Investment Data for Food-Process*
[a] United States, data for 1957.
[b] Japan, 1961, date of estimates not given.
[c] Engineering estimates based on Soviet programmin
[d] Estimates for Latin America based on U.S. enginee
[e] Japan, 1961, date of estimates not given.
[f] United States engineering estimates.